GW01158384

CURRENT LEGAL PROBLEMS 1982

Volume 35

AUSTRALIA
The Law Book Company Ltd.
Sydney: Melbourne: Brisbane

CANADA AND U.S.A.
The Carswell Company Ltd.
Agincourt, Ontario

INDIA
N.M. Tripathi Private Ltd.
Bombay
and
Eastern Law House (Private) Ltd.
Calcutta and Delhi
M.P.P. House
Bangalore

ISRAEL
Steimatzky's Agency Ltd.
Jerusalem: Tel Aviv: Haifa

MALAYSIA: SINGAPORE: BRUNEI
Malayan Law Journal (Pte) Ltd.
Singapore

NEW ZEALAND
Sweet & Maxwell (N.Z.) Ltd.
Auckland

PAKISTAN
Pakistan Law House
Karachi

CURRENT LEGAL PROBLEMS 1982

Edited by
LORD LLOYD OF HAMPSTEAD
and
ROGER W. RIDEOUT
with
JACQUELINE DYSON
as Assistant Editor

On behalf of
THE FACULTY OF LAWS
UNIVERSITY COLLEGE LONDON

VOLUME 35

LONDON
STEVENS & SONS
1982

Published in 1982 by
Stevens & Sons Limited of
11 New Fetter Lane, London.
Computerset by Promenade Graphics Limited, Cheltenham.
Printed in Great Britain by
Page Bros. (Norwich) Limited

ISBN 0 420 46540 5

All editorial communications should be addressed to:
The Editors,
"CURRENT LEGAL PROBLEMS,"
Faculty of Laws,
University College London,
4–8 Endsleigh Gardens, London, W.C.1

PREFACE

THIS volume contains eleven papers, seven of which (including the Presidential Address to the Bentham Club) formed the basis for public lectures. The subject-matter covers a wide range of topics of current interest but no attempt was made this year to group certain contributions under wide common heads.

Again the editors would like to express their appreciation particularly to those contributors from outside the Faculty at University College London who have found time to make a number of important contributions.

Professor Lord Lloyd of Hampstead who has edited this series since 1970 retires this year as Head of the Department of Laws at University College. The Editorial Committee are very pleased to know that Lord Lloyd will continue to serve as editor. The Editorial Committee and the members of the Department have asked that their appreciation of all his services should be recorded here. This would seem an appropriate place to record the same appreciation of the services of Professor E. C. Ryder both to Current Legal Problems and the Department of Laws. He also retires this year.

It is with great regret that we have to record the death of Hubert H. Monroe, Q.C. whose contributions to this volume is evidence of the extent of the loss that the legal profession as a whole has suffered. In particular the members of this faculty have lost an inspiring friend.

Finally the editors would again like to record their gratitude to Mrs. Dyson who continues her enthusiastic service as assistant editor, which can only be rewarded by the continuing success of this unique venture.

THE EDITORS

University College London
1982

CONTENTS

N.B. A paper based on the lecture on "Morality and Charity" delivered by Dr. H. Cohen at University College London on October 22, 1981 will appear in the next volume of Current Legal Problems.

TABLE OF CASES

TABLE OF STATUTES

Judicial Reflections

THE RT. HON. SIR PATRICK BROWNE

It is a daunting prospect for me to lecture to this distinguished audience of academic lawyers. I have had no formal legal education and hold no law degree. I should describe myself as mainly self-educated, but this would be grossly ungrateful to my colleagues at the Bar and on the Bench and my friends among academic lawyers who have helped in my education. What is almost as daunting is that I am very conscious that I speak under the shadow of Jeremy Bentham. He did not, I think, much care for judges, and he believed that legislation is a science. Well, I have been a judge, and like James Boswell on a famous occasion I cannot help it. And having spent a good part of my professional life trying to understand Statutes, Statutory Instruments and Regulations, I am afraid I cannot agree that legislation is a science, at any rate as practised here.

As one of Sir Walter Scott's legal characters said, I am "a mechanic, a mere working mason,"[1] while you are the architects of the law as it ought to be, and sometimes as it is. To prove the influence of academic lawyers on the law as it is, I need only mention by way of example two who, to our loss and sorrow, are no longer alive—Professor Arthur Goodhart and Professor Rupert Cross, at whose lightest word judges trembled. It seemed to me, therefore, that it would be impertinent for me to talk to you about any problem of legal scholarship, but that I could hope that it might perhaps be interesting to you to hear something about the practical problems with which a judge, and also an advocate, has to cope, especially problems with which you, as academic lawyers, are perhaps not so much troubled. I wondered whether my reflections could be said to have any relevance to *current* legal problems, but in the end I felt that some of the problems are perennial and therefore current. I will end by saying something about what certainly is a current legal problem—the recent unhappy differences between the Court of Appeal and the House of Lords.

I am not going to say much about my experience at the Bar, because my practice was mostly too specialised to be of any general interest. But I did form one idea which I hope was useful to me later. In my last few years at the Bar I did a good deal of work in the Court of Appeal, usually for appellants. I came to the conclusion that the last word was not important: what mattered was the first word. When I got to the Court of Appeal myself I tried to remember not to jump to conclusions. While I was still at the Bar I became a Deputy-Chairman of Quarter Sessions, those excellent Courts whose abolition I still bitterly regret. There, in Essex, I received from my colleagues, lawyers and lay magistrates, and from the Probation Service, my basic education in how to try criminal cases, and how to set about sentencing problems. I can never be grateful enough to them all.

In January 1965 I became a Queen's Bench judge, and after nine and a half years I went to the Court of Appeal, from which I retired in 1980. The late Mr. Theobald Mathew, the author of those instructive works "*Forensic Fables*" (under the name of "O")[2] said: "The duty of a judge of first instance is to be quick, courteous and wrong. That is not to say that the duty of the Court of Appeal is to be slow, rude and right, for that would be to usurp the functions of the House of Lords."

As a Queen's Bench judge, I spent most of my time going round England and Wales, trying cases at what were then the Assizes, and most of that time trying crime. When I did try civil cases, either on Circuit or in London, they were mostly about factory accidents or road accidents. I tried few sensational cases. So far as I remember, only one of my judgments at first instance is reported in the Law Reports, and then only in a Note,[3] and I think I only appeared once in the "News of the World." I appeared again in the "News of the World" when I was in the Court of Appeal, when they even thought it worth while publishing my photograph; unfortunately, or fortunately, they published a photograph of my brother.

I suppose that the amount of ceremonial one should have on Circuit is a problem, but that problem has now been solved under the hand of Lord Beeching by the decline of the Assizes into drab Crown Courts. I enjoyed the old ceremonial. I liked to feel that I was doing what my predecessors had done for hundreds of years, and representing the Crown to take His or Her Justice from London to the Counties. And I believe that this ceremonial had value, so that people could see the Red Judge as the symbol of that justice. For this reason, I always liked to walk in procession through the streets of the assize town.

Have you ever considered the Judicial Oath? "I will do right to all manner of people after the laws and usages of this Realm without fear or favour affection or ill will." Not, I will do my best to do right, but I *will* do right. An impossible ideal for any human being, and a burden which sometimes feels too heavy to be borne. On a more human and more attainable level, I always tried to remember that for most of the people who appeared in my Court—as parties, witnesses, jurors or merely spectators—it might well be the only time they had been or would be in a Court in their lives, and that their ideas of Law and Justice might depend on how I behaved myself. It may sound fantastical, but when I was trying crime I have sometimes felt that I was a scapegoat as well as a judge. I do not for a moment believe that all crime is caused by the defects of Society in not providing adequate housing or adequate education or adequate employment or whatever may appeal to particular sociologists, and I am a firm believer in the difference between right and wrong, good and evil. But Society has a responsibility for all its members and the judge is, in relation to each particular criminal, the representative of Society. Equally fantastical, perhaps, I have sometimes felt that by way of compensation I was being supported by some power outside myself, call it what each of you likes. Benjamin Cardozo (and who should know better) calls it "the aid of that inward grace which comes now and again to the elect of any calling."[4] I suppose there is some mythological justification for this feeling; the original Judge was the King, and the King was speaking on behalf of whoever was the relevant God.[5]

Even in crime, though, there was occasional light relief. I remember once trying a case of the rape or attempted rape of two young girls. Among my papers was a photograph of the scene of the incident—a bleak stretch of moorland, dominated by a large noticeboard in the foreground. I could not read what the notice said, but I found a magnifying glass, and what it said was "Royal Society for the Protection of Birds." True to my principle of never making a joke on the Bench I held my tongue.

My reflections as a judge of first instance have settled round four problems—jury trials; the decision of questions of fact by a judge alone; sentencing; and damages for personal injuries.

All the criminal cases I tried at Assizes were of course tried with juries. So far as I remember, I only tried two civil cases with juries, both defamation cases. From time to time one hears suggestions, based on various arguments, that juries ought to be abolished, but I am a strong supporter of juries. I think it is a great mistake to underestimate juries, though I have no recent experience of them. On the whole, I found the juries at Assizes and Quarter Sessions intelligent and very conscientious. Quite often I have had a note from the jury raising some important point which had been overlooked by Counsel and by me, and quite often at the end of a long and complicated case I have had a verdict which showed that the jury had completely understood the case and had come to what was clearly the right decision. On the other hand, I have quite often known juries produce verdicts of acquittal which seemed to me wrong and even perverse. I can only remember one conviction about which I was unhappy. It has been suggested that the reason for some particularly surprising acquittals was that half the jury cannot believe that anyone could behave as the defendant is alleged to have done, and the other half habitually behave in that way themselves. But an occasional perverse and merciful acquittal may be secretly applauded by the judge and may at least save him from an appallingly difficult sentencing problem. I remember a case long ago in which a woman was charged with what was then known as "drunk in charge . . . " She had had some kind of emotional shock and had gone to the bottle for consolation. Because of the nature of her job and the fact that she had to drive a car to do it, conviction would have been disastrous for her. The evidence was very strong, but so were the grounds for sympathy, and the jury acquitted. I was told afterwards by one of the Court officers that as the jury left the Court after the verdict one of them was heard to say to another: "This will teach her not to do it again."

The problem of the relationship of judge and jury is a fascinating and tricky one. The jury must be made to understand that the trial is a joint operation in which judge and jury each have their different responsibilities—the judge to decide the law and the jury to decide the facts—and that the judge is there to help them to discharge their responsibility but not to usurp it. I therefore thought it wrong to try to influence the jury by my own view of the case (though I think judges differ about this), except where I felt I could not stop the case but did feel they ought to acquit. But the judge has to be careful—if the jury thinks he is trying to push them too hard, they may react in the opposite direction. A judge must also learn that the habits of juries are different in different parts of the country. I found that North Country juries were more likely to convict than South Country or East Anglian juries. As to Welsh juries, I have heard a high legal authority—himself a Welshman—say that Welsh juries believe in justice but they are not dogmatic about it.

The most important responsibility of the judge in a jury trial is of course the summing-up, though before that he may have to decide vital questions about the admissibility of evidence—the most usual being a contention by the defence that admissions or confessions by the defendant were not "voluntary" (in the technical sense), which may involve a "trial within a trial" by the judge without the jury. I thought there were two main problems about a summing-up. There are some directions which a judge must give in every summing-up—explanations of the respective responsibilities of the judge and jury, the burden of proof, the standard of proof, the ingredients in law of the offence charged. The judge may have given these directions dozens or even hundreds of times before, but it is essential that the judge should not give the jury the impression that he is bored, or they will be bored too and will not attend. The other problem is the summarising of the facts. What is needed is a clear summary of the questions which the jury has to decide, and of the evidence on each side on which they have to decide them. It is no use simply reading out pages of your notes of the evidence, and I always found this the most difficult part of a summing-up. Of the problem of questions from the jury after they have retired I cannot bring myself to speak; they may be easy, they may be difficult, they may be impossible.

So far I have been talking about cases where the facts are decided by a jury, but nearly all civil cases are now decided by a judge alone, and he has to decide the facts as well as the law. If I may say so, I doubt whether academic lawyers realise that the vast majority of cases depend on the facts, and raise no point of law. You may have questions about the admissibility of evidence, in which I was tempted to follow the policy of Mackinnon L.J. when a judge of first instance. If an objection was made he used to say to counsel: "Well, yes, I know, Mr. So and so—do let's get on . . ." A more sophisticated technique is to say that you will admit the evidence *de bene esse*, and then with any luck by the end of the case the disputed evidence will have been forgotten or will have become unimportant because of other evidence.

So the main job of the judge of first instance is to decide the facts. How does he do it? When there is a conflict of evidence between witnesses, some judges believe that they can tell whether a witness is telling the truth by looking at him and listening to him. I seldom believed that. I think that in civil cases (unlike criminal cases) the witnesses are seldom lying deliberately. But I am very sceptical about the reliability of oral evidence. Observation and memory are fallible, and the human capacity for honestly believing something which bears no relation to what really happened is unlimited. Take for example an eyewitness of a motor accident. Probably it happened very quickly and very likely the witness was not paying any attention till he heard the crash. Afterwards, he thinks about it, and works out what he decides *must* have happened, and in no time he is convinced that he saw it happen. Sometimes one has the benefit of some contemporary documents, which can be invaluable. Sometimes one has to rely on probabilities and on circumstantial evidence; which I always thought was less unreliable than oral evidence. But the judge's own opinion about probabilities can be dangerous, being based on his own, perhaps limited, experience. Like all motorists, I thought I could see what the probabilities of a motor accident were, but I was quite incapable of judging the probabilities of a factory accident. As to circumstantial evidence, Sherlock Holmes said—"Circumstantial evidence is a very tricky thing . . . it may seem to point very strongly to one thing, but if you shift your own point of view you may find it pointing in an equally uncompromising manner to something entirely different."[6] But in spite of his authority I usually trusted circumstantial evidence more than direct evidence. Suppose you have a head-on collision between two motor-cars. Each driver swears that he was on his own side of the road—but tyre-marks, skid-marks and debris may make it clear where the collision happened. How often have I heard defending counsel in criminal cases say to the jury that the evidence was "only circumstantial," and how much I disagreed with the implication that it was therefore not reliable. I remember two contrasting cases which depended mainly on circumstantial evidence. Both were jury cases, and the juries must have taken different views of the weight of circumstantial evidence. One was a murder case. An old man, living alone, had been kicked to death, probably by a burglar whom he had surprised in his flat. The burglar had tried to break open the electricity meter and in doing so had cut his hand. There were three pieces of circumstantial evidence against the defendant. His fingerprints were found in the flat. There was a possible explanation for this, as he had worked as a dustman a year or two before, and might have gone into the flat, though he was not supposed to do so (we had a lot of evidence about how long fingerprints might last). The defendant had a cut finger, and the blood group of the blood found on the meter corresponded with that of the defendant. And the defendant's shoes were stained with blood of which the group corresponded with that of the dead man. The blood groups of both the defendant and the dead man were not very common, the former being found in about 10 per cent. of the population and the latter in about 15 per cent. There was one very curious feature about the case. The medical evidence was that the dead man had probably been attacked on a Monday and had died on the Tuesday: he could not possibly have gone out and walked about after he had been attacked, but four or five witnesses said they had seen him alive and well outside his flat on the Tuesday. There was no doubt that although the defendant had been wearing the bloodstained shoes on the Monday he was not wearing them on the Tuesday, so that if the witnesses were right the blood could not have come from the dead man. The jury convicted, so they must have preferred the medical and circumstantial evidence to that of the eyewitnesses. The other case was one of rape. A young man was charged with the rape in her cottage of an elderly woman who lived there alone except for six or seven cats. The defence was that the defendant had never been into the cottage, though he had been somewhere near it, but there was evidence from the forensic scientists that hairs from all or most of the cats had been found on his clothes. All the same, the jury acquitted—but they were a Welsh jury. I had no hesitation in agreeing with the first jury and disagreeing with the second.

I had meant to say something about the problems of sentencing, but there is not time to start on such an important and complicated subject. I will only say that in my opinion the object of all sentencing is the protection of the public from further offences, not only by a particular defendant but by other people, and the real problem is the best method of achieving that object with the imperfect means at our disposal. At present, the only choice is often to send the defendant to prison, but I am tempted by the vision of settlements isolated from the world, where criminals (except for dangerous or professional criminals) could be kept without too much restraint, except from escaping, and where they might learn to live as part of a community. If you are interested in sentencing problems, I strongly recommend you to read a remarkable book which was given to me by the famous Juvenile Court magistrate, the late Mr. John Watson, soon after I became a Deputy Chairman of Quarter Sessions—"*The Sentence of the Court*," by Leo Page, published by Faber and Faber in 1948. Some of the reforms he suggested have now come about (*e.g.* the training of judges and magistrates, and the need for them to visit the institutions to which they are going to send people) but much of what he says is still as important as when it was written.

The problem of damages for personal injuries is a most unsatisfactory subject. Damages for breach of contract can usually be assessed on some sort of rational and mathematical basis. So can (for example) damages for loss of earnings, and even damages under the Fatal Accidents Acts, now that by Statute one must not take into account the possibility of a widow remarrying. But how can you put into terms of money the loss of an eye or an arm or a leg, still less total or partial paralysis, and the pain and suffering and loss of the amenities of life which they involve? What Falstaff said of honour can equally be said of money—"can honour set a leg? No—or an arm? No—or take away the grief of a wound? No. Honour hath no skill in surgery then? No . . . ."[7] I am afraid that the best one can do is to have some sort of conventional bracket giving rough guidance to the amount of damages for common types of injury. Of course no two cases are alike, and in a particular case there may well be other heads of damage besides pain and suffering and loss of amenities—*e.g.* loss of past (at the time of the trial) or future earnings or the cost of past or future medical or other care. The assessment of damages sometimes involves a forecast (or guess) about whether or when something may happen in the future (*e.g.* that the plaintiff will develop epilepsy or lose his job), and one has the unhappy feeling that one's award is bound to be wrong. If the event does not happen one will have given too much and if it does one will have given too little. In *Lim Poh Choo* v. *Camden & Islington Area Health Authority*[8] a forecast turned out to be wrong between the hearing in the Court of Appeal and the hearing in the House of Lords, and the House was able to make an adjustment in the damages.

And so I come to my reflections on the Court of Appeal and on the approach to deciding questions of law. Of course a judge of first instance has to decide questions of law, but perhaps these reflections belong more to the Court of Appeal.

In the Law Quarterly Review for 1886 Lord Justice Bowen published a remarkable article on "The Law Courts under the Judicature Acts,"[9] in which he suggested various reforms, many of which have now come about, and one which has not—the amalgamation of the Court of Appeal and the House of Lords as the final appellate tribunal for English (though not for Scottish) appeals. In this article he said: "As it is, the Court of Appeal sits every day in the legal year, and seldom or never rises, except on Saturday, before four. Even with this incessant labour the fatigue of which few who have never tried it can appreciate, it is all that the Appeal Court can do to stem the current that flows in upon it." In 1950, in an address to the Society of Public Teachers of Law,[10] Lord Justice Asquith said: "When we sat at the Assizes . . . we all thought this hard work at the time. We agree now, nevertheless, that work in the Court of Appeal is about 50 per cent. more exacting . . . " All this is still true, and more so. I have no doubt that the Court of Appeal is for sheer grinding work unequalled in this country. Most of our judgments are given off the cuff, and when we do reserve a judgment it has to be written in what is euphemistically called our spare time. No doubt our judgments would sometimes be better if we reserved more of them, but the pressure of work makes this impossible, though I believe there has been some improvement since I retired. I found that to keep up I had to work almost every evening and every weekend.

In the article to which I have referred, Lord Justice Bowen said that "the multiplication of appeals tends to make the Court of Appeal the pivot of the new system" and that "The expense of appeals to the House of Lords is so large and the delay involved so substantial that practically the Court of Appeal may be said to decide the law in all but an unimportant percentage of the matters submitted to its judgment."[11] Lord Justice Asquith said that the Court of Appeal "is a final Court of Appeal for over 90 per cent. of the cases which come before it."[12] I believe that these statements are still true, in spite of the recent rash of reversals of the Court of Appeal by the House of Lords (about which I will say something later) and that the Court of Appeal is the most important, as well as the hardest worked, Court in our system.

As I have said, the main responsibility of a judge of first instance is to decide the facts. Even in the Court of Appeal there is in most cases no dispute as to the relevant law and the question is how it applies to the facts in that particular case. But of course both at first instance and in the Court of Appeal there are some cases where a real question of law has to be decided. How do judges set about deciding it? If there is an unambiguous legislative provision or a binding authority which directly covers the case, that is of course the end of the problem. But if the legislation is ambiguous or does not directly cover the case, or if there is no authority, or if there are two authorities leading to different results neither of which is the same on the facts as the case to be decided, what should the judge do? Judicial legislation is a traditional bugbear, or at least a traditional scarecrow, but in that situation the judge must in a sense legislate. He must make the law which is to decide that case and in doing so he may make a precedent which will decide future cases. Of course, the freedom of the judge is limited by the need for consistency and (so far as possible) certainty in the law and by the doctrine of precedent. As Lord Sumner and Lord Justice Scrutton have reminded us: "Whatever may have been the case [in the time of Lord Mansfield] we are now not free in the 20th century to administer that vague jurisprudence which is sometimes attractively styled 'justice as between man and man.' "[13] Benjamin Cardozo has suggested, in his brilliant lectures on "*The Nature of the Judicial Process*"[14] that, within those limits, there are four possible approaches: "The directive force of a principle may be exerted along the line of logical progression; this I will call the rule of analogy or the method of philosophy; along the line of historical development; this I will call the method of evolution; along the line of the customs of the community; this I will call the method of tradition; along the lines of justice, morals and social welfare; this I will call the method of sociology."[15] I suspect that in 1921, when Cardozo spoke, the word "sociology" did not have some of the innuendos it has since acquired. He says that these four approaches are not mutually exclusive, and the decision of a particular case may be based on a combination of two or more of them.

But, inevitably, different judges have different approaches, different temperaments, different backgrounds, and different intellectual habits, though it is interesting to note that three members of the Court of Appeal, perhaps with very different personal and professional backgrounds, usually agree. We all have our bias, not in the bad sense which that word has now acquired, but in its proper metaphorical sense from the game of bowls, of a built-in tendency to go one way rather than the other. We also all have our prejudices, conscious or unconscious. Of course, it is absolutely vital that a judge should realise what his prejudices are, and keep them in the strictest control. I will quote Cardozo again: "Of the power of favour or prejudice in any sordid or vulgar or evil sense, I have found no trace, not even the faintest, among the judges whom I have known. But every day there is borne in on me a new conviction of the inescapable relation between the truth without us and the truth within. The spirit of the age, as it is revealed to each of us, is too often only the spirit of the group in which the accidents of birth or education or occupation or fellowship have given us a place. No effort or revolution of the mind will overthrow utterly or at all times the empire of these subsconscious loyalties."[16]

I come at last to one or two problems which are certainly "current." The first was described by Professor Jeffrey Jowell in his radio broadcast—"Lord Denning, the Courts and the Administration"[17]: "Over the past few months the official law reports have contained case after case where the House of Lords has overruled the Court of Appeal. This sharp divergence between the two highest Courts in the land is most unusual in our judicial history." But Professor H.W.R. Wade has pointed out to me that it has happened before. In the 1960s the House of Lords, under the leadership of Lord Reid, decided four cases which have been described (by Professor Wade) as "four of the great landmarks of the revival of judicial review"—*Ridge* v. *Baldwin*,[18] *Conway* v.

Rimmer,[19] *Padfield* v. *Ministry of Agriculture*[20] and *Anisminic Ltd.* v. *Foreign Compensation Commission*.[21] In each of these the House of Lords reversed the Court of Appeal. It was perhaps prophetic that in three of them Lord Justice Diplock or Lord Justice Russell (as they then were) or both were members of the Court of Appeal and that in two of those Lord Denning dissented (he was not sitting in the other two). But in a brilliant address delivered at Cambridge in memory of Professor de Smith Lord Diplock refers to these cases as part of the process "when the English courts were re-discovering, not without initial hesitation, their historic but long neglected role as protectors of the private citizen against unlawful or unjust treatment by the executive branch of Government."[22] He said that in *Anisminic* the House of Lords reversed "a timorous Court of Appeal"[23] but, as Sir Robin Cooke, of the New Zealand Court of Appeal, has said: "That was a modest description indeed, for the leading judgment in the Court of Appeal was a sustained, closely argued, highly analytical presentation by Diplock L.J. of the conservative theory; the theory that jurisdiction is to be determined at the outset of the limited tribunal's enquiry, that there must be jurisdiction to decide wrongly as well as rightly."[24]

It seems to me that the spirit of the four great cases was carried on by the House of Lords in *Secretary of State for Education* v. *Tameside Metropolitan Borough Council*,[25] in Lord Wilberforce's speech in *Vestey* v. *Inland Revenue*,[26] and in *Grunwick Ltd.* v. *A.C.A.S.*[27]; and by the Court of Appeal in *Laker Airways Ltd.* v. *Department of Trade*.[28] I think the first of the series of reversals was *Gouriet* v. *Union of Post Office Workers*,[29] a case which was complicated by the controversy about the powers and duties of the Attornery-General. Thereafter came a number of cases. The classes of case which attracted most attention were the trade union cases and the administrative law cases, in which the House of Lords took a narrower view than the Court of Appeal of the control which should be exercised by the Courts. But there were also several cases in which the House of Lords took a narrower view of the powers of the Court in procedural matters. There were also reversals in a wide variety of other subjects—*e.g.* recognition of a Talaq divorce obtained by a husband on a flying visit to Pakistan[30] (the result was to deprive the English courts of jurisdiction to deal with the wife's claim to an interest in a house in England owned by the husband); time-tables in rent review clauses (held: time not of the essence of the contract[31]); formation of contract for sale of Council house (the sale had been cancelled after a change in political control and the House of Lords held there was no concluded contract[32]); exclusion of liabilities of an air carrier under the Warsaw Convention and the Carriage by Air Acts, by passenger's failure to give notice of loss within time limit[33]; the position under the Rent Restriction Acts after the death of a resident landlord[34]; the scope of the implied warranty of fitness under section 14 of the Sale of Goods Act[35]; lotteries.[36]

I will not follow the excursions of the House of Lords into Criminal Law. You will no doubt remember their views about attempts to pick empty pockets[37] and conspiracy to make a dangerous drug by a method which could not in fact work.[38] I will only quote without comment Professor J.C. Smith's rhetorical question in a recent number of the Criminal Law Review: "Can we really afford the House of Lords as an appellate Criminal Court?"[39]

I am not concerned to argue whether any of these decisions of the House of Lords are right or wrong (though I remain unrepentant about most of the decisions of the Court of Appeal to which I was a party). For the practising lawyer, the House of Lords, like the Supreme Court of the United States, is infallible because it is final, though I hope that you, as academic lawyers, do not think it is final because it is infallible. This evening I am only concerned with the effects of the decisions and, perhaps, with the reasons for the present differences between the Court of Appeal and the House of Lords.

Besides *Gouriet*,[40] the trade union cases were *N.W.L. Ltd.* v. *Nelson*,[41] *Express Newspapers* v. *McShane*,[42] and *Duport Steel Ltd.* v. *Sirs*.[43] In all of them except *N.W.L.* the House of Lords reversed the Court of Appeal. But for the later case of *Duport Steel* I think there might be an interesting argument about what was the *ratio decidendi* in *Express Newspapers* v. *McShane*, but in the later case Lord Diplock said[44] and as I understand it all the other members of the House agreed, that *Express Newspapers* had decided that "the test whether an act was 'done by a person in contemplation or furtherance of a trade dispute' and so entitled him to immunity from a part of the Common Law of tort is purely subjective: *i.e.* provided that the doer of the act honestly thinks at the time he does it that it may help one of the parties to a trade dispute to achieve their objectives and does it for that reason, he is protected by the section." I do not pause to consider how these cases may have been affected by subsequent legislation.[45] Their interest for my present purposes is in the statements made in the *Duport Steel* case (and implicit in the earlier cases) of the views of the House of Lords about the role of the judiciary. Lord Diplock said[46]:

"My Lords, at a time when more and more cases involve the application of legislation which gives effect to policies that are the subject of bitter public and parliamentary controversy, it cannot be too strongly emphasised that the British constitution, though largely unwritten, is firmly based upon the separation of powers; Parliament makes the laws, the judiciary interpret them. When Parliament legislates . . . the role of the judiciary is confined to ascertaining from the words that Parliament has approved as expressing its intention, what that intention was, and to giving effect to it. Where the meaning of the statutory words is plain and unambiguous it is not for the judges to invent fancied ambiguities as an excuse for failing to give effect to its plain meaning because they themselves consider that the consequences of doing so would be inexpedient, or even unjust or immoral . . . It endangers continued public confidence in the political impartiality of the judiciary which is essential to the continuance of the rule of law, if judges, under the guise of interpretation, provide their own preferred amendments of statutes which experience of their operation has shown to have had consequences that members of the court before whom the matter comes consider to be injurious to the public interest."

Lord Diplock accepted that a Statute might "in actual operation turn out to have injurious consequences that Parliament did not anticipate at the time the Statute was passed," but if so "it is for Parliament, not for the judiciary, to decide whether any changes should be made to the law as stated in the Acts."

Lord Keith of Kinkel[47] and Lord Scarman[48] said much the same, and Lord Scarman added this warning or threat, which to me is deeply disturbing: "But the constitution's separation of powers, or more accurately functions, must be observed if judicial independence is not to be put at risk. For, if people and Parliament come to think that the judicial power is to be confined by nothing other than the judge's sense of what is right . . . confidence in the judicial system will be replaced by fear of it becoming uncertain and arbitrary in its application. Society will then be ready to cut the power of the judges. Their power to do justice will become more restricted by law than it need be, or is today." I suspect that Lord Edmund-Davies, though he agreed in the result, was unhappy about it. He quoted[49] Chief Justice Holt: " . . . an Act of Parliament can do no wrong, though it may do several things that look pretty odd . . . " and Lord Reid[50]: "One is entitled and indeed bound to assume that Parliament intends to act reasonably, and therefore to prefer a reasonable interpretation of a statutory provision if there is any choice. . . . But I regret that I am unable to agree that this case leaves me with any choice."

It seems that the doctrine of the separation of powers applies also as between the judiciary and the executive. Lord Diplock has said that the "Officers or departments of central Government . . . are accountable to Parliament for what they do so far as regards efficiency and policy, and of that Parliament is the only judge; they are responsible to a court of justice for the lawfulness of what they do, and of that the court is the only judge."[51] I confess that I find the contrast between "policy" and "lawfulness" elusive; I should have thought that "policy" might be either lawful or unlawful.[52]

I suppose that the most sensational of the administrative law cases was *Inland Revenue Commissioners* v. *Rossminster Ltd.*[53] You will remember that that was the case in which strong forces of Revenue officials and police made early morning raids on two company offices and the houses of two directors of the companies and took away a mass of papers. They claimed to be acting under powers conferred by section 20C of the Taxes Management Act, 1970 as amended by the Finance Act 1976. The section empowers a circuit judge, if he is satisfied on the application of the Revenue that there is reasonable ground for suspecting that a tax fraud has been committed, to issue a warrant to enter premises (not necessarily the premises of the person suspected) if necessary by force and search them, and authorises the Revenue to seize and remove "any things whatsoever found there which he has reasonable cause to believe may be required as evidence for the purpose of proceedings in respect of" a tax fraud. The Revenue refused to say what offence or offences they suspected had been committed and refused to say what grounds they had for believing that the documents they seized might be required as evidence. In the Court of Appeal we held, on an application for judicial review, that the warrants issued by the circuit judge were bad because they did not sufficiently specify the offence suspected. We also held that it was not enough for the Revenue to say that they reasonably believed that the documents they had seized might be required as evidence. They must give the grounds for their belief and it was then for the Court to decide whether or not the belief was reasonable. On the facts, we held that there was a prima facie case that the Revenue had no reasonable grounds for the necessary belief, and that as they had chosen not to give any information on the point the seizure was bad. The House of Lords reversed us on both points, Lord Salmon dissenting on a point not raised in the courts below. They held that it was enough for the warrant to follow the wording of the statute—"an offence involving fraud in connection with or in relation to tax." They agreed that it is for the Court, and not for the Revenue itself, to decide whether the Revenue had reasonable cause to believe that the things seized might be required as evidence, but held that the Revenue were entitled *at that stage* to refuse to give the grounds for their belief, by analogy with the "public interest immunity" which covers information obtained by the police in the course of their investigations into possible criminal offences, and that the onus of proof in judicial review being on the applicants, they had failed to establish that the Revenue had no reasonable grounds for their belief. But the House did make it clear that the Revenue's immunity from disclosure would only continue until after criminal proceedings had been concluded or had not been taken within a reasonable time, or if it had been decided not to prosecute, and that in the civil action for trespass to goods by the applicants against the Revenue which was then (and so far as I know still is) pending, the onus would be on the Revenue to justify their seizure. The result of the decision is to exclude any possibility of effective judicial review of the actions of the Revenue under this section, but of even more general importance is the approval by the House of the decision of a two judge Court of Appeal in 1962[54] that the Court has no power to grant interlocutory declarations against the Crown (by section 21 of the Crown Proceedings Act 1947 no injunction can be granted against the Crown or its officers). There is high academic authority against this view,[55] and Lord Diplock in *Rossminster* drew attention to "a serious procedural defect in the English system of administrative law: it provides no means of obtaining interlocutory relief against the Crown and its officers."[56] It seems, however, that Lord Wilberforce, Lord Scarman and probably Lord Dilhorne, did not agree.[57] Professor de Smith calls it a "significant gap."[58]

The actual decision of the House of Lords in *Newbury District Council* v. *Secretary of State for the Environment*, reversing the Court of Appeal,[59] turned on the meaning of the word "repository" in the Town and Country Planning (Use Classes) Order, 1950, hardly a question of much general interest. The case related to two hangars on a war-time airfield on the Berkshire Downs which had been used after the War by the Home Office for the storage of civil defence fire engines. Still later, a company called I.S.R. Ltd. applied for planning permission to use them for the storage of synthetic rubber, and were granted permission subject to a condition that they should remove the hangars after ten years—in accordance with the policy of the local planning authority for restoring an area of natural beauty. When the time came, I.S.R. refused to comply with the condition, saying that it was invalid. If the use for storing fire engines was "use as a . . . repository," planning permission was not needed because the Use Classes order allowed the change of use to a "wholesale warehouse," and the condition was therefore invalid. The House of Lords so held. It is a little odd to find Lord Denning and Lord Justice Lawton saying that "no-one conversant with the English language would dream of calling these hangars a repository when filled with fire-pumps or synthetic rubber" and that "no literate person would say that the use to which the Home Office had put the hangars in the 1950s was, or that the company are now, using them as a repository . . . "[60] and Lord Dilhorne saying—"I feel compelled to say that to describe the use of the hangars when so filled as used for a repository is, in my opinion, a perfectly accurate and correct use of the English language."[60] I think the point of general interest in the case is the benevolent interpretation by the House of Lords of the reasons given by the Secretary of State for his conclusion that (assuming planning permission was necessary) the condition requiring removal of the hangars was invalid. In the Court of Appeal, we thought that his reason was that he held as a matter of law that there was no power to attach a condition for removal to a permission for change of use, as had actually been said in a Circular issued by the Ministry. If this reason was wrong in law, as we held it was, the Court of course had power to interfere. The House of Lords agreed that if this was his reason it was wrong in law, but held that his decision was not one of law but of opinion, with which the Court could not interfere.

I can only refer shortly to some other decisions of the House of Lords, reversing the Court of Appeal, which seem to me to show at least a change of emphasis from the earlier decisions: *Bushell* v. *Secretary of State for the Environment*,[61] in which the House, Lord Edmund-Davies dissenting, upheld the refusal of the Inspector at a motorways enquiry to allow cross-examination of the Department's witnesses about figures of projected traffic on which the need for the motorway was based even though it had later been accepted by the Department that the figures were unreliable; *United Kingdom Association of Professional Engineers* v. *A.C.A.S.*,[62] and *Engineers' & Managers' Association* v. *A.C.A.S.*,[63] in which the House refused judicial review, applying the *Wednesbury* principle[64]; contrast *Grunwick* v. *A.C.A.S.*[65] where the *Wednesbury* argument was rejected.

On the other hand, it seems to me that in *Inland Revenue Commissioners* v. *National Federation of Self-Employed & Small*

Businesses Ltd.,[66] the House of Lords took what may be described as a "liberal" approach to the problem of *locus standi* to apply for judicial review. You will remember that in 1977 a new Order 53 of the Rules of the Supreme Court was introduced to simplify and rationalise the procedure for applying for what had been the Prerogative Orders of Certiorari, Mandamus and Prohibition (renamed Judicial Review) and the remedies available. That Order requires the applicant to have "a sufficient interest in the matter to which the application relates," and the problem before the House was whether the Federation had such an interest. You will probably remember that the case related to a challenge by the Federation to an arrangement made by the Revenue with Unions and Employers about what were called "Fleet Street casuals"—printers who had been evading tax. The House unanimously held that the Federation had no sufficient interest, though their reasons differed, Lords Wilberforce, Fraser of Tullybelton and Roskill taking one view and Lords Diplock and Scarman another. I cannot try to summarise the speeches here, and they must be read in full by anyone interested in administrative law. But I think it is right to say that the House held that Order 53 should not be cut down by old and highly technical decisions as to the requirements of *locus standi* to apply for the Prerogative Writs and Orders, that those requirements had already been greatly relaxed since about 1950 and before Order 53 was introduced and that *Gouriet* v. *Union of Post Office Workers*[67] had no application to judicial review. Lord Diplock said[68] "To revert to technical restrictions on *locus standi* . . . that were current 30 years or more [ago] would be to reverse that progress towards a comprehensive system of administrative law that I regard as having been the greatest achievement of my judicial lifetime."

I cannot leave the subject of administrative law without reminding you of what Professor Wade has called "New twists in the Anisminic skein."[69] In *Pearlman* v. *Harrow School Governors*,[70] the Court of Appeal (Lord Justice Geoffrey Lane dissenting), on an application for *certiorari* to a County Court, held in substance that the long-standing distinction between errors going to jurisdiction (which were amenable to *certiorari*) and errors within jurisdiction (which were not) no longer existed. Lord Denning said[71] "I would suggest that this distinction should now be discarded . . . the way to get things right is to hold thus: no Court or tribunal has any jurisdiction to make an error of law on which the decision of a case depends." In *In Re a Company*[72] the Court of Appeal applied this doctrine to a decision of a High Court judge, although the statute under which the decision had been made provided that "the decision of a judge of the High Court . . . on an application under this section shall not be appealable." The House of Lords reversed this decision under the name of *In re Racal Communications Ltd.*[73] and disapproved the decision in *Pearlman*, approving the dissenting judgment of Lord Justice Geoffrey Lane. This case has nothing to do with judicial review, for the simple reason that the High Court is not a Court or tribunal of limited jurisdiction and the Prerogative Writs and Orders never went to it. If I may respectfully say so, I think that the decision of the House of Lords was plainly right but Lord Diplock, with whose speech Lord Keith of Kinkel agreed, put forward what I think was a new doctrine. He drew a distinction between "an administrative tribunal or other administrative authority however described when it is exercising quasi-judicial functions" and inferior Courts of law. As to the former, he said (echoing what he had said in the Address at Cambridge to which I have already referred[74]) that the effect of *Anisminic* was that "the old distinction between errors of law that went to jurisdiction and errors of law that did not was for practical purposes abolished," but that as to the latter it might not be, depending on the construction of the statute constituting the court. This was of course *obiter*, and the other members of the House did not say anything about this point. Meanwhile, in *South East Asia Firebricks* v. *Non-metalllic Union*,[75] in which the decision was given ten days earlier and in which two of the members of the Board were also members of the House in *Racal*,[76] the Privy Council had disapproved Lord Denning and approved Lord Justice Geoffrey Lane in *Pearlman* and apparently reaffirmed without qualification the distinction between errors going to jurisdiction and errors within jurisdiction. We can only wait for further guidance.

I have only time to say very little about the recent decisions of the House of Lords on procedural questions, which are of great importance to the practising lawyer, but probably not of much interest to the academic lawyer, except as illustrating the differences between the House of Lords and the Court of Appeal. I have therefore relegated the details to a footnote.[77] But I think it fair to say that these decisions have tended to limit or exclude the jurisdiction or discretion of the courts in a variety of matters: interlocutory injunctions; striking out actions for want of prosecution; injunctions to restrain further proceedings in arbitrations where there has been inordinate and inexcusable delay which has made a just result impossible; interim declarations against the Crown and declarations in cases involving possible criminal offences; and *Mareva* injunctions (a remedy lately developed by the Commercial Court and the Court of Appeal by which assets in this country of a defendant who is out of the jurisdiction are frozen pending the result of the action). In nearly all of the cases referred to in the footnote the House of Lords reversed the Court of Appeal and took a restrictive view of the powers of the court.

The present differences between the Court of Appeal and the House of Lords are often treated as differences between the House of Lords and Lord Denning, for example, by Professor Jowell in his radio talk to which I have already referred,[78] and to a large extent they do result from their different approaches to Law and Justice and the proper role of the courts. But I think this is an over-simplification. The other members of the Court of Appeal who sit with Lord Denning are by no means yes-men, and he was not a party to several of the decisions which have been reversed.[79] In one case the House even upheld Lord Denning's dissenting judgment.[80] One must not exaggerate these differences. There have of course been many recent cases in which the House has affirmed the Court of Appeal, some of them highly controversial—*e.g. Grunwick* v. *A.C.A.S.*,[81] *Williams & Glyns Bank* v. *Boland*[82] (right of wife with beneficial interest in matrimonial home against mortgagee to whom husband had mortgaged the house without her knowledge) to both of which Lord Denning was a party, and *Bunge* v. *Tradax Export*[83] (stipulation as to time in mercantile contract) to which he was not, but in which Lord Justice Megaw and I ventured to question some pronouncements by Lord Justice Diplock, and Lord Diplock. I must confess that I find it difficult not to be prejudiced, as I was a member of the Court of Appeal in six of the cases to which I have referred,[84] in which our decision was reversed by the House of Lords, though I was also a party to the three decisions I have just mentioned in which we were affirmed and some others.

I think that a clue to the differences may perhaps be found in a sentence in Lord Scarman's speech in the *Duport Steel* case[85]: "My basic criticism of all three judgments in the Court of Appeal is that in their desire to do justice the Court failed to do justice according to law." The "law" there in question was an Act of Parliament dealing with a subject of acute political and public controversy, and if there is any implication of a general antithesis between law and justice I do not accept it. It has often been said that hard cases make bad law, and this dogma was let out for a run in the House of Lords not long ago,[86] but whether this is true or not I have no doubt that bad law makes hard cases. I have enough faith in the justice of the law to look with suspicion on any proposition of law which seems to me to produce injustice in a particular case.

I think it emerges from the cases to which I have referred that the House of Lords now tends to take a more restrictive view of the powers and duties of the Courts than they took ten or 20 years ago and even later. The House is a firm believer in the doctrine of the separation of powers.[87] As a result, the House of Lords seeks to keep the courts out of industrial relations and trade disputes, believing that to have been the intention of Parliament[88] and tends to take a benevolent view of executive action.[89] The procedural cases tend to restrict the discretion of the courts.[90]

As to my own bias, in the sense in which I have defined bias, I am a firm (indeed passionate) believer in the right and duty and power of the courts to control what Lord Wilberforce has called "abuse of authority or jurisdiction"[91] by the Executive or administrative authorities or inferior courts. I had thought of calling this lecture "From Anisminic to Rossminster," but this would have been to admit that my judicial career began with a bang and ended with a whimper. In private law, I have already said that where there is an unambiguous legislative provision or a binding authority of course one must apply it. But where the court is not constrained by legislation or precedent I believe that it is the right and duty of the judges to develop the law to do justice. Within these limits, I have tried to give the decision which seemed to me just and sensible in the particular case, believing too that what is just and sensible in one case is likely to be just and sensible in other similar cases. Of course I fully realise that the law should so far as possible be certain and predictable, but I have never understood why it sometimes seems to be thought that justice and common sense are less predictable than their opposites.

I will end my reflections by quoting what I said in my valediction when I retired—I was sitting in the Court of Appeal with Lord Denning: "If I had my life again, there is nothing I would rather have been than a Queen's Bench judge and a Lord Justice of Appeal. Especially the last five years in this court have been the most fascinating and rewarding of my professional life . . . And still more it has been such an enormous privilege to be a member of the Court of Appeal presided over by you, my Lord. I think some people today believe, as I think James I said, that although judges should be lions, they should be lions under the throne. On the other hand, some other people say that today judges are only leaky umbrellas to protect the individual from the tyranny of the Executive. Well, we all know that there is one old lion who will never be under the throne and that there is one umbrella which will never be leaky, although it may from time to time be blown inside out by blasts from above."

Notes

[1] Paulus Pleydell, Advocate, in *Guy Mannering*, Chap. 37.

[2] Originally published by Butterworths in 1926. A good many later editions and additions.

[3] *Anisminic Ltd.* v. *Foreign Compensation Commission* [1969] 2 A.C. 147. An abridgment of my judgment is in a Note at p.223. A better abridgment with a foreword by Professor H.W.R. Wade was published in the *Cambridge Law Journal* [1969] C.L.J. Vol. 27 p.230. A few of my judgments were reported in *Lloyd's List Law Reports*. But what I think was probably my best judgment was not reported at all, though one sentence of it has now found its way into the Law Reports by way of quotation—see [1978] Q.B. at pp.169–170 and [1981] 3 W.L.R. at p.263.

[4] *The Nature of the Judicial Process* (Yale University Press, 1921, reprinted 1931), p.163.

[5] See Sir Henry Maine, *Ancient Law*, Chap. 1.

[6] *The Adventures—The Boscombe Valley Mystery*.

[7] *Henry IV*, Part I, Act V, Sc. I., lines 131–133.

[8] [1980] A.C. 174.

[9] (1886) 2 L.Q.R. 1. I am indebted to Lord Justice Stephenson for the discovery of this article and for the address by Lord Justice Asquith (note 10).

[10] "Some aspects of the Work of the Court of Appeal," *Journal of the Society of Public Teachers of Law*, New Series, Vol. 1. 1947–1951, p.350.

[11] 2 L.Q.R., 9 and 11.

[12] At p.355.

[13] Hamilton L.J. in *Baylis* v. *Bishop of London* [1913] 1 Ch. 127, 140; Scrutton L.J. in *Holt* v. *Markham* [1923] 1 K.B. 504, 513.

[14] Benjamin Cardozo, *The Nature of the Judicial Process* (Yale University Press, 1921, seventh printing 1931).

[15] *Op. cit.* pp.30–31.

[16] *Op. cit.* pp.174–175.

[17] *The Listener*, May 22, 1980.

[18] [1964] A.C. 40.

[19] [1968] A.C. 910.

[20] [1968] A.C. 997.

[21] [1969] 2 A.C. 147.

[22] "Administrative Law: Judicial Review Reviewed" [1974] C.L.J. Vol. 33, Pt. 2, p.233. He describes as the "breakthrough" *R.* v. *Northumberland Appeal Tribunal* [1952] 1 Q.B. 338. This decision was backed up by the Tribunals and Enquiries Act, 1958 which required reasons to be given.

[23] *Op. cit.* at p.243.

[24] "Third Thoughts on Administrative Law," an address to the Auckland District Law Society Seminar on May 22, 1979 (1979) 5 *Recent Law* (N.S.) 218. I am indebted to Mr. D.G.T. Williams, President of Wolfson College, Cambridge, for the discovery of this address.

[25] [1977] A.C. 1014.

[26] [1980] A.C. 1148.

[27] [1978] A.C. 655.

[28] [1977] Q.B. 643.

[29] [1978] A.C. 435.

[30] *Quazi* v. *Quazi* [1980] A.C. 744.

[31] *United Scientific Holdings* v. *Burnley B.C.* [1978] A.C. 904. At the same time, the House reversed the decision of a differently constituted Court of Appeal in *Cheapside Land Development Co.* v. *Messels Service Co.* [1977] unreported.

[32] *Gibson* v. *Manchester City Council* [1979] 1 W.L.R. 294, reversing [1978] 1 W.L.R. 520.

[33] *Fothergill* v. *Monarch Airlines* [1980] Q.B. 23 (C.A., Lord Denning dissenting); [1981] A.C. 251, H.L.

[34] *Landau* v. *Sloane* [1981] Q.B. 74, C.A.; [1981] A.C. 251, H.L.

[35] *Lexmead (Basingstoke) Ltd.* v. *Lewis* [1981] 2 W.L.R. 713.

[36] *Imperial Tobacco Ltd.* v. *Att.-Gen.* [1981] A.C. 718.

[37] *Haughton* v. *Smith* [1975] A.C. 476.

[38] *D.P.P.* v. *Nock* [1978] A.C. 979. That case was boldly distinguished by the Court of Appeal (Criminal Division) in *R.* v. *Bennett* (1979) 68 Cr.App. R. 168 and *R.* v. *Harris* (1979) 69 Cr. App. R. 122.

[39] [1981] Crim. L.R. 393.

[40] [1978] A.C. 435.

[41] [1979] 1 W.L.R. 1294.

[42] [1980] A.C. 672.

[43] [1980] 1 W.L.R. 142.

[44] At p.156.

[45] See *Hadmor Productions Ltd.* v. *Hamilton* [1981] 3 W.L.R. 139. Leave to appeal has been given by the House of Lords [1981] 1 W.L.R. 1128.

[46] [1980] 1 W.L.R. 142, 157.

[47] At pp.167–168.

[48] At pp.168–169.

[49] At p.164, quoting *City of London* v. *Wood* (1701) 12 Mod. Rep. 669, 687–688.

[50] At p.165, quoting *Inland Revenue Commissioners* v. *Hinchy* [1960] A.C. 748, 767–768.

[51] *I.R.C.* v. *Federation of Self-employed* [1981] 2 W.L.R. 722, 740.

[52] The decisions of the Executive which were upset by the Courts in *e.g. Padfield, Tameside* and *Laker Airways* might well be called "policy." *Bushell* illustrates the difficulty of drawing the frontier.

[53] [1980] A.C. 952.

[54] *International General Electric* v. *Customs & Excise Commissioners* [1962] Ch. 784, Upjohn and Diplock L.JJ.

[55] Professor H.W.R. Wade, *Administrative Law* (4th ed.), p.494.

[56] [1980] A.C. 952, 1014–1015.

[57] At pp.1001, 1027 and 1007. Although Lord Scarman described the idea of interim declarations as "absurd" and "risible" I understand that in New Zealand they may by statute be awarded against the Crown—see de Smith, *Judicial Review of Administrative Action* (4th ed.), pp.448, note 27 and 523, note 74.

[58] de Smith, *op. cit.* p.523.

[59] [1978] 1 W.L.R. 1241, C.A.; [1981] A.C. 578, H.L.

[60] [1981] A.C. at p.597.

[61] [1981] A.C. 75.

[62] [1981] A.C. 424.

[63] [1980] 1 W.L.R. 302.

[64] *Associated Provincial Picture Houses* v. *Wednesbury Corporation* [1948] 1 K.B. 223.

[65] [1978] A.C. 655.

[66] [1981] 2 W.L.R. 722.

[67] [1978] A.C. 435.

[68] At p.737.

[69] 96 L.Q.R. 492.

[70] [1979] 1 Q.B. 56.

[71] At p.70.

[72] [1980] Ch. 138.

[73] [1981] A.C. 374.

[74] See note 22 above.

[75] [1981] A.C. 363.

[76] Lord Edmund-Davies and Lord Keith of Kinkel.

[77] The procedural cases were: (a) Restrictions on discretion to grant or refuse interlocutory injunctions. In *American Cyanamid Co.* v. *Ethicon Ltd.* [1975] A.C. 396 Lord Diplock, in a speech with which all the others members of the House agreed, emphatically rejected the "supposed rule" that a plaintiff who applies for an interlocutory injunction must show a prima facie case that he will succeed at the trial. He held that it was enough for him to show that "there is a serious question to be tried." Nor should the court have regard to the relative strengths of the cases of the parties, except as a last resort. This caused consternation—see *Fellowes* v. *Fisher* [1976] Q.B. 122; 91 L.Q.R. 168. It was contrary to the previous practice in the Queen's Bench Division and in the Chancery Division, to what had been and still is the practice in Scotland (Lord Fraser of Tullybelton in *N.W.L. Ltd.* v. *Nelson* [1979] 1 W.L.R. 1294, 1309–1310) and to what had been said in the House of Lords 10 years earlier in *J.T. Stratford & Sons Ltd.* v. *Lindley* [1965] A.C. 269, especially Lord Upjohn at pp.338–339, which apparently was not cited in *American Cyanamid*; in the earlier case, however, the principle was common ground between counsel so the majority of the Court of Appeal later thought there were not two conflicting *decisions* of the House of Lords (*Fellowes* v. *Fisher*.) However, in *N.W.L.* v. *Nelson* [1979] 1 W.L.R. 1294, 1306–1307) Lord Diplock said that "properly understood there is in my view nothing in the decision of this House in *American Cyanamid* to suggest that in considering whether or not to grant an interlocutory injunction the judge ought not to give full weight to all the practical realities of the case," including the fact that the grant or refusal of an interlocutory injunction would have the practical effect of putting an end to the action. This was, however, *obiter*, because the *N.W.L.* case was governed by s.17(2) of the Trade Union and Labour Relations Act 1974 as amended, an amendment which was apparently passed specifically to exclude the application of *American Cyanamid* to actions in which the defendant claims that he was acting in contemplation or furtherance of a Trade dispute (Lord Fraser of Tullybelton and Lord Scarman in *N.W.L.* at pp.1308 and 1314–1315). It looks as if we must wait for further guidance about what "properly understood" *American Cyanamid* does mean. (b) Restriction on discretion to strike out actions for want of prosecution. *Birkett* v. *James* [1978] A.C. 297 and its logical sequel in *Tolley* v. *Morris* [1979] 1 W.L.R. 592, where it was held (Lord Wilberforce and Lord Dilhorne dissenting) that the claim could drag on for 18½ years after the accident. (c) Arbitrations in which there has been inordinate and inexcusable delay, making a just decision impossible. In *Bremer Vulcan* v. *South Indian Shipping* [1981] 2 W.L.R. 141 the House of Lords, by a majority of three to two (Lord Diplock, with whom Lord Edmund-Davies and Lord Russell of Killowen agreed without giving separate reasons, Lord Fraser of Tullybelton and Lord Scarman dissenting) overruled the Court of Appeal and the Commercial judge and held that there was no jurisdiction to grant an injunction restraining the claimant from proceeding with the arbitration. This decision was distinguished by the Court of Appeal in *Andre* v. *Marine-transocean Ltd.* [1981] 3 W.L.R. 43 and an injunction was granted, but leave to appeal was given and we can only await the result. The importance of these cases for the future has been much reduced by s.5 of the Arbitration Act 1979, but there must still be many arbitrations pending which were started before the commencement of that Act. (d) Declarations. I have already referred to the affirmation in *Rossminster* (note 53) that there is no jurisdiction to grant interim declarations against the Crown or its officers. In *Imperial Tobacco Ltd.* v. *Att.-Gen.* (note 36) it was held that, although the civil courts have jurisdiction to grant a declaration that certain conduct does not amount

to a criminal offence, it is not a proper exercise of discretion to do so after criminal proceedings have been started, unless the criminal proceedings are vexatious or an abuse of the process of the Court. (e) *Mareva* injunctions, called after *The Mareva* [1975] 2 Lloyd's Rep. 509. In *The Siskina* [1979] A.C. 210 the House of Lords, reversing the majority of the Court of Appeal, refused to extend this remedy to a case where the proceedings were going on abroad, although the defendant's only assets were in this country. Lord Diplock hinted that there might be further limitations on the remedy, though it seems that Lord Hailsham of St. Marylebone did not agree (see pp.254 and 261).

[78] *The Listener* May 22, 1980.

[79] *e.g.* the cases referred to in notes 30, 31, 34, 35.

[80] *Fothergill* v. *Monarch Airlines*, note 33 above.

[81] [1978] A.C. 435.

[82] [1981] A.C. 487.

[83] [1980] 1 Lloyd's Rep. 294, C.A.; [1981] 1 W.L.R. 711, H.L.

[84] The cases referred to in notes 30, 31, 33, 36, 53, 59.

[85] [1980] 1 W.L.R., 142, 168.

[86] *Gibson* v. *Manchester City Council* [1979] 1 W.L.R. 294, Lord Diplock and Lord Edmund-Davies at p.299.

[87] See notes 46 and 5l.

[88] The trade union cases and the recent A.C.A.S. cases.

[89] *Rossminster, Bushell, Newbury*. There seems to be some contrast between *National Federation of Self-Employed* and *Vestey* (note 26) as to the discretionary powers of the Inland Revenue.

[90] See note 77 above.

[91] In *Gouriet* [1978] A.C. 435, 483.

The Law of Scotland—Its Interest for the Comparative Lawyer

THE RT. HON. LORD EMSLIE

WHEN I was invited to become your President for 1982 I quickly realised, looking at the formidable list of my distinguished predecessors in this office, that this was probably the first time in its history that your admirable Club has exposed itself to the risk of entrusting the Presidential Address to a Scots judge still holding judicial office in Scotland. I discount Lords Normand and Kilbrandon for, at the time of their Presidencies, each was, I believe, a Lord of Appeal in Ordinary and, as expatriates, might well have been thought to have learned much to their advantage from their brethren in the Appellate Committee. In spite of an occasional foray in that Committee my roots, and my whole legal and judicial experience, have been in Scotland, and I confess at once that I found the task of choosing a subject for this address, to an audience brought up in the disciplines of a foreign jurisdiction, more than usually daunting. In the end, however, I decided to be bold and to talk to you about Scots Law as a fit subject for comparative study. For this decision I offer a few reasons or excuses—

(i) I have for long thought that the law of Scotland has received less attention from comparative lawyers than it deserves, and from my reading of the Law Reports, I have occasionally been surprised to see that rich sources of Scots law of some relevance seem to have been left untapped in a consideration of questions where the laws of our two countries are not markedly different. At all events it is, I think, certain that a Scots Court faced with such questions is unlikely to be allowed to come to judgment without reference to apparently helpful English authority;

(ii) My sole distinction on this side of the Border, at least, is that I may have the advantage of knowing more about the law of Scotland than you do.

Apart from these considerations this year seems to be a wholly appropriate one in which to recommend comparative study of Scots law because 301 years ago, when the first Viscount of Stair published the first edition of his *Institutions of the Law of Scotland*, he declared in the opening paragraph that "no man can be a knowing lawyer in any nation who hath not well pondered and digested in his mind the common law of the world." This year of 1982, further, will see the four hundred and fiftieth anniversary of the establishment of the College of Justice and the Court of Session upon a Parisian model. It will also see the three hundredth anniversary of the founding of the Advocates' library, the great library which, until 1925, was maintained and held in trust for the nation until the burden of continuing maintenance being beyond the Faculty's resources, it was given freely and without recompense and reward to the nation, and received with comparatively modest thanks. From that gift the National Library of Scotland was born.

As a national, rational and coherent system of law the law of Scotland was a relatively late developer. Not until the last quarter of the seventeenth century did it begin to deserve the serious attention of legal scholars outside its boundaries.

Until then Scotland could properly be described as a remote country which throughout its history had been bedevilled by poverty and strife. In the period which may be characterised as the somewhat disorderly formative years of its legal system the Highlands were virtually beyond the legal pale, for the King's law scarcely ran there, and in the country as a whole there was no body of generally accepted customs. Relations with Scotland's larger neighbour were antagonistic, to say the least, and no facilities for the study of the law in Scotland's ancient universities existed at all until 1710 when the first lecture upon the law was delivered in Edinburgh.

In light of this background it is not surprising that the civil private law of Scotland was notoriously hard to find. It was largely contained in individual statutes, in the collection of Statutes known as the Black Acts because of the manner of printing, and its legal literature was of the scantiest, consisting, as it did, in various manuscript collections of "Practicks" or Notes or Statutes, decisions and practical observations under alphabetical headings. There were, I need hardly remind you, no printed reports of judgments of the Court and the available records of such judgments, without opinions, were scattered throughout a number of collections in manuscript only. It is easy to appreciate why, in this state of matters, practitioners were driven to examine the texts of Roman and Canon law and to absorb their influences. The criminal law was in a no less chaotic state of accessibility although it must be said in its favour that from as early as medieval times it recognised that *mens rea* was the critical element in all crime.

I have no intention of wearying you with further elaboration of this thumbnail sketch of the dark ages of our legal system. Fortunately for us, Scots advocates in the seventeenth century began to come under the powerful influence of the great Continental civilians to which they were exposed, especially in Holland where they were forced to seek a legal education in Leyden and in Utrecht.

Let me now say something of the modern Law of Scotland which understandably retains relatively few traces of primitive native custom. It is, indeed, a system largely imported from outside which has been subsequently moulded and developed to suit the national genius. Neither a civilian nor a true common law system it found its inspiration in the wisdom and literature of both.

In the case of most modern legal systems it is far from easy to identify their foundations. Not so in Scotland for our modern law in the civil field finds its origins and its distinctive characteristics in the work of Stair—in the Institutions which were first published in 1681 while he held his first appointment as Lord President of the Court of Session.

Before attempting a somewhat slight account of Stair's importance I cannot resist the temptation to digress and to say a little about the man himself, for his life tells the story of the turbulent times in which he lived as well as any history of the period. Indeed, the more one knows of the tightrope which he walked so often amidst all the perils of revolution, dynastic changes, and constitutional upheaval, the more remarkable his great achievement can be seen to be.

He was born in 1619 and after schooling in Mauchline went to the University of Glasgow to graduate there in 1637. He then went to Edinburgh intending to become an advocate. Instead he saw military service as a Cornet of Glencairn's Horse in the War of the Covenant before returning to Glasgow and the life of a University philosopher until 1647 when he decided to go back again to Edinburgh and to the Bar.

Two years later he was in the Hague as Secretary of the Commission sent to treat with Charles II, and in 1651 he was in Breda upon the same business. Thereafter he had a few relatively peaceful years in practice as an Advocate, and in 1657 was appointed to the Bench by General Monk as one of Cromwell's Commissioners. I suppose one might call that light work, for the Courts were closed for two out of the next three years.

In 1661, after the restoration, he was reappointed to the Bench. His judicial career very nearly came to an end, however, in 1663 when he resigned, but after interview with the King he was reappointed, and in 1671 he became Lord President.

Ten years later and not long after the publication of his *Institutions*, he resigned that office, and with a little help from his friends, including advice from the King's Advocate himself, he wisely fled to Holland rather than face the consequences of refusal to take the Test. The part played by Sir George Mackenzie in this escape is described in Stair's own words—

> "I found I was in continual suspicion, that my tenants were thrown into prison and forced to give bonds on pretence of conventicles for more than they were worth, and my rents were arrested. I did ask the King's Advocate whether he thought I might be safe and free of imprisonment. He told me faithfully and friendly that he thought not, and owned to the King that he had so advised me, whereupon I was necessitated to retire to Holland."

There he stayed until 1688 when he came back with William of Orange to be reappointed Lord President in 1689.

What an astonishing and dangerous career Stair had. Most of us are content with appointment to the Bench once. In his case he was appointed three times and twice to the office of Lord President! His capacity for survival and adjustment was immense yet the political hazards of his seventeenth century life are wholly concealed by the thoughtful felicitous prose of his true memorial—the *Institutions* themselves.

In his dedication of the *Institutions* to the King, from whose wrath he was soon to flee, Stair modestly described them as a summary of the laws and customs of His Majesty's Ancient Kingdom of Scotland. They were far more than that for he was concerned not only to expound the law (the formal and proper objects of which, he saw, were the rights of men) but to handle it, as he said himself, "as a rational discipline." The result was a book which, for the first time, presented in narrative form a systematic account of the whole of the private law of Scotland. It had as its strength an essentially ethical substratum, for Stair firmly believed that "equity is the body of the law," and it was of critical importance in giving birth to the law of Scotland as a coherent system of principle which, as Professor Walker of Glasgow says, in his Introduction to the tercentenary edition of the Institutions, "was a system in which the lawyer questing for the solution to a problem could seek the appropriate principle within the ambit of whose application his case fell, and to deduce syllogistically from that principle the solution to his problem, rather than to seek a previous decision of a court on facts which can fairly be regarded as similar to those raised by his problem, and analogically to accept the judicial solution of the precedent problem as that applicable to the enquirer's problem."

Whatever be the best description of the book, but for *Institutions* and the existence of the College of Justice which provided an established judicial structure which ultimately acquired great flexibility and strength, it is open to question whether Scots Law would have developed at all after—or even survived—the Treaty of Union in 1707. Perhaps in matters of succession or land law it might but in all other fields, as Lord Cameron pointed out in his speech during the Stair Tercentenary celebrations in the University of Glasgow, it is difficult to see how it could have survived the pressures which would have come from the South. There would have been no solid foundation upon which Erskine, in the eighteenth century, and Bell, in the nineteenth century, could have built their own coherent and systematic expositions of the whole of the law as it had developed, and no *corpus* of principle upon which since the middle of the nineteenth century, the law has steadily been moulded and adapted by decisions of the Court of Session to meet the constantly changing circumstances of life in a modern world. In Lord Cameron's own words—

> "One can say that Scots law would in every probability have withered or been swallowed up in the preponderating law of England: England, the major partner with a vigorous and expanding and developing commercial law:
> England the major partner in population, in wealth, and in commerce:
> England with its developed and developing system of commercial law given added impetus by the work of Lord Mansfield and his juries:
> Scotland, with an archaic system, in every sense the junior partner, and a United Kingdom Parliament wholly unfamiliar with Scottish ideas not likely in the face of the events of 1715 and 1745, to be kindly disposed to offering support and countenance to the competitive development of the legal system of a country regarded with such misgivings and indeed distrust."

What we now enjoy in Scotland today are the twentieth century fruits of the seeds sown by Stair—a healthy system of law which can, with profit on both sides, be compared and contrasted with the law of England. In comparatively recent times, no doubt, when so much of law is the creature of United Kingdom statute and is widely concerned with commercial matters, industrial relations, and social questions, and when Scotland, subject always to the power of the Court of Session to reconsider and review its own appellate decisions in larger Benches, has for consistency and certainty adopted with some caution the rule of precedent, the old distinctions between the systems of law in the two countries have become less obvious. The background of each, however, remains fundamentally different. In so many cases the same answer to common problems is found by both systems usually, however, by different routes. To the comparative lawyer an examination of extant contrasts cannot be other than illuminating for the contrasts are, I suggest, between the two main schools of legal thought, the logical and the empirical, and between systems one of which found everything concerned with rights justiciable, and the other which, historically, at least, asked itself the initial question whether the law provided a remedy for the particular wrong which was alleged.

In both systems of civil private law the scope for judicial law-making—judiciary law—is still quite wide. Ignoring altogether the inevitability of such law-making created by the obscurities, ambiguities and silences of statutes which are so often rendered less intelligible where Parliament has been good enough to provide a definition section, the non-statutory law of both countries is in a state of constant development, and solutions for the new problems which emerge in new circumstances must be found, and are found in Scotland by the application to them of well-established principles.

In suggesting that comparative lawyers on this side of the Border might not find it a waste of time and spirit to have a look at the modern law of Scotland, its origins, how it is made to work, and its insistence, subject to a few statutory exceptions, on corroboration in proof of facts in issue, I shall end this chapter of my address by quoting Stair's own assessment of the virtues of Scots law as he saw them: "The Law of Scotland in its nearness to equity, plainness, and facility in its customs, tenors and forms, and in its celerity and dispatch in the administration of justice, may well be paralleled with the best law in Christendom." Whether this was even remotely true when it was written is open to question. The Court of Session and its procedures were, in Stair's time, ill adapted to the pursuit of celerity and dispatch in the administration of justice. Thanks in part to the influence of Jeremy Bentham, however, the Court was reconstituted early in the nineteenth century, in the form in which it exists today. The Sheriff Court system has been developed to provide local courts of almost unlimited jurisdiction, and the shackles of procedure by written pleadings have been cast off in favour of oral adversarial proceedings. Jeremy Bentham's only failure, indeed, in his advocacy of Scotch reform was that he was unable to prevent Scotland from inheriting from the English system the thoroughly unsatisfactory procedure of civil jury trial which now, I am glad to say, has almost fallen into deserved desuetude. Whether in light of these developments Stair's assessment is even true today is not for me to say. I would like to think, however, that some day his very words will be used again by someone—especially someone who is not himself a Scots lawyer. In any event I am confident that we have in Scotland now a system of civil law which, still significantly different from yours, and true to its fundamental principles, works well and with reasonable expedition. It is for that reason that it should be of interest outside Scotland. I am confident too that, like your own system, the Scottish legal system has retained its vitality, vigour and momentum. Both are, I believe, quite strong enough to resist pressures for standardisation and harmonisation of law coming from outside the United Kingdom. I distrust wholly the doctrine of standardisation of law for different communities. Let us by all means, however, harmonise but only when we must. Even where we must let us proceed with the greatest caution lest the coherence of rational systems be seriously injured. That is, I believe, the view of our own Law Commission and long may they hold it.

Whatever may be said of the virtues of the system of civil private law practised in Scotland any Scots lawyer would assert with conviction that the criminal law of Scotland today, and its administration, have little to be ashamed of. Indeed the more I see of other systems in the criminal field the more I am convinced that ours has fewer major blemishes than most, and has perhaps more to teach than to learn from them. The Criminal Law of Scotland undoubtedly works and there is, indeed, as Stair might have said, had he been prepared to have anything to do with criminal law, a genuine measure of celerity and dispatch in the administration of criminal justice generally.

The native criminal law of Scotland, and the system by which it and the statutory criminal law are administered, are markedly different from the criminal law practised and administered in England. Just as we can find the foundation and the inspiration of our modern civil law in Stair, and attribute its development to the existence of the College of Justice and the work of Erskine and Bell in the eighteenth and nineteenth centuries, we can with confidence attribute our modern criminal law and its administration primarily to Hume in the eighteenth century and the establishment in 1672 for the first time, of a professionally manned High Court of Justiciary.

The first serious attempt to set out the criminal law of Scotland in a systematic way was made by the great King's Advocate Sir George Mackenzie, the moving spirit in the establishment of the Advocates' Library in 1682. In 1678 he published his treatise on "The Laws and Customs of Scotland in matters criminal" and that treatise which reached a second edition in 1699, became the manual of the criminal law of Scotland for 100 years or more.

It is, however, not Mackenzie's work which is recognised as the true foundation of the modern criminal law of Scotland. The true foundations on which that law has been erected were laid down by David Hume, Baron Hume, in 1797, when he published the first edition of his "Commentaries on the Law of Scotland respecting crimes." Hume was one of the great public teachers of law holding the Chair of Scots Law at Edinburgh in succession to Erskine. Sir Walter Scott was one of his students. The last edition of the Commentaries was published in 1844. It was then reviewed by James Craufurd, Lord Ardmillan, a former Advocate-Depute, and Solicitor General, and one of the Lords Commissioners of Justiciary. That review was described in Stair Gillon's article on the criminal law in the Publications of the Stair Society, as a panegyric upon a work which brought order out of chaos, and the author went on to say—"The importance of Hume, therefore, consists in the acceptance among all lawyers which his *magnum opus* has won, since it first appeared in 1797 down to the present day, and the fact that he brings us in direct contact with the sources and repositories. His sturdy nationalism was roused by the insinuating influence of English legal notions alien to those on which Scottish life had been built up. His historic sense rebelled against the loose generalities of Erskine and his references to the Roman Law. And so he resolutely turned to the records. One cannot do better than gather from his own words the stupendous task which he set himself." After telling us how disappointing to him were Forbes' Institutes of the Criminal Law, and Erskine's handling of the subject in the fourth book of the Institute, and pointing out how greatly times had changed since Mackenzie, he proceeds: "In this penury, therefore, of information having, in the course of my duty as Public Teacher of the Law, particularly directed my attention to the department of Crimes; and having gone over the whole series of the Books of Adjournal (so the records of the Court of Justiciary are called), I hope I may at least be excused for the attempt to save others the labour of the like research, for which not many persons can be supposed to have either leisure or inclination."

Hume's work was truly prodigious in providing for us in admirable prose a systematic treatment of the whole field of our native criminal law. The other main general treatise on crimes was the work of Alison—a work which does not measure up as a rival to Hume's but which provides a most valuable supplement to his Commentaries.

The other great influences in the creation of the modern criminal law of Scotland were, I think, four.

1. The unique position of the Lord Advocate as public prosecutor to which I shall return in a moment.

2. The establishment of the High Court of Justiciary in 1672. From 1503 until then the administration of the criminal courts was in the hands of the Justice General, a layman who, with the assistance of his clerk, the Justice Clerk who, after 1532 was always a Senator of the College of Justice and was known as the Lord Justice Clerk, and with the aid of Deputes whom he appointed, tried crime in Edinburgh and on circuit in a wholly unsystematic way, even in those parts of the country where the King's law could be said to run. In 1663 the Lord Justice Clerk was called from the clerk's table to the Bench. In 1671 the office of Justice Depute was abolished, and the constitution of the High Court of Justiciary thereafter consisted of the Lord Justice General (still a layman), the Lord Justice Clerk and five Senators of the College of Justice. It was not until 1830 that the Lord Justice General became a professional lawyer. What was done was simple, for the Lord President became an *eodem officio* Lord Justice General. The last lay holder of that office was the Duke of Montrose who died in 1836.

The final major steps forward were taken in 1887 when the High Court was reconstituted to consist of the Lord Justice General, the Lord Justice Clerk and all the other Senators of the College of Justice who then became Lords Commissioners of Justiciary and, in 1926, when criminal appellate jurisdiction was introduced.

3. The Sheriff Court system. The Sheriff Court is primarily the Scots local court of summary jurisdiction but Sheriffs have jurisdiction also to try on indictment almost every common law crime (with the obvious exceptions of treason, murder and rape) which is suitable to be tried by a court with a power of punishment restricted to two years' imprisonment.

4. The Criminal Procedure Act of 1887, the base legislation upon which successive statutory provisions governing criminal procedure have been constructed.

In what I have said so far I have already mentioned some of the many distinctive features of our criminal law system. Fundamentally, unlike your own criminal law which has suffered statutory intrusions—not all of them happy ones—Scots criminal law has remained based on the common law throughout its history and the Supreme Criminal Courts have long been considered to have "an inherent power, as such, competently to punish every act which is obviously of a criminal nature though it be such which in time past has never been the subject of prosecution!" So said Hume (i. 12), and I do not believe that this proposition has ever been seriously questioned. The scope for judiciary law has been unrivalled. Notwithstanding the Benthamite view that the function of evolving the law is too important to be conceded to the Judiciary, that all legal change must be brought about by the legislature alone, and that a system must find its regularity only in statute, our native criminal law has evolved primarily by judicial law-making which I hope will continue. That being so it is fortunate that we are able to correct our own mistakes by re-examination of doubtful judicial doctrine by convening larger benches of judges. This we do often enough when we are persuaded that decisions of the High Court have taken our law along the wrong track, and when we do it is far from unusual for us to start again at the beginning with Hume himself. Recent examples of this kind of exercise can be found in the cases of *Lambie* v. *H.M. Advocate*[1] and *Brennan* v. *H.M. Advocate*.[2] In the first of these the Court exposed as heretical a practice which had crept in since 1946 of telling juries that there was an *onus* upon an accused person to establish a special defence of alibi, self defence or incrimination. In the second, the Court, after a thorough review of the authorities beginning with *Hume*, held that the Law of Scotland had strayed from the true path in 1921 when it was lightly assumed, following the House of Lords decision in the English case of *Beard*, that if a man accused of murder is shown to have been incapable by reason of self-induced intoxication of forming the intention to kill or to do serious injury to his victim, he will be guilty only of culpable homicide. *Beard* was thus singed from the face of the Law of Scotland. The Court also held that the Law of Scotland did not admit as the sole foundation of a defence of insanity or diminished responsibility, evidence of the transitory effects of self-induced intoxication of whatever degree.

Not only may the substantive law be contrasted with the substantive criminal law of England. Leaving out of account altogether statutory crimes and offences common to both systems, the law of Scotland is to be distinguished, too, most sharply in our system of prosecution and in the unique office of the Lord Advocate. Save for one or two unimportant statutory exceptions the Lord Advocate is alone responsible for all criminal prosecutions in Scotland, and prosecutions are conducted in the High Court by himself, and his Advocates Depute including the Solicitor General, and in the Sheriff Court by his procurators-fiscal. Private prosecution in Scotland, while still competent in certain very limited circumstances, is virtually unknown. You will not, of course, be unaware that as the result of certain recent well publicised events an application is now before the Court for leave to mount one. The Police in Scotland are not concerned at all with prosecution. Their role is the investigation of crime and the reporting of the results to the appropriate Procurator-Fiscal for consideration. The Lord Advocate, further, is, in our law, the master of the instance. Just as he and he alone decides, independently and impartially, whether or not to prosecute and, upon the contents of all indictments and complaints, he and he alone, subject only to the new statutory power of the Court at the close of a Crown case to acquit an accused if there is no case to answer, may bring a trial or prosecution to a premature end.

The function of the Lord Advocate, the Courts, and the Police are distinct and complementary. The boundaries of the role of each are sharply defined. As a result there is no question in Scotland of the Courts ever becoming involved in plea-bargaining or of attempting to interfere with the Lord Advocate's discretion in the matter of who shall be prosecuted to a verdict on what charges—a verdict which may be returned by a simple majority of a jury of fifteen.

Other differences abound. Not least are the differences in procedure. In particular there are in Scotland no committal proceedings. Indictments must be served within 12 months after the first appearance of an accused in court on being arrested on Petition. In particular the power to detain an untried prisoner is severely restricted. When he has been committed and detained an indictment must be served within 80 days and his trial must begin within 110 days. If there is a failure to observe either time limit, which may only be extended by the Court in exceptional circumstances not attributable to fault on the part of the prosecutor, the accused goes free for ever from prosecution for the offence in question. There is a similar safeguard in summary proceedings. No person detained for more than 40 days may be tried upon summary complaint. There is no pre-trial publicity. In trials themselves there are no opening speeches from Counsel, and there is no obligation on a judge in charging a jury to rehearse the evidence. A judge will only deal with evidence in his charge if, in the particular circumstances of any case, it is desirable to do so for the jury's assistance. Further, no conviction may be returned save upon corroborated evidence a rule which I regard as of major importance in reducing the risk of the wrongful conviction of the innocent. Lastly, I might mention the apparent difference in the length of trials as between Scotland and England. Criminals in Scotland and England commit similar crimes and Scots lawyers read with some mystification that trials of persons accused of crimes of relatively commonplace character—and murder, alas, is one example—appear to last for months rather than days or, at the most, a week or two, which would be the norm in Scotland. In Scotland one expects trials to be completed in days rather than weeks and if a trial lasts more than a week or two one becomes concerned immediately to ask why. Why there should be this apparent difference in the length of trials is not obvious. In any event it is not for me to hazard an answer and one can only admire the English Judges and juries who appear to be possessed of a fortitude and patience far beyond the call of duty. Lengthy trials on any view are not calculated to promote the return of sound verdicts, and, as a judicial realist with an interest in trying as far as possible to avoid tiring and confusing juries, I wholly support the determination of Scots Judges—all of whom have had criminal law experience before elevation to the Bench—to curb, when they detect it, any unnecessary elaboration of evidence or any form of time-wasting at all.

There are two further observations which I would like to make. The first is that the Sheriff Court in its summary jurisdiction makes an interesting study in itself. With the possible exception of the Sheriff Court at Glasgow, which has special problems attributable to inadequate accommodation and resources, it is certainly expeditious in its disposal of minor offences both at common law and under statute and, on the whole, in the hands of its professional judges, the Sheriffs, and subject to the rights of appeal by stated case in much improved form since the Criminal Justice (Scotland) Act 1980, it works reasonably well.

The second is that, as a result of the Social Work (Scotland) Act 1968 the prosecution of children in the Courts of Law has been restricted. The system of dealing with child offenders which the Act created has, I think, now proved its value and it is interesting to observe in the criminal statistics for 1979 that the number of children prosecuted for crimes and offences fell to 1,055, the lowest figure since the Act came into operation in 1971.

I am conscious that in this paper I have laid myself open to the charge that I have done little more than to offer a child's guide to the legal history of Scotland together with a necessarily selective account of some of the distinctive features of the law of Scotland. If anything I have said, however, encourages a single scholar of this great Club to think that Scots Law may be worthy of some comparative study, I shall be content.

Notes

[1] 1973 J.C. 53.
[2] 1977 J.C. 38.

Fiscal Finesse: Tax Avoidance and the Duke of Westminster

HUBERT H. MONROE, Q.C.

IN his amusing collection of essays, *Essays in Satire*, Father Ronald Knox included one entitled "The New Sin." This told how an announcement appeared in the Morning Post to the effect that on a particular evening in the year a lecture would be delivered in the Albert Hall entitled "The New Sin." Came the evening and naturally the Albert Hall was packed. The vast audience awaited the arrival of the lecturer in a mood of suppressed excitement. A short, stocky middle aged man, apparently of European origin came on to the platform. He had endured, he explained, great torment of mind. Should he, or should he not, disclose to his audience, so obviously eager to learn, the details of the New Sin. After much heart searching he had reached the reluctant conclusion that it would be morally indefensible to expose them to the temptations inherent in such knowledge. He would bid them good-night. He had nothing more to say.

Similar disappointment must await those who entertained any expectation of a searching denouement of the latest fashions in tax avoidance, as also those who nourished more modest hopes of at least hearing a coherent exposition of the current state of the law. The truth is that just at present the law relating to tax avoidance is in what can only be described as a Heraclitan state of flux. Questions rather than answers abound. How has the law got to the point which it has reached? In what direction is it likely to proceed from here?

The *Westminster*[1] case provides a starting point since it is frequently, if perhaps rather unfairly, identified as some kind of tax avoider's charter. Recently Lord Diplock acknowledged the pervasive influence attributed to the case when he spoke of the blinkers that the court is enjoined to wear by the *Westminster* decision in revenue cases. The case itself involved no more than modest reliance on a relieving provision expressly included in the tax code. By committing himself for a period capable of exceeding six years the taxpayer could effectively at that time transfer a slice of his income from himself, a high surtax payer, to another less fortunately circumstanced who would pay income tax on the income so transferred at a less exacting rate. The taxpayer suggested to several of his personal servants that they might accept such transfers of portions of his income as adequate acknowledgment of the value of their services without looking for wages as well. Once it was accepted that wages could have been demanded, the rest followed. The covenants were for tax purposes effective transfers of income. There was no obvious reason why the legal effect of the covenants should be displaced in favour of the alleged substance of the transactions. At best, the proposition that the covenanted payments were payments of wages was dubious. The authorities reacted predictably. The war occasioned some delay but at an early opportunity, 1946 in fact, the gap was plugged.

Meanwhile, however, their Lordships had discharged some weighty sentiments and for these, perhaps, the price to be paid was rather more than just the cost of plugging a hole. "Every man is entitled if he can," declared Lord Tomlin, "to order his affairs so that the tax attaching under the appropriate Acts is less than it otherwise would be. If he succeeds in ordering them so as to secure this result, then, however unappreciative the Commissioners of Inland Revenue or his fellow taxpayers may be of his ingenuity, he cannot be compelled to pay an increased tax. This so-called doctrine of 'the substance' seems to me to be nothing more than an attempt to make a man pay notwithstanding that he has so ordered his affairs that the amount of tax sought from him is not legally claimable." Ringing sentiments, roundly expressed. All the pent-up dislike of tax and taxing authorities characteristic of judges no less than of other citizens expressed in a resounding constitutional declaration and the real legal problem quietly shelved for another 40 years or so. Just how is the legal effect of a contrived series of transactions designed to exploit some relieving provision in the tax code to be determined? Must each step be regarded quite separately and as a transaction taking effect independently of the scheme as a whole? Is it proper to take note of the result which the parties to the series of transactions intended to achieve? Or must the effect of each separate step according to its declared form prevail over the aggregate result of the series of steps?

The question left unanswered in the *Westminster* case had received no comprehensive answer by the time the *Plummer*[2] case reached the House of Lords in 1979. There were not lacking citizens to accept Lord Tomlin's implied invitation to order their affairs with a view to reducing the incidence of tax, nor were there lacking citizens who, for a fee, would assist them in threading their way through the maze of the tax code and demonstrate how best to take advantage of the relieving provisions so thoughtfully provided by the authors of the code. How schemes devised to take advantage of such provisions were to be approached and the legal effect of the steps taken pursuant to such schemes determined, remained unresolved questions.

The *Plummer* scheme, as so often in such cases, was positively breath-taking in its neat simplicity. It exploited the same relieving provision as had been relied on in the *Westminster* case, an application of the notion that annual payments reduce a taxpayer's total income. The taxpayer would undertake to make a series of annual payments in return for a lump sum. The scheme purveyor would arrange for a company with charitable objects to be the recipient of the annuity. The purveyor would also arrange for the necessary lump sum to be produced. It would not be handed over to the taxpayer but would be made available in the form of a series of promissory notes each equal to the annuity payment due to be paid in successive years. These would conveniently be retained as security for the taxpayer's undertaking to pay the annuity. The purveyor would arrange overdraft facilities and the taxpayer would then make each annuity payment on overdraft and the corresponding promissory note would be released and the overdraft would be repaid. Reduced to essentials the scheme came to this: for a fee the purveyor purported to make available a lump sum representing the price of the taxpayer's undertaking to pay an annuity. As each annuity payment was made an instalment of the lump sum was moved in to fill the gap. The money went quietly round in a circle. At the end of the selected period of circulation the taxpayer was no richer and no poorer save that he could claim to have made annual payments which reduced his total income and the recipient charitable company could claim to have received annual payments on which tax was recoverable. (This particular aspect of the scheme broke down but that was coincidental.)

The Revenue attacked the scheme under a number of heads. For present purposes one only is significant. It was argued that the so-called annuity payments were no more than instalment repayments of the deposited lump sum. "If it were possible to disregard the legal form of the documents and to look beyond them for an underlying substance," said Lord Wilberforce, "there would be attractions—beyond those of ingenuity—in this argument." Lord Wilberforce felt constrained to reject the argument. He did not mention the *Westminster* case by name, but presumably it was that case which dictated the result: the answer to the question what was the legal effect of the arrangement entered into by the taxpayer was the effect which the documents purported to achieve. The taxpayer signed an agreement to pay an annuity: so, he paid an annuity. The arrangement for dealing with the lump sum was something separate, a matter of convenience. The lump sum was paid to the taxpayer. It became his money. He could deal with it as he chose. He chose to apply it in acquiring the promissory notes which would finance his annuity payments. Lord Fraser of Tullybelton agreed with Lord Wilberforce. "In practice, of course," he said, "the £2,500 invested in promissory notes was the obvious source from which the annuity payments were to be made, but it was only a matter of convenience and if the respondent had chosen to make all or any of the payments from some other source, he was free to do so." Lord Keith of Kinkel concurred and that carried the day for the scheme on that point, the agreement to make annual payments must be taken at its face value.

What, if any, conclusion is to be drawn from this first part of the *Plummer* decision? The decision appears to represent a final flowering of the unalloyed *Westminster* principle: you are to take a taxpayer's document at its face value. If he signs an agreement to make annual payments, that is the legal transaction he effects. The payments which he makes pursuant to that agreement must be identified as annual payments regardless of the context and without reference to the arrangements made for discharging the payments. Lord Fraser dismissed those arrangements as only a matter of convenience. Is it to be worldly wise—a form of wisdom to be distinguished perhaps from judicial wisdom—to suggest that in the context of a tax avoidance scheme the manner in which the scheme is carried out may indeed be presented as no more than a matter of convenience but usually it is also of the essence of the whole arrangement? Consider the scheme in all its simple brilliance. Apart from the fee, and possibly a small topping-up figure, the taxpayer did not have to pay a penny piece. Purveyor provided lump sum: lump sum provided annual payments: annual payments went back round to repay lump sum. Lord Dilhorne took a different view to that taken by his colleagues. He looked at the arrangements made for implementing the scheme and found each annual payment of £500 to be nothing other than repayment of part of the £2,500 received as the price of the annuity and applied in purchasing promissory notes. Did Lord Dilhorne then substitute his view of the substance of the scheme for the legal effect of the agreement made? Or does the key lie in the extent to which the manner in which it is agreed to implement an agreement may affect the agreement itself?

In *Ramsay*[3] Lord Wilberforce identified the *Plummer* case as a case in which it was legitimate to have regard to all the arrangements as a whole. The conclusion, however, was that there was commercial reality in the arrangements and accordingly they should be upheld. The arrangements amounted to a covenant, for a capital sum, to make annual payments, coupled with security arrangements for the payments. The critical question seems now to be: what more was there in *Ramsay*?

Ramsay also involved a scheme under which, apart from the fee, the taxpayer company would not have to find any money. The object of the scheme was to provide the taxpayer company, which had realised a real gain, with a loss which could be set off against that gain. The capital gains tax code exempts from charge debts not being debts on a security. The essence of the scheme, therefore, was that the taxpayer company should make the required loss on the liquidation of a company provided for the purpose for shares in which it would have subscribed, and that this allowable loss should be matched by a non-chargeable gain on a loan for which the taxpayer company would also subscribe of which the terms could be so manipulated that the holder could collect a substantial and, it was hoped, tax-free gain. In fact, the scheme failed for the House of Lords held the loan—the gain on which had been confidently expected to be tax free—to be a debt on a security. On that basis there was indeed a loss but instead of a tax-free balancing gain, a taxable gain and no relief to set against the real gain which it was the object of the scheme to relieve. The importance of the case for present purposes, however, is the success of the argument, advanced quite independently of the successful assertion that the scheme was technically defective, that the scheme should simply be disregarded as artificial and fiscally ineffective.

Lord Wilberforce prefaced his statement of the new approach with a valuable reassertion of certain long standing principles, four in number.

(1) *The first principle*. When a taxing act has to be construed, the courts are not confined to literal interpretation. There may, indeed, should, be considered the context and scheme of the relevant Act as a whole, and its purpose may, indeed should, be regarded.

This is indeed a welcome new approach or, if that be an emotive phrase, a welcome restatement of the proper approach. There is still, and will still be, ample scope for disagreement and diverging views, but at least it will be a relief not to be exposed to the unabated fire of the critical purists if one supposes that those who framed the code had a coherent purpose and contemplated that the tax would work out in a reasonable and comprehensive manner.

(2) *The second principle*. The taxpayer can still organise his affairs to reduce the incidence of tax. What he does is to be judged according to its legal effect.

In fact it may in due course be found that the new approach does impinge upon this principle. For a distinct change in the technique of analysing the legal effect is inherent in the new approach. The tax avoiding context is not to be ignored. Once the existence of a scheme is recognised as designed to produce tax consequences without producing other significant economic consequences, the legal effect of the various steps involved in the scheme is, according to the new approach, to be analysed accordingly.

(3) *The third principle*. Documents and transactions are either genuine or sham. Those that are genuine are, in law, what they purport to be. Those that are sham profess to be one thing but, in fact, are something different. It is for the fact-finding commissioners to find whether a document or transaction is genuine or sham. This is a different principle even if it has been part of the law for a very long time. In the absence of any reported cases where the fact-finding attempts of commissioners have received appropriate correction from the courts, the system does not permit us to know whether there are any circumstances in which scheme documents and transactions can or should be classified as sham. What arguments the authorities habitually advance or what reactions they obtain from the fact-finding commissioners, all these matters must remain a closed book until the vagaries of the system throw up a reported case in which the issue, genuine or sham, is raised on appeal and illuminated by judicial wisdom. There is just this difficulty in the concept. The pattern of many avoidance devices is predictable. Allowable loss, allowable deduction, allowable relief to be matched by a non-chargeable gain, non-taxable receipt or tax free accretion. The purpose of the scheme's purveyor is to present a genuine loss or payment. His purpose will not be served by a sham loss or payment, by some other document or transaction masquerading as, say, a disposal at a loss or as a payment of interest. He is, therefore, unlikely to rely on a sham document or transaction. It seems possible that the sham principle will remain unexplored for the time being and the fact-finding commissioners uninstructed in how to distinguish between genuine and sham documents and transactions. The more fruitful way ahead may lie with the modification to the fourth principle involved in the new approach.

(4) *The fourth principle*. Given that a document or transaction is genuine, the court cannot go behind it to some supposed underlying substance. But if it can be seen that a document or transaction was intended to have effect as part of a nexus or series of transactions, or as an ingredient of a wider transaction intended as a whole, so to regard the transaction is not to prefer substance to form.

It is in modifying the proposition that you cannot go behind a transaction, that you must take it at its face value, that the House of Lords in the new approach would seem to have broken significant new ground. If all the steps taken in a planned series of transactions may be considered together rather than one by one in isolation, and if their effect in law may be taken to be the effect of the series, then the chances of arriving at a realistic assessment of any average tax avoidance scheme must be greatly increased.

It may be questioned whether the *Westminster* case ever did impose on courts the blinkers which it is alleged to have imposed. There was no series of transactions involved in that case with one transaction at one end of the series expressly designed to cancel out another transaction at the other end. There was a simple deed of covenant and a simple act of forbearance by the recipient of the covenanted sums. But, of course, it is not what was decided that matters, rather what is thought to have been decided. The myth is the message. And tax myths can be strong and emotive. In this case the message was strong: transactions had to be accepted as they were presented. If the transaction in question was not challenged as a sham transaction but accepted as genuine, there was no looking to the context, just as time and again there was no looking to the context to discover what a statutory provision meant. The strength of the precedent and the inhibitions which the system imposes are not far below the surface when the speeches in the *Ramsay* case are read. Lord Wilberforce, having cited robust American authorities which use such frank phrases as "sham" and "facade" to describe features frequently found in tax avoidance schemes, refers almost wistfully to our different system allowing less legislative power to the courts than the U.S. courts claim to exercise. In fostering a system under which judges in the House of Lords must continually guard against legislating and confine themselves rigorously to the legitimate judicial activity of interpreting the law, may we not be in danger of unnecessarily depriving ourselves of a sensitive and flexible technique for tempering the law to the shorn body of taxpayers?

Again, the system requires the judges in the House of Lords to lay claim to an infallibility which many of them might well be reluctant to acknowledge. When the tax avoidance device of dividend stripping engaged the attention of the House of Lords in the sixties the same evident dislike of tax and the same rigidity of analysis set the scene. In 1960, in the *Harrison (Watford)*[4] case, the Special Commissioners had found the dividend strippers' cunningly contrived transactions not to be trading. But that was patently absurd: there was a purchase, there was a strip, there was a sale. Obviously there was trading. It was eleven years before the absurdity of the sixties became the orthodoxy of the seventies. In the *FA and AB*[5] case some distinguished the earlier case, some declared it to have been wrongly decided. While the techniques of tax avoidance had progressed and been technically improved, the courts had not been obliged to stand still. And so again today, the time lag between *Plummer* and *Ramsay* is shorter. The *Westminster* case has not been reversed or distinguished. But a new approach has been adopted: the *Westminster* myth has been exploded.

The basis of the *Ramsay* decision would seem to be this: there was a cunningly contrived scheme; money would be provided to enable the taxpayer seeking relief to invest in shares; money would be provided to enable the taxpayer to invest in loans; one loan would be vastly inflated in value as the other subsided; the inflated loan would be disposed of at a gain and the shares realised at a corresponding loss; the money would move round the circle; the taxpayer, apart from the fee, would be no richer and no poorer but he could claim a capital loss for tax purposes. Taking the scheme as a whole, there was no gain and no loss. The claim to have created a capital loss for tax purposes consequently failed.

If the new approach advanced no further, if *Ramsay* ended with the triumph of reality and the discomfiture of the purveyors of avoidance devices, those whose task it is to apply the law of tax to everyday human situations in unfashionable obscurity might heave a sigh of contentment and return to their unglamorous task knowing, at least, what to look out for.

But the new approach does not stop at *Ramsay*. It sweeps on to *Burmah*,[6] identified as a case involving a preordained series of transactions (whether or not they include the achievement of a legitimate commercial end) into which there are inserted steps that have no commercial purpose apart from the avoidance of a liability to tax which in the absence of those particular steps would have been payable. *Burmah* had a subsidiary. The subsidiary owed *Burmah* a substantial sum of money. As matters stood, there was little chance of the subsidiary paying the sum owed and no chance of *Burmah* obtaining tax relief for the loss which the debt represented since the debt was not a debt on a security. *Burmah* accordingly put additional money into its subsidiary by way of taking up a rights issue of shares. The money was used to pay off the debt and having been used for that purpose was gone from the subsidiary which consequently on liquidation threw up a loss. Could there be tax relief for that loss? No—said the House of Lords—it must be disregarded as artificial.

The decision was represented as an application of the *Ramsay* principle. The claim to have suffered a loss failed because the loss was not a real loss. The subsidiary had originally become indebted to *Burmah* in 1969 in an amount of approximately £380 million representing the price agreed to be paid for a holding of BP shares. In 1971 *Burmah* repurchased the BP shares but by that time the value had fallen and the price was no more than £220 million or so. The subsidiary was left owing *Burmah* approximately £160 million. There were other transactions involving other subsidiaries but, in essence, *Burmah* put up £160 million for additional shares and that money discharged the debt, moving back round the circle. At the end of the series of planned transactions *Burmah* was no richer and no poorer than previously but whereas previously it had had a valueless debt owed by its subsidiary and representing a non-allowable loss of £160 million, now it had some valueless shares representing, it hoped, an allowable loss of similar amount. The House of Lords put emphasis on *Burmah*'s retention of the BP shares. As to them *Burmah* had suffered a real but unrealised loss: as to the subsidiary's indebtedness and shares there was a realised but seemingly unreal loss.

The disturbing feature of the *Burmah* case is not so much the result as the implications. The rules relating to groups of companies are no less capable of operating harshly than in this case they were seemingly capable of being manipulated to the group's advantage, if indeed to register the loss which *Burmah* had incurred in relation to its subsidiary was to manipulate the rules to the group's advantage. Had there been a profit on the liquidation of the subsidiary one would take leave to doubt whether hesitation would have been displayed in taxing the profit because the BP shares were still retained in the *Burmah* group and might—the emphasis is on the possibility—subsequently be realised at a profit. Experience suggests that there is a wealth of difference in real life between the sort of steps taken by *Burmah* and the scheme purchased by *Ramsay*. The difference is not easy to define, some will doubtless argue that it is too refined to detect. But must every planned course of action undertaken for commercial reasons be scrutinised for fear that it contains a step designed to avoid an avoidable liability for tax? Can we dispense with section 460 of the Taxes Act and tax simply by eliminating artificial steps? What, if any, is the limit of the new approach?

In a penetrating, careful and much to be valued judgment in *Furniss* v. *Dawson*[7] Mr Justice Vinelott provides an answer, at least temporarily. He offers a reconciliation of the *Burmah* decision with the *Ramsay* decision which, at least until it is displaced, will restore to some of us a measure of confidence in the touching belief that rational analysis of tax decisions is possible. *Ramsay* was a case of no real loss. Obviously so since the whole point of the scheme was that the purveyor provided the taxpayer with the means of recording a tax loss (similar to the loss sustained by *Burmah*), while at the same time receiving a non-taxable gain (or, at least, so it was planned to be) to balance the loss. The essence of the scheme was that there should be no real loss.

It is less obvious that there was no real loss in *Burmah*. As between *Burmah* and its subsidiary there was a potential loss of £160 million. Mr Justice Vinelott offers an explanation when he points out that the new approach is not to be confined to cases where the steps taken in the furtherance of a single composite scheme are circular or self-cancelling. The Court, he points out, may disregard a transaction and treat it as fiscally a nullity even though there is a change in the legal position of the parties before and after the scheme is carried through if that change can be regarded as a mere change of form with no enduring legal consequences. When the *Burmah* scheme was completed the subsidiary no longer owed *Burmah* £160 million. The debt had been repaid and replaced by money subscribed on the issue of additional shares in the subsidiary. The subsidiary was no longer a debtor. But this was a change which could be treated as a mere change of form. The change in *Burmah's* position from creditor to contributor could not affect third parties and could have no enduring effect since it was all part of the scheme that the subsidiary should be wound up. Consequently the loss on the liquidation was not a real loss.

Should the transactions in question in *Furniss* v. *Dawson* be regarded as fiscally ineffective because no more than a mere change of form? The transactions consisted of an exchange of shares in X Ltd. by A for shares in B Ltd. which A controlled and the sale on by B Ltd. of the shares in X Ltd. to C Ltd. A claimed, quite properly, that the exchange of shares in X Ltd. for shares in B Ltd. was a transaction which the capital gains tax code expressly contemplated should be free of tax. The sale on by B Ltd. threw up no taxable gain and the effect of the transaction was simply that A had postponed payment of capital gains tax for the time being on any gain derived from the disposal of the shares in X Ltd.

The tax authorities, however, clearly regarded the whole transaction as very much more sinister. Amongst other arguments advanced was one to the effect that the entire transaction looked at as a whole was so invaded by fiscal considerations as to lose its character, and because of the fiscal considerations the corporate identity of B Ltd. should be pierced and B Ltd. recognised as the alter ego of A. Tax, is, as I have already mentioned, an emotive subject; but if *Ramsay* and *Burmah* are to be regarded as justification for piercing a company's corporate identity and identifying the company as the alter ego of its shareholders, then the *Westminster* case is indeed overthrown and the anathematised doctrine of the substance rides again with a vengeance.

Mr Justice Vinelott, however, thought not. The transfer by A of the shares in X Ltd. to B Ltd. and the subsequent sale of those shares by B Ltd. to C Ltd. produced legal results which differed from what would have been the legal results of a direct sale by A of the shares in X Ltd. to C Ltd. Merely because the sale on of the shares by B Ltd. to C Ltd. was in contemplation from the outset, the judge declined to substitute for the legal agreements which the parties were found actually to have made, the substance of an agreement which they might have made and which would have produced a different legal result.

So far, so good. There at least is a limit to the process of excising intermediate transactions which have been introduced into a series of transactions to produce a fiscal result. Not the least valuable part of Mr Justice Vinelott's judgment is his discussion of what conclusions are to be drawn from *Floor* v. *Davis*.[8] Seemingly a minority view expressed in the Court of Appeal has received approval in two speeches in the House of Lords. Interpretation of the law, clearly falling short of legislation, in such an indirect and inferential manner introduces a new hazard for those of us who must discharge their judicial function beneath three layers of appellate courts by whose experienced wisdom we must at all times be guided to correct conclusions. Lord Justice Eveleigh seems to have been attracted by the alter ego theory of the intermediate purchaser/vendor. He reckoned that in similar circumstances the shares in X Ltd. were sold by A to C Ltd. because at all times A controlled B Ltd., the intermediate purchaser/vendor. The transfer of the shares to B Ltd. was but a step in the process of transferring the shares from A to C Ltd.

Mr Justice Vinelott has pointed out that in *Floor* v. *Davis* the proceeds of sale of the shares in X Ltd. emerged as part of the whole scheme and were in effect at the disposal of A. To treat the intermediate steps, the disposal by A of the shares to B Ltd. and the disposal on of the shares by B Ltd. to C Ltd., as steps to be left out of account on the *Ramsay* principle was, therefore, consistent since in *Floor* v. *Davis* those intermediate steps had no enduring effect on the rights and obligations of the parties after the completion of the scheme. It was otherwise in the case with which the Judge was concerned. It was no part of the scheme that the proceeds of sale of the shares when sold by B Ltd. the intermediate purchaser/vendor, to C Ltd., the ultimate purchaser, should be put at the disposal of A. For the moment A remains untaxed. It will be interesting to learn in due course whether he continues to enjoy that state or whether the authorities, restlessly seeking the real, will succeed in taxing him on the unreal gain which he has not yet realised.

Are there any conclusions to be drawn from this troubled review of the uncertainties which presently surround the law relating to tax avoidance?

As the history of dividend-stripping showed, the most effective counter to avoidance is not always ad hoc legislation, not always even a consistent and coherent campaign conducted through the courts, but sometimes a recasting of the tax code. The exploitable reliefs, allowable losses, deductions for interest or annual payments, tax-free disposals of interests under trusts, are all reasonably predictable. Indeed, there must have been occasions over the past twenty years or so when some of the more ingenious purveyors of schemes must have wondered whether they were not shooting at sitting ducks. In that same period many suggestions have been made for engaging those of diverse expertise to come together to keep the tax code under constant review. Might there not be merit in subjecting the code to a continuous public scrutiny with a view to considering suggestions for eliminating features which lend themselves to exploitation through schemes? May it not also be the case that through such a scrutiny some proponents of sophisticated systems might learn that the price to be paid for an intelligible, workable code may sometimes be a rougher and readier justice than they are accustomed to claim?

As to the decisions of the Courts, there have, of course, been proposals put forward by responsible bodies from time to time urging a reduction in the number of levels of appeal. The uncertainty introduced by the inevitable time lag between the dawn of doubt when a case is first decided by appeal commissioners and the final setting to rest of all doubts by the illumination of the House of Lords must make difficult tasks for many concerned, even more difficult. A reduction of the flux period would find a high place on my list of reasons for urging that England might take a leaf from Scotland's book in the matter of appeals.

For the rest, it is much to be hoped that the new approach to statutory interpretation will catch on and that comprehensive consideration of the code's purpose will become a legitimate exercise in tax cases.

Finally, and at the risk of repetition, I must express the hope that these difficult tax avoidance cases, so often destructive of normal standards of mutual trust and mutual confidence between those concerned with them in their various professional capacities, will be approached, argued and decided in an atmosphere of that indifference to which the Book of Common Prayer refers as a desirable ingredient, along with truth, in the proper administration of justice.

Notes

[1] *I.R.C.* v. *Duke of Westminster* [1936] A.C. 1; 19 T.C. 490.
[2] *I.R.C.* v. *Plummer* [1980] A.C. 896; [1979] S.T.C. 793.
[3] *W.T. Ramsay Ltd.* v. *I.R.C.* [1981] S.T.C. 174.
[4] *Harrison (Watford) Ltd.* v. *Griffiths* [1963] A.C. 1; 40 T.C. 281.
[5] *Lupton* v. *F.A. & A.B. Ltd.* [1972] A.C. 634; 47 T.C. 580.
[6] *I.R.C.* v. *Burmah Oil Co. Ltd.* [1982] S.T.C. 30.
[7] *Furniss* v. *Dawson* [1982] *Simon's Tax Intelligence*, p.7.
[8] *Floor* v. *Davis* [1980] A.C. 695.

Restitution and Wrongs

PETER B.H. BIRKS

THIS is an intractable subject. Which is why treatments of it multiply. Of recent contributions I want to single out the well-known article by J. Beatson of Merton College, Oxford.[1] I am going to disagree with it, and quite radically. But, as often happens, the scholar with whom one publicly disagrees is the very one from whom one has learned most. Right or wrong my different views on the subject owe much to his.

My limited aim is to try to prove that some of our difficulties are due to the fact that, in a way which we have failed to recognise, "Restitution and Wrongs" is really two subjects, not one. The essential preliminary is to stabilise some aspects of the meaning of "wrong" and "restitution." Each requires more space than it can have.

First, "wrong." The subject of the paper is chiefly the phenomenon traditionally called waiver of tort, but what is said applies no less to breaches of equitable and statutory duty, and also, in principle, to breaches of contract. "Wrong" is chosen as a word which includes but has a rather wider sweep than "tort." There is no use trying to define a wrong in terms of blameworthiness. Conversion, which occupies the centre of this stage, is an obvious example of a wrong which can be committed without fault. So the sense I have in mind is "any event which triggers legal consequences between plaintiff and defendant by reason of being characterised as a breach of duty."[2]

Next, "restitution." The vital point is that, differently from "contract" or "wrong" or, on the lower level of generality, from "tort," "breach of equitable duty" and "breach of statutory duty," the word "restitution" does not denote a composite event in the world which causes legal consequences to happen. Another way of putting this is to say that "restitution" is not a cause of action, not a cause for asserting that legal consequences favourable to oneself have been generated. It belongs in the series of words which includes "compensation" and "punishment," a response and not a trigger. If you draw out a grid on a sheet of paper and then, choosing your level of generality, enter causative events along the top, responses such as restitution, compensation and punishment will belong down the side, naming the horizontal columns.[3]. The horizontal column labelled "restitution" will cut across the vertical columns labelled "contract," "wrongs" and so on. In each square formed by the intersection the question will be whether the law does actually include examples of restitution triggered by the event named at the top, contract, wrongs and so on.

The point of labouring this is to be proof against statements of this kind: "Our claim arises not in tort but in restitution."[4] The two terms in supposed opposition come from different series. At the zoo one might as well say of a particular tawny animal, "It is a meat-eater, not a lion."

If restitution is not an event but a response, similar to compensation but differently measured, we have to say briefly what its nature is. This has to be done here dogmatically, without argument. So, restitution consists in the creation and enforcement of rights such as cause a defendant to give up to a plaintiff a benefit received at his expense or its value in money.[5]

I. *TWO CLASSES OF CASE*

In *United Australia* the question was whether the bringing of an action for restitution of the proceeds of a conversion was enough, without judgment or recovery, to bar a second action for compensation in respect of the same tort.[6] Answered negatively. One argument to the contrary had been that the first action rested on a genuine waiver which once and for all extinguished the wrong. Part of the reply to that argument went like this: the plaintiff who claims restitution cannot be said to extinguish the wrong because he has no cause of action but the wrong; the basis of his claim, whether he seeks compensation or restitution, is one and the same, the tort itself.[7]

As a general proposition that is not correct. Beatson's article proves that, conclusively. But nor is it true—and this is where we part company—that a plaintiff claiming restitution always has a cause of action independent of the wrong. There is one class of case in which he need not rely on the wrong, because he has an alternative cause of action. There is a second class in which he does base himself on the wrong but nevertheless goes for restitution rather than compensation. *United Australia*, as it happens, has facts which belong to the former category. That has practical consequences but does not touch the actual decision that an unsatisfied claim for restitution leaves open a later action for compensation.

A. *The First Class: Two Separate Causes of Action*

Here the victim of an acquisitive wrong can make out his claim to restitution without relying on the event in its character as a wrong. If he takes this course he does not extinguish or waive the wrong any more than he relies upon it. He simply ignores it. The fact that the event happens also to be a tort or other breach of duty is irrelevant. I shall give examples—they are only examples not an exhaustive list—and then conclude this section with an attempt to generalise the principle which they illustrate.

1. *Cases within the ratio of restitution for mistake*

If I pay you £100 by mistake then, subject to detailed and continually disputed tests and exceptions, you come under a restitutionary obligation to pay me an equivalent sum. Nobody will say that that obligation is triggered by a wrong. There need be neither blame nor technical breach of duty in your receiving the money.[8] Beneath the mass of detail, mostly meant to stop this kind of restitution being too easy and in that way to recognise the interest which recipients have in the security of their receipts, the reason for restitution is that I did not mean you to have the money. My intent to transfer it to you was vitiated by my false supposition.

It is not necessary to go beyond this simple outline to see that many wrongful acquisitions will come within its ratio. That is to say, they will also be cases of transfer without, or with vitiated, consent. Suppose you come to my house while I am away and break my door and steal £100.[9] If I can have restitution of a mistaken payment where my intent to give was vitiated, then *a fortiori* I must be entitled to restitution of a sum which has moved across absolutely without my knowledge. The claim to restitution does not have to rest on the trespass. It can be based simply on the non-voluntary transfer.

There are many versions of this same story. In *United Australia* itself[10] the fraudulent secretary of the appellant company had received a cheque payable to the company and had secretly endorsed it in favour of another company in which he had an interest, M.F.G. Ltd., the defendant in the first action. The effect was that funds of the appellant company were directed to M.F.G. Ltd. absolutely without the appellant company's knowledge. The secretary converted the cheque. So did M.F.G. Ltd. So did the collecting bank, defendant to the second action. But to show that there was a non-voluntary transfer within what is routinely exemplified by a mistaken payment the appellant company had no need to rely on these events in their character as conversions.

The same is true of a finder. Suppose I lose my wallet. You find it and after keeping it for a while you decide that you might as well spend the money. Again it is *a fortiori* from mistake and I can therefore recover without having to say that you committed any wrong. In the little case of *Moffatt* v. *Kazana*[11] a vendor left a biscuit tin full of pound notes in his loft when he moved house. He completely forgot it. In the course of time a man who came to fit a new cooker for the purchaser found the tin. Its contents were taken to the police and ultimately returned to the purchaser. He put the money into his bank, nearly £2,000. The vendor then made his claim and obtained judgment for that sum. On those facts it is tempting to start thinking of waiver of tort. The judgment rightly does not do so. It is not even necessary to break one's head asking what sort of mistake the plaintiff made. Though within its ratio the facts lie beyond mistake.[12] They make a clear case of transfer without knowledge, the elementary example of non-voluntary transfer.

So far we have been considering transfers of wealth of which the plaintiff was unaware, and the point has been that if one believes in restitution for mistake one has to believe that there is a cause of action in these cases which has no more to do with wrongdoing than does recovery for mistake. The same can be said of a quite different kind of case. Suppose that I insure a cargo of lemons with you. In the false belief that the lemons have perished you pay me their value. That is a payment by mistake, and we know that I must make restitution.[13] Your claim has nothing to do with wrongdoing. Nor do the facts as stated reveal any trace of a wrong. But they might. Let it be given that I concocted the story of the loss. I committed the tort of deceit. But you have your restitutionary claim whether I induced your mistake or not. The addition of the fact of my deceit cannot prevent your ignoring my tort and sticking to the action available to you for mistake. You have two separate causes of action.[14]

This example can be made more complicated. Suppose that the mistake induced by fraud is one of law, not fact. Had it been a spontaneous mistake there would be no recovery, at least not according to traditional orthodoxy. But the deceived payor is entitled to restitution.[15] Does his claim depend on the wrong or can it still be said to be analytically independent? I think the claim can still be based on non-voluntary transfer alone. There is room for long argument. The case for my position is this. The payor spontaneously mistaken as to law is no less a non-voluntary payor than one who is mistaken as to fact. His intent is no less vitiated. In principle he ought to recover. But he comes up against a policy-motivated exception. In a world in which people do not know the law no payment would be safe from recall if such mistakes grounded recovery. So in the interests of stability this kind of restitution, though available in principle, is barred. But where the mistake is induced by fraud the fear of a flood of claims abates, since unlike ignorance of law fraud is not universal. Hence the policy-motivated inhibition of recovery can be limited to the area of its own mischief. Viewing the matter in this way we can say that a payor deceived as to law has the same claim, based not on the tort of deceit but on the neutral fact of non-voluntary payment, as is in principle available to a payor whose mistake is spontaneous. But unlike the latter's his claim is outside the mischief of the *ignorantia iuris* maxim. Undeniably he will in the end have to show that he was deceived, but only for the purpose of dealing with the secondary question whether he is caught by an artificial bar to the claim based on non-voluntary transfer.

2. *Cases within the ratio of restitution for compulsion*

The pattern of argument having been established it should now be possible to proceed more quickly. And besides, Beatson has already done this work.[16] There are many situations in which restitution is available to a plaintiff who has conferred a benefit on a defendant under the influence of some pressure. Sometimes the pressure is inflicted on the plaintiff by the defendant himself, by threats or deeds. Then it is usually called duress or actual undue influence. Sometimes it arises simply from the circumstances, as where an emergency constrains a man to intervene. That can be called moral compulsion, for the pressure operates on the conscience: a decent man cannot hang back when without disproportionate risk to himself he can ward off or reduce some evil eventuality.[17] Sometimes the pressure emanates from a third party, as where he brings the law to bear on the plaintiff[18] for a performance primarily due from the defendant. That is legal compulsion.

In all these cases the underlying reason for restitution, beneath the mass of detail, is the same as in the case of restitution for mistake: non-voluntary transfer. The factor vitiating the plaintiff's intention is different and carries a different set of complicating secondary questions, but the basic idea is the same.

In moral and legal compulsion there is no question of resting the claim to restitution on a wrong. Unless in freak circumstances, there is no trace of one. However, cases of duress frequently disclose two distinct causes of action, one for a wrong and one simply for non-voluntary transfer. Suppose, for example, that you lock me up until I pay you £5,000. That is the tort of false imprisonment. But I can ignore the trespass and have the £5,000 as money had and received relying on the imprisonment not as a wrong but simply as the factor negativing the voluntariness of my payment.[19] Exactly the same can be said when you withhold my goods to make me pay a charge which I do not owe.[20] Or where you refuse to perform a contract with me until I have paid an increased price.[21] I could sue you for the tortious interference with my goods or for the breach of contract, but I can alternatively rely on those stories not as actionable wrongs but simply as compulsion vitiating my consent to the payment. In developing that cause of action nobody ever paused to predict that one day these acts might also be regarded as the tort of intimidation.

In relation to duress there is a complication with a structure similar to the one relating to mistakes of law. There we saw that practical considerations can inhibit a cause of action which in principle should be available. With duress the problem is that some pressures—often strong ones (like threats to sue and refusals to trade at the buyer's price)—have to be tolerated as part of normal life and therefore exempted from the law of restitution. If the position were ever reached in which the test of an unacceptable pressure became whether the pressurising act was itself actionable as a wrong[22] then, for at least as long as that test lasted, it might create the illusion (despite the survival of restitution for moral and legal compulsion) that the cause of action based on compulsion had ceased to be independent. But it would be an illusion, for only the scope of an expedient inhibition of liability would be in question. However, it is neither likely nor desirable that the question whether the pressure amounts to an actionable wrong will ever become more than a guideline. For pressures which are not wrongs cannot safely be regarded as invariably exempt, incapable of triggering restitution. In the criminal law it is clear, in relation to blackmail, that lawful actions and threats, such as the disclosure of discreditable but true facts, can be regarded as unacceptable when used to obtain money. Also, there is a continuum between duress and actual undue influence, and there is no suggestion under the latter head that the conduct complained of must be a wrong actionable as such outside the claim for restitution.[23] The right approach is to ask whether according to the standards of the time the species of pressure applied to the plaintiff ought to be regarded as an acceptable incident of normal life. If yes, it ought to be exempt, otherwise not.

3. *Claims within the ratio of free acceptance*

Free acceptance happens where the recipient of a benefit knows that it is being conferred on him otherwise than as a gift and, having an opportunity to reject, chooses to accept. The reason why it triggers restitution is that the recipient has himself to blame for the transfer of value to him. He could have stopped it. Suppose for example that the owner of a house hangs back in the kitchen when he spies an uninvited window-cleaner. He lurks there till the job is done and then rushes out to protest that he neither wanted nor asked for it to be done. He had his chance. He should have gone out earlier.

Claims based on free acceptance differ markedly from those based on non-voluntary transfer. In free acceptance the cause for restitution is found in the conduct of the defendant recipient. In non-voluntary transfer it is found in the motivation of the plaintiff. Many claims can be put in both ways. If you pay me money by mistake and I know you are mistaken there is non-voluntary transfer on your part and free acceptance on mine. This applies to those cases of secret and fraudulent taking discussed above. I take your money when you are not looking. That too is both non-voluntary transfer by you and free acceptance by me, the strongest possible example of both.

Free acceptance comes into its own where the benefit transferred is not in money but in kind.[24] This is because benefits in kind are prone to the phenomenon of subjective devaluation, and free acceptance renders them immune. So, in the example of the window-cleaner the householder cannot say that the work was something he did not want and as such valueless to him. He chose to accept it. Free acceptance thus goes not only to the reason why he should make restitution of his enrichment (because he has only himself to blame) but also to scotching doubts he might raise as to whether it was an enrichment in the first place (because he cannot say he did not want it). By contrast a window-cleaner who came while you were out and had to rely on non-voluntary transfer would run into difficulties. Suppose he meant to be in Smith Crescent but came to Smith Square instead. His mistake will show the non-voluntary transfer. But of what? You will say you like dirty windows or at least that you always clean them yourself. Your point is that the cleaning is not valuable, not to you whatever may be the case for the generality of mankind. Even against an absent or otherwise non-accepting recipient there are some ways of showing that some benefits in kind are incontrovertibly enriching; but neither window-cleaning nor clean windows is likely to qualify. So this claim will falter on the enrichment issue.

This much orientation enables us to consider tortious acquisition of benefits in kind. Suppose I eat your cake or use your land or lock you up and make you work for me. These are all cases of free acceptance, just like the stealing of money which was mentioned above. So there are quite separate causes of action. Take the cake. There is conversion, perhaps also trespass to goods. And I accept the benefit knowing that you do not intend it as a gift. "Accept" is odd, of course, but only in the sense that it is too mild to describe what I do. If one is liable for free acceptance, *a fortiori* one must be liable if one goes out and seizes the benefit. To make out the claim for restitution on the basis of the free acceptance it is wholly unnecessary to rely on the facts in their character as a wrong. Hence there are indeed two separate causes of action. That proposition makes one vital assumption, namely that I knew the facts. If I was an innocent tortfeasor and thought that the cake was mine, I never had opportunity to stop the transfer of value to me, so that there could not then be said to have been any free acceptance.

This is one way in which *Phillips* v. *Homfray*[25] can be understood. The defendant's *de cuius* (*i.e.* testator) had used the plaintiff's land. He had carried coal over it without asking. The plaintiff ignored the trespass[26] and sought restitution in respect of the benefit thus usurped. The action failed. The reasoning is difficult to follow, but subject to one qualification the conclusion seems right. The trespass was innocent. Because of the mistake there could not be any free acceptance. That is the difference from the earlier cases in which defendants had had to pay reasonably for the services of apprentices tortiously seduced away from their masters.[27] They knew what they were doing and therefore had every opportunity to stop the transfer of value. Against them there were therefore two cases of action, *per quod servitium amisit* and free acceptance.[28]

The qualification is that on the facts of *Phillips* v. *Homfray* it might after all be possible to make out the non-tortious cause of action on the basis of non-voluntary transfer. Since the plaintiff did not assent to the user there is no difficulty under "non-voluntary," so that the question would be whether even without a free acceptance there could be held to have been an incontrovertible economic benefit to the trespasser.[29]

4. *Generalisation*

These examples show that acquisitive wrongs sometimes contain within their facts a wholly separate cause of action of the same kind as is found in cases of mistake, compulsion and free acceptance. The crucial question is whether there is any formula which will alert us to the circumstances in which this duality occurs.

We have already slipped into one degree of generalisation by taking mistake and compulsion together as non-voluntary transfer. One further step can be taken by putting non-voluntary transfer and free acceptance together[30] in the still more general description "unjust enrichment at the expense of another." Thus, payment by mistake is a sub-species of the cause of action in non-voluntary transfer which is in turn a species of the cause of action in unjust enrichment at the expense of another. That is the generic conception of the event which triggers the restitutionary response.

The study of restitution cannot manage without habitual and disciplined recourse to the words of that generic conception. Intellectual chaos is the price of ignoring it. There has to be a stable pattern of reasoning, and only the text of the generic conception can provide one. For instance, every time a claim to restitution is rejected the court must say whether the reason is (i) that contrary to first appearances the defendant was not enriched, or (ii) not at the expense of the plaintiff, or (iii) that the decided cases reveal no ground for characterising the enrichment as unjust and therefore reversible,[31] or (iv) that some other factor inhibits the claim. And every inquiry into a restitutionary problem should be phased according to the same scheme. Only in that way can we hope to find out what the old cases have been doing. It must be said at once, with the maximum emphasis, that in the scheme the word "unjust" has its nose to the cases, not in the air. An enrichment is only "unjust" if the cases show it to be reversible. Fears of appeals to abstract justice are groundless. Yet they are the reason why the words of the generic conception are not regularly used and why there is therefore no shared pattern of thinking in this field. An irony. The fear of chaos has bred chaos.[32]

This is not a digression. The analysis cannot continue except in the framework of this scheme. Our question arises after an acquisitive wrong. It is this. When can you find against the wrongdoer the independent cause of action which is exemplified in restitution for mistake, compulsion and free acceptance? We know that the cause of action so exemplified is, generically stated, unjust enrichment at the expense of another. Or, restated without changed sense but more conveniently (a) enrichment of the defendant (b) at the expense of the plaintiff (c) in circumstances held in the cases to render its retention unjust. It follows that the independent cause of action can be made out against the wrongdoer whenever (a) (b) and (c) can be established against him without relying on the story in its character as a wrong.

As for (a), whether a defendant's acquisition amounts to an enrichment has nothing to do with its being well- or ill-gotten. Then (b), at the plaintiff's expense. There is more in this than meets the eye. The phrase has two senses. In the case of payment by mistake, for example, the defendant is enriched "by subtraction from" the plaintiff. Here "at the expense of" merely indicates movement from one to the other. Suppose, by contrast, that I get £500 from X for beating you up. That £500 can be said to have been obtained at your expense. But it is not obtained "by subtraction from your wealth," only "by doing you wrong." I shall refer to "the subtraction sense" and "the wrong sense" of the phrase. It is obvious that a plaintiff who has to rely on the wrong sense of "at the expense of" will never be able to establish a cause of action which is independent of wrongdoing. Not surprisingly all the examples which have been given of facts which contain two separate causes of action involve a flow of wealth to the defendant from the plaintiff. That is, "at the expense of" always bears the subtraction sense.[33]

At this point we can affirm that the separate cause of action in unjust enrichment will only be available against wrongdoers who are (a) enriched (b) by subtraction from their victims.

That leaves (c), the factor going to "unjust" and calling for the enrichment to be reversed. Prima facie a plaintiff might have to rely on the wrong as that factor. But I do not think that there is any such case. It appears to be correct to assert that, on all facts on which authority actually or arguably allows restitution, when (a) and (b) are satisfied without reliance on a wrong there will always be found to be a non-voluntary transfer or a free acceptance, with the effect that (c) will also be satisfied without relying on the facts in their character as a wrong.

If that is right, the key is simple. It is found in the seemingly innocuous phrase "at the expense of." If that phrase can bear its subtraction sense the plaintiff can ignore the wrong as such and claim restitution in autonomous unjust enrichment.[34]

B. *The Second Class: The Wrong as the Cause of Action*

There is no *a priori* reason why wrongs should not themselves generate restitutionary claims, so that a plaintiff relying on the wrong *qua* wrong would nevertheless assert a remedial right which was restitutionary, not compensatory. Compensation is not ordained as the natural, universal and invariable measure of response. Take the case in which you are paid for beating me up. I might get your reward rather than my loss. It would have to be, though, by relying on the wrong done to me. For I could connect myself to the money only by saying it had been earned by doing me wrong. There is no flow of wealth from me to you, no question of relying on the subtraction sense of "at my expense." Or, suppose that you made a fortune by defaming me in print. If I tried to make out an independent cause of action in unjust enrichment I would come unstuck. But I might try relying on the wrong sense of "at the expense of." I certainly could not ignore that trivial phrase altogether. I would cut myself off from my title to sue. As Goulding J., recently observed, the words "unjust enrichment," standing alone, fail to identify any plaintiff.[35]

1. *A logical trick*

Perhaps these are not cases in which one can have restitution anyhow. Nobody says there is restitution for every gainful wrong or, in the old vocabulary, that every such tort can be waived. There is a logical trick here which can dangerously suggest the contrary. It comes from allowing "unjust" to float up in the clouds. In the down to earth and case-bound version, the rule against unjust enrichment at the expense of another only says that where one is enriched at the expense of another there are some circumstances in which the law reverses that enrichment, "unjust" being the generic qualification of those case-documented circumstances. That leaves no doubt that over and above the enrichment of A by subtraction from or through a wrong to B, there must also be further circumstances recognised as calling for restitution. But if you let "unjust" float away from the cases, the proposition that the law reverses unjust enrichment at the expense of another implies a startling consequence for all cases in which "at the expense of" bears its wrong sense. For every acquisition gained by doing wrong to another is "unjust" in the vague acceptation of that word. So the proposition implies that there is restitution of all gains by wrongdoing. Which is incorrect.

2. *Examples of restitution for wrongs*

However there are some indisputable examples of restitution for wrongs *qua* wrongs. The clearest are cases of corruption. My agent or employee who accepts a bribe to betray me gains by breach of duty to me. He is enriched at my expense, i.e. by doing me wrong. It cannot be said that he is enriched by subtraction from me unless we are prepared to hold that exactly his gain would have accrued to me if it had not been intercepted by him.[36] Sometimes it is certain that it would not have done. In *Reading* v. *A.-G.*[37] a British army sergeant was bribed to help smugglers through road-blocks in Cairo. The Crown could never have acquired that money. The sergeant had been enriched by his breach of duty to the Crown but not by subtraction from it. The Crown's claim to the money was upheld.

The commonest restitutionary claim arising (to use neutral language) in association with a wrong is for the proceeds obtained by the defendant through the sale or use of the plaintiff's property. I sell your car for £5,000 or earn £5,000 by carrying loads in your lorry. These are not subtraction cases. The only cause of action for restitution is the wrong itself. As with the bribe, I did not take the £5,000 from you and it is not certain that you would have got it if I had not intervened. Hence it cannot be said that I enriched myself by £5,000 subtracted from your wealth. There are other points tending to the same conclusion. Perhaps I paid £6,000 for the car or lorry and dealt with it believing it mine. In that case I am down £1,000 and not enriched at all. The contrary can be maintained only if the focus is kept narrowly on the conversion itself. By that wrong against you, it is true, I have obtained £5,000. Again, very probably the car remains yours in the hands of the man who paid me £5,000 for nothing. *Nemo dat quod non habet.* So your wealth has not been reduced at all.

The conclusion must be that when a plaintiff goes for the proceeds of a converted chattel he cannot dispense with the wrong as his cause of action. He cannot get within the subtraction sense of "at the expense of." It is different with a cheque, which is only a vehicle for moving the plaintiff's money. Also, there is an important difference between claims to proceeds and claims in respect of the thing itself. When I eat your cake or use your car, the value of the thing or its user flows straight from you to me. Subject to what was said above about establishing "enrichment" in relation to benefits in kind, those are enrichments by subtraction. But the remoter proceeds of conversion are not. They are obtained at your expense only in the other sense, through wrongdoing. The same must be said of exploitations which are technically not conversions, as where one sells another's confidential information.[38]

Two other areas should be briefly mentioned. A trustee or other fiduciary who makes an acquisition in breach of his duty to avoid conflicts of interest is, analytically albeit often not morally, in the same position as one who corruptly takes a bribe. That is, the facts are unlikely to add up to a subtraction from the beneficiary, but in all cases the fiduciary is enriched at his expense in the wrong sense. *Boardman* v. *Phipps*[39] exemplifies.

The other case is *English* v. *Dedham Vale Properties Ltd.*[40] There Slade J., compelled the defendants to disgorge a sharp profit. They were developers who had bought the plaintiff's land. Only they got much more than they paid for because they covertly obtained planning permission to build on it. To achieve this end they had to short-circuit the statutory machinery[41] which would have given their vendor notice of the planning application. That involved submitting false certificates and working through a nominee who purported to be agent of the vendors. Slade J., was able to find that they had infringed not only the statute but also an equitable duty cast on self-appointed agents. Not an easy conclusion, since it involved putting a purchaser into a fiduciary relation with his vendor and a predator with his prey. We will come back to that. Was this a subtraction case? The land was obtained from the plaintiffs, but the added value came from the community as a whole (or the next purchasers). It was not taken from or intercepted *en route* to the plaintiffs. I think the added value was therefore only obtained at the plaintiffs' expense in the sense of by doing them the wrong of making the undisclosed application. So here too there was restitution based directly on a wrong.

If even some of these examples are secure cases of restitution within only the "wrong" sense of "at the expense of" I think that Beatson's thesis that all restitutionary claims arise from a cause of action distinct from the wrong can only stand if one is prepared to affirm that compensation somehow enters into the definition of a wrong, a proposition not easily defended unless from authority rather than common sense. Wrongs actionable *per se* and those which give punitive damages sufficiently show that there is no necessary link with compensation. The proposition that loss is an element in most tortious causes of action really means no more than that, when the claim is for compensation, a court will give you nothing merely for being the victim of a breach of duty. It was not formulated with a view to creating a theoretical bar against the perfectly sensible notion of restitution for wrongs. If this is right it only means that Beatson must give up some part of the large territory which he gained.

3. *Which wrongs generate restitutionary claims?*

Examples of this phenomenon do not reveal what it is that makes restitution possible. For which instances of acquisitive wrongdoing can the plaintiff maintain a restitutionary claim? There are no clear answers, though for certain the clues are there in the cases. There are, as it seems to me, (at least) two tests.[42] I shall deal first with the one which once identified is more conveniently applied second.

(i) ANTI-ENRICHMENT WRONGS. The key to this is the commandment, Thou shalt not steal. Within the legal system that simple injunction becomes complex, divides between civil and criminal law, and breaks down into families of related wrongs. In some the element of fault becomes attenuated or even disappears. But they are all concerned with the prevention of disapproved enrichment. The commandment is too. It places a duty on everyone to abstain from unjust enrichment; and the families of stealing wrongs are breaches of that duty. Restitution is the reversal of disapproved enrichment. It comes into play when the preventive mechanisms have failed.[43]

These observations knit together in this way. The wrongs for which restitution is an appropriate response are those which group themselves together under Thou shalt not steal—those, that is to say, which by their commission infringe primary duties to abstain from disapproved enrichment. The policy which explains why those wrongs are forbidden then coincides exactly with the operation of the restitutionary response. Thus, when restitution of the enrichment is awarded after the wrong, precisely the same end is being pursued as is sought by the imposition of the duty which the wrongdoer broke.

Of course it is not always easy to say whether a particular wrong belongs in this way to the machinery for preventing unjust enrichment. Some wrongs are compendious, like trespass, and, considered generically, express mixed policies. Breach of confidence is aimed against infringements of privacy as well as against a species of disapproved enrichment and may have to be divided according to the nature of the confidence in each case. Yet many wrongs are clearly in or clearly out. The duty not to hit people is, for example, not aimed against a disapproved mode of enrichment but against the mischief of bodily insecurity. Hence I should not have restitution under this head against the man paid to beat me up. Similarly, defamation is not a stealing wrong. The duty not to defame is aimed at preventing harm to reputation, not some kind of disapproved enrichment.[44] And the duty of care above the tort of negligence is aimed at preventing losses, not gains. On the other side of the line, since the routine temptation of those who manage the wealth of others is the interception of profitable opportunities, the fiduciary's duty to avoid conflicts of interest manifestly has as one of its main purposes the prevention of that mode of enrichment. And this is all the more clear in the case of duties, legal and equitable, not to misappropriate assets already belonging to another or to usurp their enjoyment over a finite period of time.

The shortest statement of this test is: Has the defendant committed an anti-enrichment wrong? An anti-enrichment wrong is one which consists in the breach of a duty which itself has, as a main purpose underlying its recognition by the law, the prevention of some mode of enrichment.[45]

(ii) DELIBERATE EXPLOITATION OF WRONGDOING.[46] The other and easier test is: Did the defendant set out to make a gain through the commission of the wrong? Battery is not an anti-enrichment wrong; but, if you earned £500 by beating me up, under this test you would have to disgorge your reward to me. The same applies where you knowingly publish sensational untruths about me to increase the circulation of your magazine. If you sell my car knowing it to be mine you are caught under both heads, for the conversion is an anti-enrichment wrong and you have deliberately committed it in order to gain.

The last example also serves to illustrate why it is better in practice to apply the second test first. It can take care of all cases of deliberate exploitation of wrongdoing for profit, leaving the more difficult test to discriminate only between other cases.

Thus, in *Reading* v. *A.-G.* the sergeant deliberately broke his duty to the Crown in order to earn money from the smugglers whom he helped. It is more doubtful whether he also committed an anti-enrichment wrong. For there is an argument, applicable alike to *Boardman* and to *Reading*, that the general duty broken, namely to avoid conflicts of interest, is aimed at two distinct mischiefs, interception of profits and infliction of other types of harm; and further, that, although the duty can generally be said to have the prevention of enrichment as a main purpose, nevertheless once there is no "real and sensible"[47] possibility of the gain in question accruing to the beneficiary the policy in play cannot be against the fiduciary's enrichment but only against his inflicting harm, as for instance, by damaging the other's reputation or taking incautious risks. Hence, this argument would say, on such facts the duty to avoid conflicts of interest survives only as a prophylaxis against loss, not against enrichment. *Boardman* shows how fierce the law is. Its rigour consists in refusing to ask (a) whether the risk of harm materialised, or (b) whether the fiduciary succumbed to the temptation to run a risk (but got away with it), or even (c) whether he was tempted to run a risk (but resisted the temptation). Enough that he might have been tempted. Or, more fully, that there was more than a fanciful possibility[48] that his own interest might, as he began to pursue it, tempt him to take risks with the safety of the trust. *Reading*, more wicked, belongs in the same segment of the circle. It exemplifies the non-hypothetical case. He actually was tempted, did succumb and did inflict harm, damaging the Crown's reputation and objectives in Egypt, just as a trustee actually inflicts harm who keeps a fund in a failing investment or is habitually dilatory in trust business. Put deliberate exploitation for profit on one side and suppose them doing these things from unrewarded malice or indifference or extraneous loyalty. In that light the duties broken by their wrongs do seem to be aimed solely at the prevention of loss, not against a disapproved mode of enrichment.

A similar discussion can be had of *English* v. *Dedham Vale Properties Ltd.*[49] Without the effort of discovering the unprecedented fiduciary relationship Slade, J., could have reached the same conclusion by finding that the defendants had deliberately violated the statute with a view to profit. Only if there were doubt about that would it have been necessary to ask whether the obligations imposed by the statute had as a main purpose the prevention of the mode of enrichment used by the developers.[50]

4. *Remoteness of gain*

The field of "deliberate exploitation" is contested between restitution and punishment.[51] It may turn out that a plaintiff can choose between the actual profit made by the wrongdoer or penal damages with no fixed relation to the amount of that gain. Penal damages have the merit of avoiding the need to work out what the profit was or where to stop.[52] But where a wrong does *qua* wrong give restitution and there is no right to penal damages (and therefore certainly in every case where it qualifies only under the anti-enrichment test) these difficulties cannot be escaped. For example, suppose a defendant has wrongly used the plaintiff's materials to obtain and complete certain valuable contracts.[53] There are bound on such facts to be awkward issues of principle and quantification in calculating the amount, if any, of the profit attributable to his wrong.

In the law of compensation the lengthening cone of loss is cut off by the principles of remoteness of damage. The case law explicitly on remoteness of gain still has to develop. In "subtraction" cases the question is settled by the fact the the plaintiff identifies himself as having a claim only to the value subtracted from him. But in the "wrong" cases that nexus is broken. There the plaintiff identifies himself as the victim of a breach of duty and claims all the enrichment, however the court will assess it, obtained by doing him wrong. "At the expense of" imposes no natural limit on the measure. Suppose that defamatory statements increase the sale of your magazine and that we manage in the first instance to quantify the immediate yield of your wrong at £1m. You then put that money into your publishing business where it represents 20 per cent. of your capital. Are the profits of your business to be counted, as to one fifth, as the product of the tort?

At the moment there is no coherent answer. A trustee who sold a trust asset and put the proceeds into his business would indeed be accountable for the share of his business profits[54] but it cannot be finally said whether the same consequences do or do not attend a stranger's conversion of a car or even (which is an intermediate case) the "conversion" of confidential information.

In America there is some authority for awarding restitution of all profits in the case of deliberate exploitation of wrongdoing while confining claims against unintentional wrongdoers to the reasonable value of the asset or, if it has been returned after user for a time reasonable rental for its use (*i.e.* the same measure as in "subtraction" cases).[55] For example, if I unknowingly use your machine to produce goods I must pay you a reasonable hire for the use of the machine, but if I know the machine is yours I must give up all the profit earned on the market by manufacturing with it. That gives a measure of remoteness against the unintentional wrongdoer, but against the deliberate wrongdoer it leaves the ultimate cut-off point still unclear.

5. *Cases in both classes*

We have been speaking of situations in which the wrong is the sole cause of action but gives rise to a remedial restitutionary right. By contrast, the first class comprised those situations in which facts amounting to a wrong also disclosed an alternative cause of action in autonomous unjust enrichment. At this point it is possible to come to terms with the fact that a given wrong may fall in both classes. That is, the plaintiff may be able to re-analyse the facts and dispense with the wrong; or, basing himself solely on the wrong, he may yet have a choice whether to go for restitution or compensation. The choice between the two routes to restitution has practical implications.[56]

This relationship between the two classes is expressed in the fact that even when a wrongdoer gains by subtraction from his victim it is at the same time also true that he gains by doing his victim wrong. That is, the two senses of the crucial phrase coincide.

II. *NOMENCLATURE AND SCHEMATIC SUMMARY*

"Waiver of tort" has all sorts of objections. It does not reach all wrongs. It suggests that the tort is extinguished. It does not distinguish between cases where there is an independent cause of action in unjust enrichment and those where the cause of action is the wrong itself. It is appropriate only for genuine ratification of tortious dispositions made by a purported agent,[57] but to retain it even there would allow the roots of confusion to survive. It is best eradicated.

1. *A restricted sense of "unjust enrichment at the expense of the plaintiff"*

There are two ways of pinning down the main division discussed in this paper. The first is to restrict the use of "unjust enrichment at the expense of another" to the subtraction sense of "at the expense of" and thus to draw a distinction between restitution for unjust enrichment (meaning by the abbreviation only unjust enrichment by subtraction) and restitution for wrongs. That usage allows statements of this kind: the victim of an acquisitive wrong may be able to seek restitution either for unjust enrichment or for the wrong itself. And, on the grid which has events at the top and responses down the side, the renunciation of the wrong sense of "at the expense of" makes for a coherent and distinct series at the top: contract wrongs, unjust enrichment, others. The restitution column cutting across these will then certainly be found to have content in the second and third squares (the first and fourth being outside the scope of this paper).

2. *Primary and secondary restitutionary rights*

Lord Diplock has recently disinterred this Austinian terminology in the context of contract.[58] Breach triggers a secondary obligation to pay damages, secondary because its coming into being necessarily supposes the anterior existence of another obligation. That other obligation, born of the contract itself, is primary, because its existence does not entail the earlier existence of any other. Secondary rights are sanctioning or remedial, in the sense that they are the response to infringements of primary rights. The restitutionary rights born of non-voluntary transfer and free acceptance and all other cases of unjust enrichment (by subtraction) are primary. Take a mistaken payment. The right to restitution stands on its own. It is not the sanction for a pre-existing right infringed. By contrast, if "unjust enrichment at the expense of the plaintiff" is allowed to include even the cases within the wrong sense of "at the expense of," every case within only that second sense will create restitutionary rights which are secondary and stand in a sanctioning relationship to pre-existing rights and duties. For example, as a trustee you are under a duty to avoid conflicts of interest. If you acquire in breach of that duty, you incur a restitutionary obligation. It stands in a fixed relationship, secondary and sanctioning, to the prior duty.

This terminology allows a different statement to be made, in function the same as that which used the restricted sense of unjust enrichment: facts amounting to an acquisitive wrong may generate either primary or secondary restitutionary rights.

3. *Summary using the above nomenclature*

(i) Wrongdoers either gain or they do not. (ii) Where they do not, no question of restitution arises. (iii) Where they do, the victim may be able to obtain restitution by either primary or secondary restitutionary rights. (iv) By primary restitutionary rights, where, choosing to ignore the characterisation of the facts as a wrong, he can make out an unjust enrichment. (v) By secondary restitutionary rights, where, choosing to rely on the facts in their character as a wrong, he can show either (a) that the wrongdoer deliberately sought to profit from wrongdoing, or (b) that a main purpose of the duty breached was to prevent a mode of enrichment.

To make assurance doubly sure, it is safest to reiterate that proposition (iv) uses "unjust enrichment" in the restricted sense, as short for "unjust enrichment by subtraction from the plaintiff."

III. *PRACTICAL IMPLICATIONS*

The most important practical consequences come under these heads: 1. Measure of Recovery; 2. Actionability; 3. Procedural Rules.

1. *Measure of recovery*

This has been touched on already. The plaintiff who brings his action in autonomous unjust enrichment can only get the value which was subtracted by the defendant from him. But when he does rely on the wrong, the wrong itself creates a nexus between him and any improvement in the wrongdoer's position which (subject to a test of remoteness) is capable of being attributed to the wrong. One who pays over £1,000 through a mistake induced by fraud may know that the rogue managed to put that money to work and raise it to £1,500. Ignoring the wrong and proceeding just as though for spontaneous mistake he cannot expect to recover more than the £1,000; but relying on the wrong he can make a prima facie case to be allowed the whole £1,500. So secondary restitutionary rights may give the plaintiff more.

It must be emphasised that this has nothing to do with the possibility of tracing. Let it be assumed that after turning the £1,000 into £1,500 the rogue used the whole sum to buy a quantity of caviar. Which he then ate. That puts paid to the issue of tracing, too large for this paper.

2. *Actionability*

If the plaintiff ignores the wrong and sues only in unjust enrichment no problem arises for him if on closer inspection a doubt emerges whether the facts do after all add up to a tort or other actionable wrong. Does a public authority commit a tort if it refuses to issue a licence until paid an *ultra vires* sum of money?[59] Such a question is irrelevant in the context of a plaintiff's claim in independent unjust enrichment. He is not relying on the wrong and his claim is not touched by arguments relating to the status of the event *qua* wrong. Correspondingly, if he does rely on the wrong he must be willing to argue about its actionability as such. At the very least he must be prepared to argue that the event should be recognised as actionable, for restitutionary damages if for nothing else.

It is not easy to think of examples of the same phenomenon the other way around, allowing a restitutionary claim for the wrong to escape an objection to one in unjust enrichment. If the premiss were still right that a minor's incapacity was a defence to claims in unjust enrichment but not in tort, against a fraudulent minor one would obviously base a claim to restitution on the wrong even on facts otherwise admitting of alternative analysis. *Bristow* v. *Eastman* shows this being done.[60] Again, suppose I use your machine (or your land) for months thinking it to be mine. Because of the mistake there is no free acceptance and therefore, failing the difficult proof of incontrovertible benefit, no claim in unjust enrichment. Yet, relying on the wrong (exactly what the plaintiff could not do in *Phillips* v. *Homfray*) perhaps you can get the value of the user, for the wrong might be held to bar me from the luxury of subjective devaluation.[61]

3. *Procedural rules*

This is really a special variety of the last point. Suppose that a statute regulating the business of litigation imposes a particular requirement or restriction on claims for "torts" or "wrongs" or "breaches of duty." A plaintiff who ignores the wrong and proceeds in unjust enrichment must be outside that bar, unless the court deliberately extends it for reasons of expediency or by other arguments of a non-logical kind. For example, a claim in unjust enrichment (by subtraction) cannot logically be caught by a limitation period attached to wrongs. The other side of that penny is this: a plaintiff relying on a wrong cannot logically escape the limitation period merely by claiming restitution rather than the more usual compensation. For it is given that the limitation is attached to the event (wrongs) not to the response (compensation).[62]

The last paragraph takes the standpoint of a plaintiff under a statute already in operation. There is another perspective. Those who draft future statutes must deal expressly with unjust enrichment. It needs its own rules. So also restitution, if the draftsman prefers to deal in categories of response.

CONCLUSION

The last words are only about the general nature of what has been attempted. In one respect I know the work may seem slovenly. Dozens of questions are left open. There is no fine tuning. Within the area loosely denominated "Restitution and Wrongs" I wanted to establish the *summa divisio* between restitution for wrongs and restitution for unjust enrichment, an independent event latent in some wrongs. On the way I have had to make a case for habitual and disciplined use of the language of unjust enrichment, with "unjust" downward-looking to the cases and with the often suppressed but never to be forgotten phrase "at the expense of" given only its subtraction sense. Without these changes I do not think we will ever see the subject clearly enough to do the fine tuning which I know I have not done.

Notes

[1] J. Beatson, "The Nature of Waiver of Tort" (1978–79) 17 Univ. of W. Ontario L. Rev., 1. This is cited hereafter as Beatson, "Waiver." Citations to Goff and Jones refer to R. Goff and G. Jones, *The Law of Restitution*, (2nd ed., London, 1978).

[2] *Cf.* P.H. Winfield, *The Province of the Law of Tort* (Cambridge, 1931), p.32; *Letang* v. *Cooper* [1965] 1 Q.B. 232.

[3] "Damages" also, though at a higher level of generality than these three, at least if taken as "unliquidated money award."

[4] *Strand Electric and Engineering Co. Ltd.* v. *Brisford Entertainments Ltd.* [1952] 2 Q.B. 246, 251 *per* Denning, L.J.; Beatson, "Waiver," p.15.

[5] Restitution can be of a thing to a person or of a thing or person to a condition. The second sense should be eschewed if the line with compensation is to be clear: *Barlett* v. *Barclays Bank Trust Co. Ltd.* (*No.* 2) [1980] 2 All E.R. 92; *Re Dawson* [1966] 2 N.S.W.R. 211. "Give up" is preferable to "give back" since all writers suppose that there can be restitution to X from Y of a receipt from Z: *e.g. Shamia* v. *Joory* [1958] 1 Q.B. 448 and cases cited in note 33 below.

[6] *United Australia Ltd.* v. *Barclays Bank Ltd.* [1941] A.C. 1.

[7] *Ibid.* p.18, *per* Lord Simon, p.35, *per* Lord Romer. *Cf.* A.L. Corbin, "Waiver of Tort and Suit in Assumpsit" (1910) 19 Yale L.J. 221, 235–238; G.E. Palmer, *The Law of Restitution* (Boston and Toronto 1978) Vol. 1, p.71; Goff and Jones, p.469.

[8] *Kelly* v. *Solari* (1841) 9 M. & W. 54.

[9] *Neate* v. *Harding* (1851) 6 Exch. 349.

[10] *Loc. cit.* note 6 above. The same of *Banque Belge* v. *Hambrouck* [1921] 1 K.B. 321.

[11] [1968] 3 All E.R. 271 (Nottingham Assizes).

[12] *Cf.* excess payment from computer malfunction: *Commonwealth of Australia* v. *Burns* [1971] V.R. 825.

[13] *Norwich Union Fire Ins. Soc.* v. *Wm. H. Price Ltd.* [1934] A.C. 455.

[14] Beatson, "Waiver," p.16.

[15] *Kettlewell* v. *Refuge Insurance Co.* [1909] A.C. 243; *Hughes* v. *Liverpool Legal Friendly Soc.* [1916] 2 K.B. 482; *Harse* v. *Pearl Life Assurance Co.* [1904] 1 K.B. 558.

[16] Beatson, "Waiver," pp.15 *et seq.*

[17] "The impulsive desire to save human life when in peril is one of the most beneficial instincts of humanity. . . . " *Scaramanga* v. *Stamp* (1880) 5 C.P.D. 295, 304 *per* Cockburn, S.J.,—a truth witnessed across the world in the rescuer seen entering the frozen Potomac to save a victim of the Air Florida disaster in Washington in January, 1982. This compulsion (which extends beyond danger to life) is called in Goff and Jones "necessitous intervention."

[18] Either to his property (*Exall* v. *Partridge* (1799) 8 T.R. 308; *Johnson* v. *R.M.S. Packet Co.* (1867) L.R. 3 C.P. 38) or to his person (*Brook's Wharf and Bull Wharf Ltd.* v. *Goodman Bros* [1937] 1 K.B. 534).

[19] *Duc de Cadaval* v. *Collins* (1836) A. & E. 858.

[20] *Astley* v. *Reynolds* (1731) 2 Str. 915.

[21] *Sundell T.A. and Sons Pty. Ltd.* v. *Yannoulatos Pty. Ltd.* (1956) 56 S.R. (N.S.W.) 323; *The Atlantic Baron* [1978] 3 All E.R. 1170.

[22] As might be inferred from *Smith* v. *Charlick Ltd.* (1924) 34 C.L.R. 38; *cf. Eric Gnapp Ltd.* v. *Petroleum Board* [1949] All E.R. 980.

[23] *Williams* v. *Bayley*, (1866) L.R. 1 H.L. 200; *Re Craig* [1971] Ch.95.

[24] Goff and Jones, pp.14 *et seq.*; G. Jones, "Restitutionary Claims for Services Rendered" (1977) 93 L.Q.R. 273; P. Birks, "*Negotiorum Gestio* and the Common Law" [1971] C.L.P. 110.

[25] (1883) Ch. D. 439; *cf. Morris* v. *Tarrant* [1971] 2 Q.B. 143; *Raven Red Ash Coal Co.* v. *Ball* (1946) 185 Va. 534, 39 S.E.2d 231.

[26] An action based on the tort would have been caught by *actio personalis moritur cum persona*.

[27] *Foster* v. *Stewart* (1814) 3 M. & S. 191; *Lightly* v. *Clouston* (1808) 1 Taunt. 112; *cf. Hambly* v. *Trott* (1776) 1 Cowp. 371.

[28] In the old language, implied contract for reasonable recompense.

[29] For a remote third possibility (no subjective devaluation permitted to even an innocent tortfeasor) see below, text to note 61.

[30] It is essential not to suppose these species finally exhaust the genus: *cf.* Birks, [1980] C.L.P. 191, 206 *et seq.*

[31] *Cf.* note 5, above. This useful word has also to be deprived of the natural sense of its prefix, on account of triangular situations.

[32] This irony is identified by Palmer, but not its root cause: for his use of "unjust" remains vague and upward-looking, G.E. Palmer, *The Law of Restitution* (Boston and Toronto, 1978), Vol. 1, pp.5 *et seq. Cf.* Goff and Jones, pp.11 *et seq.*; P.S. Atiyah, *The Rise and Fall of Freedom of Contract* (Oxford, 1979), pp. 767 *et seq.*

[33] This sense can be satisfied by an interception from a third party provided the value would certainly have accrued to the plaintiff if not cut off by the defendant, as where the plaintiff was already entitled to it: *e.g. Howard* v. *Wood* (1679) 2 Lev. 245, 2 Show.21; *Asher* v. *Wallis* (1707) 11 Mod. 146, Holt K.B. 36; *Shamia* v. *Joory* [1958] 1 Q.B. 448; *Cook* v. *Deeks* [1916] A.C. 554; *Caskie* v. *Philadelphia Rapid Transit Co.* (1936) 321 Pa. 157, 184 A.17.

[34] Hence, of the phenomenon in Class A, but not Class B below, Keener was right to insist on "not only a plus but a minus quantity": W.A. Keener, *Quasi-Contracts* (New York, 1923, reprinting 1983), p.163.

[35] [1981] Ch.105, 125.

[36] *Cf.* note 33 above. Possibly, this finding of fact could have been made in *Mahesan s/o Thambiah* v. *Malaysian Govt. Officers' Cooperative Housing Soc. Ltd.* [1979] A.C. 374.

[37] [1951] A.C. 507.

[38] In *Seager* v. *Copydex Ltd.* [1967] 1 W.L.R. 923; (*No.* 2) [1969] 1 W.L.R. 815 the defendants, unconscious plagiarists, were confined to the value subtracted; contrast *Peter Pan Mfg. Corpn.* v. *Corsets Silhouette Ltd.* [1964] 1 W.L.R. 96, where defendants had to account for profits of selling goods made through the confidential information, value obtained by breach of duty to the plaintiff but not subtracted from them.

[39] [1967] 2 A.C. 46; *cf. Regal (Hastings) Ltd.* v. *Gulliver* [1942] 1 All E.R. 378; *Industrial Development Consultants Ltd.* v. *Cooley* [1972] 1 W.L.R. 443—in which it was found that a slight possibility still survived that the plaintiff could have obtained the intercepted gain; *Boston Deep Sea Fishing & Ice Co.* v. *Ansell* (1888) Ch. D. 339; *Williams* v. *Barton* [1927] 2 Ch. 9.

[40] [1978] 1 W.L.R. 93.

[41] Town and Country Planning Act 1962, s.16.

[42] "At least" leaves room for tests to meet specialised needs: *e.g.* if the law, concerned to prevent loss not enrichment, nevertheless determines to impose a liability as soon as danger threatens, the compensatory measure is excluded (because no actual loss will have materialised) so that, apart from injunctive relief and imposition of penalties, restitution is the only available measure of the prophylactic liability: see below, text to notes 47 and 48.

[43] Another *preventive* mechanism is preservation of title through catastrophic interruptions of possession: through loss, theft, fundamentally mistaken sale, my bicycle stays mine, its possessor gaining nothing except user for a time.

[44] *Hart* v. *E.P. Dutton & Co. Inc.* (1949) 98 N.Y.S. 2d 773. Similarly nuisance: *Kirk* v. *Todd* (1882) 21 Ch. Div. 484.

[45] This test has much in common with D. Friedmann's "property principle" except that (i) he does not first distinguish Class A, independent cause of action, from Class B, restitution for the wrong, and (ii) he gives "property" so wide a sense as to turn even defamation into—in my terms—an anti-enrichment wrong: Daniel Friedmann, "Restitution of Benefits Through the Appropriation of Property or the Commission of a Wrong" (1980) 80 Columbia L. R. 504, 510 *et seq.*

[46] This approximates to Friedmann's "deterrence" category: *Ibid.* pp.551–556.
[47] The language of Lord Upjohn's dissent in *Boardman* [1967] 2 A.C. 46, 124.
[48] *Ibid.*
[49] [1978] 1 W.L.R. 93.
[50] The Town and Country Planning Act 1962, s.16 imposed duties to the authority, not the vendor-plaintiff; but that technicality should not matter if they were constructed in the latter's interest.
[51] *Rookes* v. *Barnard* [1964] A.C. 1129; *Broome* v. *Cassell & Co. Ltd.* [1972] A.C. 1027; *cf.* U.S. authority cited below, note 55.
[52] Faced with a not dissimilar choice equity inclines slightly against the difficult business of a full account of profits and welcomes a decision to take interest in lieu: *Docker* v. *Somes* (1834) 2 My. & K. 655; *Jones* v. *Foxall* (1852) 15 Bear. 388; *Vyse* v. *Foster* (1874) L.R. 7 H.L. 318; *Re Davis* [1902] 2 Ch. 314.
[53] *Re Sims* [1934] Ch. 1.
[54] *Heathcote* v. *Hulme* (1819) 1 Jac. & W. 122; *Williams* v. *Stevens* (1866) L.R. 1 P.C. 352; *Re Davis* [1902] 2 Ch. 314; *Re Jarvis* [1958] 2 All E.R. 336.
[55] *Olwell* v. *Nye and Nissen Co.* (1946) 26 Wash. 2d, 282; *Edwards* v. *Lee's Administrators* (1936) 265 Ky. 418; G.E. Palmer, *op. cit.* note 7 above, pp. 157–166.
[56] See below, section III.
[57] *Verschures Creameries Ltd.* v. *Hull and Netherlands S.S. Co. Ltd.* [1921] 2 K.B. 608.
[58] *Photo Production Ltd.* v. *Securicor Transport Ltd.* [1980] A.C. 826, 848; *Moschi* v. *Lep Air Services Ltd.* [1973] A.C. 331, 346 *et seq.*, 350, *cf.* J. Austin, *Lectures on Jurisprudence* (5th ed., London, 1885), Lecture XLV, pp.760 *et seq.*
[59] *Brocklebank Ltd.* v. *R.* [1925] 1 K.B. 52. Similarly, is usurpation of the profits of office a tort? *Arris* v. *Stukely* (1677) 2 Mod. 260; *Howard* v. *Wood* (1679) 2 Show. K.B. 21; Goff and Jones, pp.446, 469.
[60] (1749) 1 Peake 291; *cf. Cowern* v. *Nield* [1912] 2 K.B. 419. But even where the restitutionary claim is "in substance *ex delicto*" it is now obstructed by *Leslie Ltd.* v. *Sheill* [1914] 3 K.B. 607.
[61] Difficult otherwise to explain any measure of recovery against an innocent and therefore not freely accepting tortfeasor: note 52 above. This coincides with "mesne profits" as a head of compensation damages, as in *Morris* v. *Tarrant* [1971] 2 Q.B. 143.
[62] Hence the opinions cited in Goff and Jones, p.482, are correct of Class B claims, incorrect so far as they purport to include Class A. *Semble*, *Chesworth* v. *Farrer* [1967] 1 Q.B. 407 belongs in Class B (restitution for wrongs). Though the court treats it as though in Class A (claims in unjust enrichment). *Cf.* the contrary position taken *obiter* by Denning, J., in *Beaman* v. *A.R.T.S. Ltd.* [1948] 2 All E.R. 89.

Judicial Notice and Personal Knowledge in Magistrates' Courts and Tribunals[1]

CLIFFORD F. PARKER

It can be no exaggeration to say that this topic is one which is involved every day in dozens of magistrates' courts and tribunals throughout the country, even if, like M. Jourdain's prose,[2] it is not recognised. Even on those occasions when it is recognised, even then, fortunately for the prompt administration of the judicial process it is rarely treated as a problem. When it does emerge as a problem it is virtually insoluble; certainly this paper does not seek to offer a solution, because there is a real risk that any solution which is attempted will bring with it even worse problems.[3] My treatment of the topic will be essentially practical, drawing on my experience both as a Justice of the Peace and as a Chairman of a Regional Supplementary Benefit Appeal Tribunal, and theoretical considerations will be raised only insofar as it is necessary to do so in order to put the topic in context.

To state briefly the function of the doctrine of Judicial Notice, when judicial notice is taken of a fact, it dispenses with the need of proof of that fact.[4] Time and expense are thereby saved, both because the obvious need not be proved by evidence and also because, at least according to what may be called the prevailing view, the obvious cannot run the risk of being disputed since judicial notice excludes the possibility of evidence being called in rebuttal.[5]

The first group of facts usually listed of which judicial notice may be taken consists of what are sometimes called "legislative" facts, statute law and case law, which do not have to be proved by evidence before the judge because he is deemed to know it all.[6] Then there are those facts which are so notorious that any proof thereof is utterly superfluous, matters of common knowledge, among the popular examples of which are that Christmas Day falls on December 25, that Queen Victoria, not to mention Queen Anne, is dead. As a slight extension to this latter category there are those facts "which are capable of accurate and ready determination by the court by reference to sources whose accuracy cannot reasonably be questioned,"[7] for example, that a particular date in the past fell on a particular day of the week, the time of sunrise on a particular day at a particular place which is listed in a reputable almanac.[8]

But over and above these categories of facts which are generally accepted as falling under the umbrella of judicial notice, there are those grey areas of facts which are known, especially in the case of lay magistrates and lay members of tribunals, because of their own personal knowledge of local geography or other local matters or because of their own personal knowledge and experience acquired in their own trade, career or profession. Are these also facts of which the bench or tribunal may take judicial notice without the need of evidence for their proof? Or, to re-phrase the question from another standpoint, are these matters "non-adjudicative facts" or "non-evidence facts" in the terminology of Professor Kenneth Davis. "Every case involves the use of hundreds or thousands of non-evidence facts. When a witness in an automobile accident says 'car,' everyone, judge and jury included, furnishes from non-evidence sources within himself, the supplementing information that the 'car' is an automobile, not a railroad car, that it is self-propelled, probably by an internal combustion engine, that it may be assumed to have four wheels with pneumatic rubber tyres, and so on. The judicial process cannot construct every case from scratch . . . . These items could not possibly be introduced into evidence, and no one suggests that they be. Nor are they appropriate subjects for any formalised treatment of judicial notice of facts."[9] Do these observations apply also to such supplemental information supplied by lay magistrates or tribunal members from non-evidence sources within themselves, arising out of their personal knowledge and experience?

I shall take as my text, as it were, the phrase we quite often hear as magistrates when trying a disputed case of, say, careless driving, when the defendant is alleged to have emerged from a side road, controlled by a "Give Way" sign, on to the main road, without having exercised due care and attention so that an accident has resulted. "Your Worships are no doubt familiar with this junction." We nod, flattered perhaps by this recognition of our worldly wisdom, eager to identify ourselves with the community. After all, we are often told that one of the great advantages of the system of the lay magistracy is that we are a cross-section of the local community, with local knowledge and experience in such matters as local employment and housing and traffic. Are magistrates, of all people, to be presumed ignorant of what everybody else in the locality knows?[10]

But even when we are asked this question as to our familiarity with the road or junction in question, there is already some divergence of opinion as to what precisely we are being asked to do. Some justices' clerks and prosecuting solicitors have no doubt but that we are being invited to take judicial notice of, at least, the existence and general lay-out of the road or junction. Indeed, one prosecuting solicitor phrases it explicitly: "Your Worships are entitled to take judicial notice of this junction arising out of your personal knowledge." Against this is the view that all we are being asked to do is to use that background knowledge in the interpretation of the evidence we are about to hear. Certainly, if it were necessary for us to be given any precise measurements and details of the stretch of road or junction, a proper plan would have to be produced and proved.

Wigmore tells us, in an oft-quoted passage, "It is therefore plainly accepted that the judge is not to use on the Bench, under the guise of judicial knowledge,[11] that which he knows as an individual observer. The former is in truth 'known' to him merely in the peculiar sense that it is known and notorious to all men, and the dilemma is only the result of using the term knowledge in two senses.[12] Where to draw the line between knowledge by notoriety and knowledge by personal observation may sometimes be difficult, but the principle is plain."[13]

However, one may be forgiven for thinking that the great man was over-optimistic when he wrote that even the principle is plain, at least in magistrates' courts and tribunals, when one considers firstly the problems arising with regard to facts which, even if they are "notorious," are notorious only locally, *i.e.* arising from the actual knowledge of the bench or tribunal in the particular locality or activity, and secondly the problems arising with regard to a multiple bench or tribunal.

As far as judicial authority is concerned, there are not many reported cases on this use of local knowledge in magistrates' courts, but it may be useful to examine some of them, to see how the issue has arisen and how it has been dealt with.[14]

Ingram v. *Percival*[15]

In this case, which is often cited as an authority in support of the ability of magistrates to use their local knowledge, the defendant was charged with a fishery offence in that he was alleged to have placed a fixed net in tidal waters for catching salmon and trout. The only evidence produced was a map on which the siting of the net was marked. He was convicted by the magistrates who, when they subsequently stated a case for the Divisional Court, recorded: "We considered that tidal waters consist of waters affected by a lateral or horizontal flow of water . . . and it is within our knowledge that such a flow extends beyond the low water mark and is experienced at more than one hundred yards from the shore. We therefore held that in this case the net was within tidal waters." In the opinion of Lord Parker C.J., the appeal turned on whether the justices were entitled to make use of the knowledge which they said they had. "In my judgment they were fully entitled to do so. It has always been recognised that justices may and should—after all they are local justices—take into consideration matters which they know of their own knowledge and particularly matters in regard to the locality, whether it be on land, as it seems to me, or in water."[16]

The actual phrase "judicial notice" does not occur in the judgments and it may be said that the proposition enunciated by Lord Parker, that justices may and should take into consideration matters known to them of their own knowledge, relates only to the weighing up and interpretation of the evidence actually before them, in that case the map with the position of the net marked. However my next case hardly lends itself to this explanation.

Clift v. *Long*[17]

The charge here was attempting to drive a motor-car in a public place under the influence of drink, the place being a car park adjacent to the Pier Pavilion in Felixstowe. At the close of the prosecution's case, the defence submitted No case to answer, on the basis that no evidence had been given to establish that the car park was a public place, and that in the absence of any such evidence the inference to be drawn was that the car park was reserved for the hirers, and guests and invitees of the hirers, of the Pavilion on the particular night. The justices were indeed invited to view the car park, but said that that was not necessary because they knew it well; it was visible from the window of their retiring room. They were of the opinion that it was a public car park and so ruled; consequently there *was* a case to answer. The defendant gave and called no evidence and was convicted. On appeal the Divisional Court said that the justices were entitled to make use of their general local knowledge[18] and as prima facie the car park was a public place within the meaning of s.15 of the Road Traffic Act 1930 they had come to a correct decision. And so in this case the personal knowledge of the justices was used, and its use was upheld on appeal, presumably as evidence in itself, to resist a submission of No case to answer on the ground that the prosecution had brought no evidence to support its assertion that the car park in question was a public place.

Borthwick v. *Vickers*[19]

The defendant was charged with unlawfully using on diverse roads an overladen goods vehicle. The vehicle had been loaded at a company's south works in Hartlepool and the goods delivered to premises adjacent to the company's north works. No evidence was given as to the precise route taken by the vehicle; indeed that was not known to the prosecution. Here too there was a submission of No case to answer in the absence of any evidence as to the use of the vehicle on any road within s.257(1) of the Road Traffic Act 1960, "any highway or any other road to which the public has access." The justices stated that they knew from their own knowledge that the north works were about a mile and a half from the south works and that to get from one to the other it was necessary to use several different roads and they concluded that the vehicle must have travelled over some public roads, and so rejected the submission. Here too the defendant gave and called no evidence and was convicted. In dismissing the appeal by way of case stated, the Divisional Court declared that justices dealing with local geography in the sense that they were dealing with matters which were notorious locally and within their own knowledge were entitled to supplement the evidence in such a case by their own knowledge that the journey inevitably involved travelling on public roads. But the court added that if the defendant had elected to give evidence, a different picture might have emerged, but since there was no evidence that the vehicle had pursued the particular journey it was open to the justices from their own local knowledge to draw the inference that it had used public roads in the course of the journey.

Again in this case, at least according to the only report available in the *Criminal Law Review*, it does not seem that the phrase Judicial Notice was actually used, although the Commentary starts with the remark[20]: "It has frequently been held that justices are entitled to take Judicial Notice of local geography including the lay-out of roads and streets in their locality," with reference to *Clift* v. *Long*, the car park case just discussed, and to *Johnstone* v. *Hawkins*,[21] to be next discussed. However, in *Borthwick* v. *Vickers*, any proper use of the doctrine of judicial notice should surely be limited to the distance between the two works of some one and a half miles which they knew from their own personal knowledge. It could hardly be appropriate to speak of their taking judicial notice that a particular journey was made at least partly on a public road. The proper interpretation of the case, as is explicit in the words of the Divisional Court, at least as reported in the

Criminal Law Review, is that the justices, from whatever evidence they had before them, including the fact of which they could take judicial notice by reason of their personal knowledge, namely, the distance between the start and end of the journey, were entitled to draw the inference that the lorry must at some time have travelled on a public road.

Such a distinction between the knowledge which a justice or judge has or the judicial notice which he may take of a fact, on the one hand, and the inference which he may draw from such knowledge or notice, on the other hand, is supported by the comments on Judicial Notice made by the High Court of Australia in *Burns* v. *Lipman*.[22] On a "second stage" appeal against the verdict of a trial judge without a jury, the High Court said: "His Honour said he could take judicial notice of the habits of motorists in relation to the sounding of the horn when passing or commencing to pass another vehicle. We would point out that whilst a juryman or judge may bring to the resolution of a case his knowledge of what usually occurs on a highway, that knowledge is not properly to be regarded as judicial notice. Use of that knowledge in this case was appropriate rather to the question of what a motorist is entitled to expect when being overtaken,"[23] *i.e.* relevant to a finding of negligence in an overtaking driver who failed to sound his horn.

Johnstone v. *Hawkins*[24]

Although, as just mentioned, this case is often referred to in connection with justices and judicial notice, once again we do not in fact find the phrase judicial notice used in the case, at least according to the *Criminal Law Review* note, and indeed, in this respect, the case would present some difficulties of its own.

On charges of dangerous driving and careless driving, the justices found simply that the defendant was driving a motor-cycle at some 85 to 90 m.p.h. along a main road across a junction where the side-road was controlled by a "Slow—Major Road Ahead" sign. There was no other traffic about at the time. The justices dismissed the two informations and the prosecutor appealed to the Divisional Court. In their case stated the justices recorded that they were very familiar with the road; it ran through woodland; there were no buildings adjacent to it; there was only the one side-road. There was a clear view some 20 yards from the junction of both roads, with visibility a quarter of a mile along the main road and three hundred and fifty yards along the minor road.

The Divisional Court remitted the case to the justices for further findings of fact. Had they taken into account both actual and potential danger? What traffic was to be expected? Did the view down the side-road start 20 yards from the junction? If not, when did it start? It is not surprising that there was no mention of judicial notice in these circumstances, because it would be pushing the doctrine beyond its limits if it were to embrace such details as were involved in the facts given in the case stated, going far beyond the existence and general lay-out of the junction; and, when the case was remitted for further findings of facts, surely evidence would have to be produced to enable the justices to answer those further questions; they could not draw further upon their "judicial knowledge."

After these references to the cases, one may already feel that the dividing line between knowledge by notoriety, which may be judicially noted, and knowledge by personal observation, which may not be, is not as clear as Wigmore would like to think,[25] and indeed that, at least with regard to magistrates' courts, the dividing line may not exist at all, since how, otherwise than by personal observation, have the justices acquired their local knowledge?

This is an appropriate point at which to revert to my "text," "Your Worships are probably familiar with this junction," because this elaborates the difficulties of this so-called distinction and it also illustrates the complications which emerge in a multiple bench. It may well be that at least some of the Bench—let us assume that it is composed of the usual three, being a disputed case—*are* familiar with the junction. But what if they are not *all* familiar with it? What happens about the third one if only two are? In the nature of things, he or she is unlikely to admit to his ignorance of the junction. If he does so acknowledge, then, if the party really must establish the facts as part of his case, it is incumbent on him to call evidence to the extent of the detail which he requires, although, *ex hypothesi*, if he has already invited the bench to take judicial notice without calling any evidence, he would seem to be asking only for a knowledge of the existence and general lay-out of a junction without any detail, and this might well be supplied by means of a photograph agreed with the other side or proved in the usual way. Of course, there is always the possibility of a "view,"[26] but it requires little imagination to realise the effect on expense and time if such a procedure were regularly adopted.

But how well is the junction really known even to those who profess "knowledge" of it? As a matter of personal experience, I have several times been discomfited by my realisation that the evidence produced before us did not seem to correspond exactly with my own particular recollection of the particular stretch of road or of the particular junction, only to find later, perhaps when deliberately driving over it in order to check "the truth," that it was my own recollection that was at fault. Fortunately, in no case, to the best of my knowledge, information and belief, has my decision been conclusively affected by such a discrepancy, but clearly the danger is always there, difficult to avoid and impossible to detect externally, as far as any individual magistrate is concerned.

And what about the situation where the *locus in quo* is well-known to, say, two of the bench, but from different angles? Thus, the one magistrate knows the junction well, but only as a traveller on the main road on which the side-road emerges; he or she barely notices it when driving into court, only semi-consciously being aware of the queue of cars waiting in the side-road until there is a gap in the main road traffic. But the home of the other magistrate may be situated in the side-road itself, so that every time he comes into court he is in one of those cars waiting in the side-road for the main road traffic to thin out, being mainly aware of the high speed of that traffic and its lack of concern for the patient side-road users. In our case of careless driving, based on the emergence of the defendant from the side-road, allegedly without due care and attention, it is true that both these magistrates have some first-hand personal knowledge of the junction, but from very different standpoints and starting, quite possibly, from very different sympathies. All right, one may say, in that event, these differing standpoints, these differing prejudices, if one dare use that word and if that is in fact what they are, will cancel each other out, leaving it, ironically, one may think, to the third magistrate in his or her innocence, or ignorance, to tilt the scale one way or the other, acting properly solely on the evidence produced before the court.

But what if the two "knowing" magistrates are both "main road" drivers, or both "side-road" drivers, as the case might be? Can they be relied on to judge the evidence impartially and reach their decision on that evidence alone? Indeed, if in such a case the two of them were emphatic in their conclusions, the third magistrate, who might have been better placed to have reached a truly impartial and "just" decision on the evidence actually produced, might well yield to the "better information and experience" of the other two so as to produce in the end a unanimous verdict!

These then are some of the difficulties which can, and surely do arise, when magistrates make use of their own local knowledge in reaching decisions, when they feel able to dispense with the production of evidence since the facts are sufficiently notorious within their own local knowledge. Now we shall consider another area where personal knowledge can be involved, where the magistrate or the tribunal member possesses his knowledge and experience because of his own training, trade or profession. Usually these cases can be differentiated from those involving local knowledge since this can normally be attributed, rightly or wrongly, to all members of the bench or tribunal, whereas in these cases of specialised knowledge or expertise it is more usual, in the nature of things, for only one member of the bench to possess them.

The case which often provides a starting point for a discussion of this issue in magistrates' courts is *Wetherall* v. *Harrison*,[27] where the offence charged was one of failing without reasonable cause to provide a specimen for a laboratory test, contrary to s.9(3) of the Road Traffic Act 1972. The defence consisted in the assertion that the defendant was unable to give a sample because he had some sort of fit. The doctor who had been called by the police to take the sample ruled out all medical reasons for the defendant's behaviour and expressed his opinion that he was simulating a fit. There was no medical evidence in rebuttal, but one of the magistrates, a Dr. Robertson, was a practising medical practitioner. The defendant was discharged and the prosecutor appealed to the Divisional Court by way of case stated. In the words of Lord Widgery, L.C.J., delivering the judgment of that court: "Counsel for the appellant, in putting the matter before us, is really inviting us to say, for the advantages of justices hereafter, what should happen when a justice has specialised knowledge of this kind: should he use it or should he not? . . . I do not think that the position of a justice of the peace is the same, in this regard, as the position of a trained judge. If you have a judge sitting alone, trying a civil case, it is perfectly feasible and sensible that he should be instructed and trained to exclude certain factors from his consideration of the problem . . . "[28] "Justices are not so trained. They are much more like jurymen in this respect. I think it would be wrong to start with the proposition that justices' use of their local or personal knowledge is governed by exactly the same rule as is laid down in the case of trained judges. I do not believe that a serious restriction on a justice's use of his own knowledge or the knowledge of his colleagues can really be enforced. Laymen (by which I mean non-lawyers)[29] sitting as justices considering a case which has just been heard before them lack the ability to put out of their minds certain features of the case. In particular, if the justice is a specialist, be he a doctor, or an engineer or an accountant, or what you will, it is not possible for him to approach the decision in the case as though he had not got that training, and indeed I think it would be a very bad thing if he had to. In a sense, the bench of justices is like a jury, they are a cross-section of people, and one of the advantages which they have is that they bring a lot of experience into the courtroom and use it. So I start with the proposition that it is not improper for a justice who has special knowledge of the circumstances forming the background to a particular case to draw on that special knowledge in interpretation of the evidence which has been heard in court. I stress that last sentence, because it would be quite wrong if the justice went on, as it were, to give evidence to himself in contradiction of that which has been heard in court. He is not there to give evidence to himself, still more is he not there to give evidence to other justices; but that he can employ his basic knowledge in considering, weighing up and assessing the evidence given before the court is, I think, beyond doubt . . . . Furthermore, I do not see why he should not, certainly if requested by fellow justices, tell his fellow justices the way in which his specialist knowledge has caused him to look at the evidence . . . he can explain the evidence they have heard; he can give his own views as to how the case should go and how it should be decided; but he should not be giving evidence behind closed doors which is not available to the parties . . . . Applying these principles to the instant case, there was certainly no reason why Dr. Robertson should not, when forming his own conclusion about this case, have referred to his own knowledge, and his own knowledge and experience was that this kind of fit was genuine, and knowing that it would be right that in reviewing and considering the evidence in this case he should have that knowledge on the background and use it if he thought fit. Since his fellow justices knew he was a doctor, and I think asked him for the benefit of his views, I see no reason at all why he should not tell them what his views were." In the result, the appeal was dismissed, *i.e.* there was nothing improper in the proceedings.

Now, one may readily accept that it is impossible and impracticable, and indeed undesirable, to expect an individual justice to put out of his mind any specialised knowledge he may possess when assessing the evidence produced before him. But if he decides to find against that evidence because of his knowledge and experience, it is difficult to see how he has not in fact given evidence to himself which outweighs the court evidence. Even so, no one can in reality complain about such a process as long as he keeps it to himself, if for no other reason than that no one will know. They are entitled to assume that he did not find that the evidence submitted satisfied him to the requisite standard of proof. It might indeed be better for him to intimate some of his misgivings regarding the evidence which is produced by posing some questions to the witness who is proffering it, although he must surely be careful not to phrase any such questions in a way which suggests that he is putting them from a firmly held viewpoint which is not likely to change. Equally he would have to be careful not to dismiss with any sign of impatience or incredulity the answers offered by the witness to his questions.

The course of action which is sometimes held out as the proper one where a member of the bench has such evidence to offer is that he should descend from the bench and take the witness-stand to give his evidence under the sanction of the oath and subject to the check of cross-examination and evidence in rebuttal. But in that event it is submitted that he should certainly not resume his seat on the bench after having given his evidence,[30] because "What would a litigant think if he saw one of the justices come down from the bench, give evidence against him and then resume his place on the bench?"[31]

To revert to Dr. Robertson in *Wetherall* v. *Harrison* and to consider his position *vis-à-vis* his fellow justices, it would seem acceptable for him to inform his colleagues of the way in which his own knowledge and experience had led him to interpret the evidence brought before them. We can also agree that "he should not be giving evidence behind closed doors which is not available to the public."[32] But between these two extreme positions there are a number of intermediate propositions which may be difficult fully to accept, especially "he can give his own view on how the case should be decided." Of course, he can give his own view on how he would, or will, decide the case in the light of his own training, knowledge and experience, but to go further and to suggest that that is the decision which his colleagues too should reach, seems to pre-empt the individual personal judgment of those colleagues who, presumably, lack that specialised knowledge, so that he is in reality telling them how the case should be decided, *i.e.* how *they* should decide the case, and in that event is he not indeed imposing his own knowledge and experience, *i.e.* his own evidence, upon them?

This particular situation can also arise in the case of lay members of tribunals, where very often the so-called "wing" members, *i.e.* the two members apart from the chairman, are only "lay" insofar as they are not lawyers, being very often very experienced and knowledgeable in some aspect of the tribunal's work. Indeed that experience and knowledge are some of the reasons for their appointment; examples are Industrial Tribunals and, perhaps to a lesser extent, Supplementary Benefit Appeals Tribunals. While there have been a number of cases over the decades involving arbitrators and country court judges and their use of their personal local knowledge of, for example, rates of pay and working conditions,[33] there are very few cases so far dealing specifically with tribunal members. One of these is *Dugdale* v. *Kraft Foods Ltd*.

An industrial tribunal had dismissed an application by female employees for equality of pay under the Equal Pay Act 1970, as amended by the Sex Discrimination Act 1975. On appeal to the Employment Appeal Tribunal by the employees, the tribunal of first instance included in the reasons for its decision the following passage: "In this matter, as in many other aspects of the decision, our unanimous view is reinforced by the invaluable shop-floor experience of our lady member who works in a similar food manufacturing industry." On this point, Phillips J., delivering the judgment of the E.A.T., had this to say: "It is suggested that this indicates a wrong approach, and that the decision is based on evidence wrongly obtained. The members of industrial tribunals are appointed because of their special knowledge and experience, and we have no doubt that they are entitled to draw on it in playing their part in assisting the tribunal as a whole to reach a decision. The main use they will make of this knowledge and experience is for the purpose of explaining and understanding the evidence which they hear. Certainly they are entitled to use their knowledge and experience to fill gaps in the evidence about matters which will be obvious to them but which might be obscure to a layman. More difficult is the case where evidence is given which is contrary to their knowledge and experience. If such an occasion arises, we think that they ought to draw to the attention of the witnesses the experience which seems to suggest that the evidence given is wrong, and ought not to prefer their own knowledge or experience without giving the witness an opportunity to deal with it. Provided that this opportunity is given, there seems to us to be no reason why they should not draw on their knowledge and experience in this way also. But it is highly desirable that in any case where particular use is made by an industrial tribunal of the knowledge and experience of one or more of its members in reaching its decision this fact should be stated and that particulars of the matter taken into account should be fully disclosed."[34] In this case the judgment had already indicated that the case would be remitted for rehearing for other reasons, and so it is impossible to deduce how these remarks would in themselves have affected the decision in the instant case—whether the inclusion of the matters taken into account in their statement of the reasons would have been a timeous and sufficient disclosure. Perhaps the later case of *Hammington* v. *Berker Sportcraft*[35] indicates that it would not have been.

In that case, similarly before the Employment Appeal Tribunal, the question was the assessment of compensation for unfair dismissal. The claimant had been employed as general manager of the defendants' bridal division for one year from December 1, 1977, at £7,000 per annum with the use of a car and up to £500 contribution to a pension scheme. He was dismissed and, in the view of the industrial tribunal, unfairly, on November 30, 1978, but he was awarded damages only for his loss up to the date of the order, nothing for further loss in the future. He appealed to the E.A.T. against the amount.

Here again, in the reasons given by the tribunal at first instance for their decision, occurs the following passage: "Drawing on the knowledge and experience of one of the members of the tribunal, Mr. Apter, who made known his expertise when questioning the employee, we are satisfied that with the varied experience which the employee had in New Zealand including an apprenticeship lasting five years, he should, had he used his fullest endeavours, have obtained employment by now as a pattern cutter, designer or factory manager at a total remuneration at least commensurate with that which he received from the company, including the car or its equivalent in cash terms and a non-contributory pension scheme entitlement. We do not accept that £5,000 is the most he can expect to earn in the immediate future."[35]

On the appeal, the point of law was raised: Whether it was proper for the tribunal to draw on the knowledge and experience of one of its members, Mr. Apter, who was said by the chairman to have possessed expertise in certain trades connected with the employee's former employment, in coming to the conclusion that the employee, who was general manager of a retail shop, should, had he used his fullest endeavours, have obtained employment by the date of the hearing.

Talbot J., giving the judgment of the E.A.T., commented thus: "The point therefore is whether, improperly in the sense that it was wrong to do, reliance was placed upon matters about which Mr. Apter knew which were not given in evidence. We would like to make it clear at the outset that the knowledge, experience and expertise of a member of an Industrial Tribunal is plainly something that should play its part in the assessment of evidence and in its interpretation. That is, in part, why members are appointed, but there are limits." He refers to several cases where the question has been considered, including *Wetherall* v. *Harrison*,[36] and continues: "The essence therefore of the use of specialised knowledge and information and experience is that it is to be used, as can be seen from all these authorities, for the purpose of weighing up and assessing the evidence and, if necessary, interpreting it. What must not be done is using that knowledge to substitute for the evidence given in court evidence derived from such knowledge nor must it be used for producing some facts of evidence which is not evidence before the court, with which the parties have not had an opportunity of dealing. Here the tribunal went too far . . . "[37] His Lordship then cites the particular questions asked by Mr. Apter of the claimant and his answers, and concludes that the facts should have been brought to the attention of the employee or, in this particular case, to his Counsel so that, if they were facts relied upon, Counsel could have dealt with them, or, if necessary, as was submitted in the case, if unable to deal with them, he could have asked for an adjournment. It was not put to Counsel in this way and so the case was remitted to the industrial tribunal.

Since this paper was read, the report of another Employment Appeal Tribunal case has appeared in The Times, *Williams and Others* v. *Compair Maxam Ltd*.[37] Four employees had appealed to an Industrial Tribunal claiming that they had been unfairly dismissed by the company, but the claim was dismissed by a majority of the tribunal. To quote Browne-Wilkinson J., giving the judgment of the E.A.T.: "One of the grounds of appeal was that the decision (of the industrial tribunal) was perverse and therefore wrong in law. In the legal sense a decision was perverse only if no reasonable tribunal, properly directing itself, could have reached that decision. In considering whether a decision was perverse in the legal sense there was one feature which did not occur in other jurisdictions where there was a right of appeal only on a point of law. Industrial tribunals were industrial juries which brought to their task a knowledge of industrial relations from the viewpoint of both the employer and the employee. Matters of industrial relations practice were not proved before an industrial tribunal: the lay members were taken to know them. In considering whether the decision of an industrial tribunal was perverse, it was not safe to rely solely on the common sense and knowledge of those who had no experience in the field of industrial relations. Accordingly, the correct approach was to consider whether an industrial tribunal, properly directed in law and properly appreciating what was currently regarded as fair industrial practice, could have come to the decision reached by the majority of the industrial tribunal in the present case." It appeared that the E.A.T. had little difficulty in concluding that the dismissals had been carried out in blatant contravention of the standards of fair treatment generally accepted by employers; the decision of the industrial tribunal was perverse and so the appeals were allowed.

Some reflections on these dicta may now be offered in an attempt to reach some conclusions on the rather untidy and amorphous material brought together in this paper, always bearing in mind the dangers of trying to "button up" this area in an uncomfortable and unworkable straitjacket.[38]

In those cases where a magistrate or a tribunal member has some specialised knowledge or experience, one may well think that the principle is reasonably clear, namely that he can, and should utilise that knowledge and experience in the interpretation and assessment of the evidence produced before the tribunal, but that he should stop short of giving further, additional, evidence to his colleagues. Ideally he should not even give such additional evidence to himself, but then the line between unacceptable additional evidence and acceptable knowledge and experience in interpreting the evidence which has been produced becomes extremely thin and uncertain, because on what is that knowledge and experience based if not upon incidents, experiences, which could in turn themselves be regarded as additional evidence? Moreover as Lord Widgery impliedly acknowledged in *Wetherall* v. *Harrison*,[39] it is realistically impossible to do anything about it anyway if the individual keeps it to himself. Where he does communicate with his fellows, giving them the benefit of his knowledge and experience, even there the dividing line is often tenuous, and it must very largely be entrusted to the good sense and sense of propriety of the member himself to determine, so to speak, where experience stops and evidence begins. Also it behoves his fellow members not to tempt him to supplement the evidence properly presented with additional evidence which should itself have been given during the hearing of the case.

With regard to the use by a bench or tribunal of its personal knowledge, using that phrase in this context in a collective sense, whether or not this is truly an application of the doctrine of Judicial Notice or rather of some analogous principle easily confused therewith,[40] the same difficulties and dangers seem to exist whether the knowledge imputed is "general local knowledge" as in the case of magistrates or specialised knowledge and experience as in the case of, say, members of industrial tribunals.

There can be no guarantee of the equality and impartiality, or should one say, objectivity, of that knowledge, whether it be the "knowledge" of the main-road user or that of the side-road user in my earlier example, or the "knowledge and experience" of the members of the industrial tribunal in *Williams* v. *Compair Maxam* in assessing fair industrial practice as they saw it. Matters of industrial relations practice may not have to be proved before an industrial tribunal but how can one be sure of the validity and consistency of the knowledge which the members are presumed to have?

As far as lay magistrates are concerned, if they are entrusted with the difficult, often thankless, task of administering justice according to the law and to the best of their ability, and if society wishes to enjoy the benefit of their judgment and experience and good sense and impartiality, society must be willing to rely on them to negotiate, without too many accidents—and in any event with the safeguard of an elaborate appeal system—the gray and narrow path between that "general local knowledge" which they are permitted to call in aid in order to discharge their duties with the greatest possible saving of time and expense, and that personal, one may say, perhaps fortuitous knowledge in any given case which may qualify him to give evidence himself as a witness in the case, or which may disqualify him from sitting as judge in it.

At the outset of this paper I confessed to having no solution to put forward to correct or remedy some of the weaknesses which may have been revealed here in the acceptance of personal knowledge as evidence. Certainly I would not want to see any elaborate attempt made to hamstring the magistrates and tribunal members by means of regulations or rules of court, or even judicial precedents on appeal. The trouble with such safeguards is that eventually they tend to obscure the fact that the human agencies which operate the system, and are the most important component of it, are simply not up to the task, and I hope that not many responsible critics would make that allegation concerning our lay magistrates' courts and lay membership of tribunals, which on the whole serve the community reasonably well and which are still capable of further improvement within their present framework by means of improved selection and improved instruction.

Notes

[1] This topic was prompted by an earlier article, published in the commemorative volume of the Exeter University Law Faculty in 1980, on "Fundamental Duties," when I took as my theme the fundamental duties of magistrates to do justice according to the law, a duty formulated in their judicial oath. I tried to point out

how, to some extent at any rate, their ability to discharge their judicial duties is hampered by the adversarial system which deters them from asking too many questions and from calling their own witnesses, in their desire to arrive at "the truth." An associated question is to what extent can and should magistrates draw on their personal knowledge and experience in arriving at their decision, in discovering "the truth," and it is this question which is the subject-matter of this present article, widened to embrace also the question of lay members of tribunals.

[2] Molière, *Le Bourgeois Gentilhomme*: Act II, Scene IV.

[3] Very much in mind is the monstrous system of statute law and statutory regulation now governing supplementary benefit since November, 1980, partly as the result of academic criticism as to the amount of discretion previously available to supplementary benefit officers and appeal tribunals: see Dr. Carol Harlow, 44 M.L.R. 546.

[4] See any textbook on evidence: *e.g.* Cross (5th ed., 1979), Chap. V, section 1.

[5] *Cf.* Wigmore, *A Treatise on the Anglo-American System of Evidence, 2567.* (3rd ed., 1960).

[6] An English lawyer will find it interesting, and surprising, that the Rule relating to Judicial Notice (r. 201) of the Federal Rules of Evidence in the United States Codes Annotated deliberately omits all reference to "legislative facts," influenced by the writings of Professor Kenneth Davis: "those facts which have relevance to legal reasoning and the lawmaking process, whether in the formulation of a legal principle or ruling by a judge or court or in the enactment of a legislative body." The reason for this omission is said to lie in the need to retain some flexibility in the legal process, whereas the essential prerequisite for the application of the doctrine of judicial notice is a high degree of indisputability.

Insofar as judicial notice is taken of such legislative facts in magistrates' courts in this country, the knowledge is clearly that of the magistrates' clerk whose knowledge is then "imputed" to his lay magistrates so as to enable them to take judicial notice.

[7] R. 201, note 6 above. This description usefully meets that somewhat casuistic dispute as to whether a case where the judge has to consult a reference book before taking cognisance of a fact really constitutes an example of taking judicial notice or whether the reference book should not rather be regarded as being tendered in evidence. *Cf. McQuaker* v. *Goddard* [1940] 1 K.B. 687. Cross, *op. cit.* p.158.

[8] *Aliter*, it seems, if the particular place is not so listed, *R.* v. *Crush* [1978] Crim. L.R. 357. But see the commentary there on the decision.

[9] Professor Kenneth Davis, *A System of Judicial Notice Based on Fairness and Convenience in Perspectives of Law* (1964).

[10] Adapting a phrase quoted by Professor J.N. Morgan, "Judicial Notice" in 57 Harv. L. Rev. (1943–44) 269, 272 n.3.

[11] The phrase used here is "judicial knowledge," but it is presumed that judicial knowledge is what enables a judge to take judicial notice of a fact, so that the two phrases, at least in the present context, are synonymous.

[12] One is reminded of the similar analysis of "knowledge" in a very different area of law, that of measure of damages in Contract law, by Asquith L.J. in *Victoria Laundry (Windsor) Ltd.* v. *Newman Industries Ltd.* [1949] 2 K.B. 528, 539; where he relates imputed and actual knowledge to the first and second rules, respectively, of *Hadley* v. *Bexendale* (1854) 9 Ex. 341.

[13] Wigmore, *op. cit.* para. 2569.

[14] Just as there are only a few cases reported on the topic, so also there is little to be found in textbooks with special reference to magistrates' courts. One exception is Carter, *Cases and Statutes on Evidence* (1981) pp.108–109.

[15] [1969] 1 Q.B. 548.

[16] At p.555.

[17] [1961] Crim. L.R. 121.

[18] This is the phrase as given in the *Criminal Law Review*.

[19] [1973] Crim. L.R. 317.

[20] At p.318.

[21] [1959] Crim. L.R. 459.

[22] (1965) 132 C.L.R. 157.

[23] At p.161.

[24] [1959] Crim. L.R. 459.

[25] See note 13.

[26] As was offered, and refused, in rather special circumstances, in *Clift* v. *Long*, note 17, above.

[27] [1976] 1 Q.B. 773.

[28] At p.777. One may however cite the well-known dictum of Wills J. in *R.* v. *Field*, *ex. p. White* (1895) 64 L.J.M.C. 158, where a magistrates' court, consisting of a retired Admiral, Admiral Field, as chairman and two other justices who had also served in the Royal Navy, had dismissed a complaint brought under the food and drugs legislation relating to the sale of allegedly adulterated cocoa. The complaint had been based on the certificate of a public analyst. The defence offered no evidence, but the bench dismissed the case since they considered it a matter of public knowledge that cocoa, as an article of commerce, must necessarily contain a large proportion of other ingredients, and this fact would bring the case within one of the exempting provisos. A rule *nisi* had been made calling on the justices to show cause why they should not state a case for the opinion of the High Court. Admiral Field did show cause, in person: "The Justices will certainly state a case if any point of law be involved. But no point of law arises. Naval officers are expert in cocoa. No one can consume pure cocoa." It was however ruled that a case should be stated and, although the justices' decision was upheld, Wills J., expressed some misgivings about the way in which the bench had dealt with the matter; and in the course of these remarks he utters the dictum which, with respect, throws some doubt about the validity of Lord Widgery's confident declaration of the "professional judge's" ability to exclude "non-evidence" from his considerations. "However," said Wills J., "They decided the case as they did on their own knowledge; and in the nature of things, no one, in determining a case of this kind, can discard his own particular knowledge of a subject of this kind. I might as well be asked to decide a question as to the sufficiency of an Alpine rope without bringing my personal knowledge into play . . . " But the personal knowledge professed by the Judges of the Provincial Division in the South African case of *R.* v. *Tager* as to the method of mixing milk-shakes was firmly and eloquently rejected by Watermeyer C.J. in the Appellate Division [1944] A.D. (S.A.) 339, 342–345.

[29] One wonders how the increasing number of "academic" lawyers who are magistrates would be classified.

[30] Pace Holmes J., in *R.*v. *Antrim Justices* (1895 2 Ir.R. 603, Q.B.D. at p.657).

[31] To adapt a dictum of Rowlatt J. in *Mitchell* v. *Croydon Justices* (1914) 30 T.L.R. 526.

[32] *Wetherall* v. *Harrison*, at p. 778.

[33] See, *e.g.* Manchester, 42 M.L.R. 22.

[34] [1977] 1 A.E.R. 454.

[35] (1980) Industrial Case Reports 248.

[36] *Supra*, (27).

[37] The Times, January 27, 1982.

[38] *Supra*, (3) and (9).

[39] *Supra*, (27).

[40] *Cf.* Carter, *Cases and Statutes on Evidence* (1981), pp.108–109.

The Structure of the Employment Contract

PATRICK ELIAS

THE late Sir Otto Kahn Freund, in one of his typically striking metaphors, once described the contract of employement as "the cornerstone of the edifice of labour law."[1] But this assertion did not go unchallenged. Professor Rideout, in a lecture delivered in this series 16 years ago,[2] contended that far from occupying this pivotal position the contract had come to play an incidental and largely irrelevant role in the regulation of the rights and duties of employers and workers. It has suffered a decline, he argued, both because of the dominating influence of collective bargaining, and also because contract rules were fundamentally unsuited to regulate the modern employment relationship. They had singularly failed to provide effective protection for the worker. He believed that the contract should be decently buried, and it should be recognised that the employment relationship, though rooted in contract, created in reality a form of status.[3] This latter observation has indeed since been recognised, perhaps to a greater extent even than Professor Rideout would have envisaged. The inadequacy of common law principles to protect the interests of employees had led to the creation of a whole series of statutory rights relating to such matters as redundancy, unfair dismissal and maternity, which has resulted in a further decline in the importance of contract as a source of rights. The almost total eclipse of the law of wrongful dismissal by the statutory concept of unfair dismissal graphically illustrates this fact.

Yet curiously, far from being cowed by this statutory assault, the contract of employment has emerged more resilient, and has proved to be infinitely more relevant, than could possibly have been foreseen even a dozen years ago. The explanation of this apparent paradox is that the statutory rights have been built upon the common law contractual framework, so that whilst the contract is of diminishing importance as a direct independent source of rights, it remains central to the operation of these statutory provisions. This importance is manifest in two rather different ways. Sometimes the employment contract provides the vehicle through which the statutory right takes effect, such as the equality clause which, under the terms of the Equal Pay Act, has become part of every worker's contract of employment.[4] More significantly, recourse often has to be made to contractual concepts in order to determine the scope of the statutory rights. Such questions as when the contract is terminated, or whether the employer can, within its terms, lawfully require the employee to work overtime, or on a different job, or transfer to another place of work—all these regularly arise in industrial tribunals in the context of deciding whether the employee's statutory rights have been infringed. Furthermore, the relative ease with which employees can bring cases before tribunals has meant that they—and perhaps more importantly for the elucidation of the law of the employment contract, the appellate courts—have had to determine controversial points of contract law far more frequently than the courts had to do in the past. So far from gradually fading away, the contract of employment has been rejuvenated by Parliament's industry. With remarkable tenacity it has adapted itself to a new legal environment.

Yet despite its long-standing importance, there are still certain basic issues going to the heart of the structure of the contract which continue to puzzle labour lawyers. Such questions as defining the nature of the obligations arising under the contract, the point when the contract ceases and, perhaps most importantly, the legal significance of the fact that the contract creates a social relationship as well as an economic nexus, can still not be answered with any confidence. An analysis of these issues also inevitably raises the question of how far the employment contract has been influenced by special features considered peculiar to it and how far it reflects the application of general contract principles. This arises because the judges' perception of the structure of the contract, and the legal rules they apply to it, will depend upon how they see its role as a social phenomenon, and also by how far they believe it should be moulded to achieve particular policy objectives in the field of labour relations. In short, questions of structure are ultimately rooted in questions of policy: the two cannot be separated.

The nature of contractual obligations

Dr. Mark Freedland, in his seminal work on the contract of employment, considered that the contract has a two-tier structure: at the first level is what may loosely be described as the wage-work bargain, the exchange of labour for remuneration; at the second level is the exchange of mutual obligations for future performance, the promise to employ on the one side and be employed on the other, which gives the relationship its continuity.[5] To these it may be useful to add a third tier which, to a greater or lesser extent, is a feature of all employment contracts, namely the employee's obligation to serve the employer honestly and faithfully and not to deliberately damage the employer's interests. This duty, which reflects the continuing dependent nature of the employment relationship, will impose restrictions on the employee's freedom of action. For example, no employee is entitled to work in his spare time for a competitor knowing that it will seriously prejudice his employer's business.[6] Another rule, equitable in origin, is that an employee cannot disclose to a third party confidential information which he gains by virtue of his employment, nor can he use it for his own benefit.[7] Admittedly for many employees these duties will not be onerous; they will be virtuous out of necessity since the opportunity for infringing the contract in these ways will be remote. Nevertheless these obligations are important because they emphasise the negative element in the contract, the restrictions on his freedom of action which an employee is deemed to accept as part of his bargain. Frequently these negative undertakings will extend beyond the period of the employment relationship itself. The duty not to disclose confidential information does so automatically as a matter of law,[8] and the restrictions on working in competition can also be extended in this way, at least within the limits set down by public policy, provided there is a specific contractual restraint of trade clause to this effect.[9]

The duration of contractual terms

One of the more interesting features of the contract of employment is that the obligations arising thereunder can, and frequently will, endure for different periods of time. Although in common parlance we talk of the termination of the contract, that does not necessarily mean that all the rights and obligations arising under the contract then end simultaneously. This is obvious when certain common contractual terms are considered: as just mentioned, a restraint of trade clause may bind the employee even though he had severed all his connections with his former employer and is perhaps even working for a new employer; again, a retired worker may draw a pension to which he is contractually entitled years after the relationship with his employer has ceased. Yet it would be misleading in these cases to say that the contract is in force because a particular term arising under it remains in operation. The very nature of these terms envisages that they will operate only when the body of the contract, in the sense of the employment relationship and its principal terms, have come to an end. But the fact that some terms may survive a termination raises the question of precisely which terms of the contract must come to an end before the contract as such can be considered in law to have terminated. What exactly is the core of the contract whose destruction brings the whole edifice to the ground? It must be emphasised that usually this will be an irrelevant question: a court will simply have to determine whether a particular contractual obligation is in force, and it will be unnecessary to decide whether the contract itself lives or not. But occasionally the question may be crucial. This may occur at common law where certain rights are made contingent on the continued existence of the contract itself[10]; and in the statutory context, the concept of dismissal—so important in the operation of the unfair dismissal and redundancy laws—is defined in terms of the termination of the contract,[11] and also the date when the contract terminates is crucial to the operation of these rights.[12] So the point of termination has to be established, and in the course of this the interrelationship of the various contractual terms has to be considered. For this reason, theories of termination have much to say about the structure of the contract.

Policy considerations

But as has been argued, theories of termination are not simply logical abstractions. They have been developed in the course of judges having to decide practical questions and seeking to achieve particular policy objectives. It is possible to distinguish three policy considerations which have tended to dominate the judicial perception of the contract of employment, particularly when they are dealing with its termination. Indeed, so deeply rooted are these in judicial consciousness that they frequently tend to be asserted as self-evident propositions, and it is easy to forget that they conceal value judgments at all. The first is that an employee should not receive wages unless he has worked, so that even if the failure to work is because of the employer's refusal to provide him with tasks to do, still he should be prevented from claiming remuneration and be limited to a claim in damages. This is closely related to, and indeed is a necessary condition for, the operation of the second policy, namely that the employee should be under an obligation to mitigate his loss by seeking to find alternative employment. This duty to mitigate arises only if the employee is obliged to claim damages: if he could claim wages then he would be under no duty to mitigate since it is trite law that a party must mitigate damages but not debt.[13] Consequently the debt has in some way to be converted into damages before this objective can be realised. The third policy objective is that no employer should be compelled against his will to continue an employment relationship with any worker.[14] The general denial of the remedies of specific performance or injunction secures this objective.

These policies in turn reflect certain more fundamental assumptions about the employment contract. Taken together, they involve a perception of the contract in purely economic terms.[14] The refusal to require specific performance of the contract, coupled with the obligation to mitigate, ensures that the employee will be compensated only for unavoidable loss. Furthermore—and this is true of contract principles generally—the restriction of compensation to the innocent party's loss rather than the guilty party's gain positively encourages the latter to break his contractual obligations when a more profitable enterprise presents itself. The law of equity recognised that these principles could work harshly and the remedies of specific performance and injunctions were developed specifically to ensure that in some circumstances the party would get what he bargained for rather than simply compensation for losing it.[15] But these will apply only where damages are an inadequate remedy and the courts have not, barring a few limited exceptions which are considered below, been willing to accept that a worker's interest in his job justifies these remedies being granted.[16]

In short, the effect of these policies is that the common law has applied the principles of free enterprise to the labour market no less than to the commodity market. A justification for this is that it helps to avoid economic waste, promotes the maximisation of profit and permits the exploitation of commercial opportunities.[17] But the fundamental weakness is that it has failed to recognise any legitimate interest in job security. In seeing a man's job in purely economic terms, the common law has ignored the important social and psychological benefits which form an integral part of the employment relationship.[18]

Rationalising the policies

How, then, have the legal rules operated to secure these policy objectives? And more importantly, how have the rules been justified? The answer is complicated because they have not been explained by any single formula. Take the wage-work bargain: a number of reasons have at various times been proposed to explain why the refusal of the employer to continue the employment relationship will destroy the employee's right to claim wages. Until recently the orthodox answer would have been that a wrongful dismissal automatically terminated the contract and that the wage-work bargain lasts only as long as the contract subsists.[19] It was recognised that this was an exception to the usual contractual rule that a repudiation requires acceptance, and different grounds have been suggested for justifying this departure. One is that the inability of the employee to obtain an order to force the employer to continue the contract should itself automatically prevent the contract continuing.[20] On this analysis the third policy objective outlined above, the refusal to grant specific enforcement of the employment contract, is considered to automatically require the courts to treat the other two objectives as implemented. This is unsatisfactory: it assumes that a contract cannot be kept in force following a repudiation unless it is capable of specific enforcement, but as Lord Hodson pointed out in the leading contract case of *White and Carter (Councils) Ltd.* v. *McGregor*,[21] this is manifestly wrong. There is no logical reason why an innocent party should not keep the contract alive even if, once dead, the contract cannot be resurrected. The objectors to this approach are surely right to say that the question of which remedies are available should not dictate the substantive law principles to be applied.

A second justification for the automatic termination theory is that the continuation of the contract depends upon the personal relationship subsisting. Sometimes this in turn is explained on the grounds that the maintenance of trust and confidence, or, in a slightly different vein, harmony and co-operation, is fundamental to the contract, so that its destruction must bring the contract to an end.[22] But this latter emphasis is not an adequate rationalisation of the automatic termination theory either. It is clear that conduct which is objectively inconsistent with the maintenance of trust and confidence does not immediately terminate the contract. This follows from the decision in *Healey* v. *S.A.F. Rubastic*.[23] The employee had sent false reports to his employer and was dismissed when this fact was subsequently discovered. He was not paid his wages for the period following his deceitful conduct and he sued for them. His claim was upheld. The contract did not terminate until the employer chose to accept the repudiation and bring it to an end.[24] So the personal relationship must at least be severed before the contract is terminated. Does this mean that the personal relationship must be severed together with trust and confidence before the contract terminates? Some support for this proposition might be found in *Hill* v. *C.A. Parsons & Co. Ltd.*,[25] where unusually the Court of Appeal issued an injunction to prevent an employer from dismissing his employee on the grounds that the trust and confidence between the parties continued to exist notwithstanding the wrongful dismissal. The employee in that case had been dismissed because he refused to join a particular union which had entered into a closed shop arrangement with the employer, and so the union pressed for his dismissal. Without that pressure, the employer would have happily continued the employment relationship.

But it is important to understand precisely what is meant by the loss of trust and confidence in this context; it simply means that the employer wishes of his own accord to terminate the contract. It does not necessarily mean that there are personal conflicts or animosities at all. For example, an employer may summarily dismiss an employee because he wishes to replace him by another who will accept a lower wage. It is surely misleading to say that he has lost confidence in the dismissed employee; he has simply found a better bargain. Yet on the theory of automatic termination it is clear that the contract is terminated by the employer's action. So to emphasise the loss of trust and confidence is confusing. This may, and often will, be the reason for the relationship being terminated, but it is not inevitably so. The logic of the automatic termination theory then, is that the employer's desire to terminate the employment relationship for whatever reason will, when he has implemented that desire, terminate the contract. To automatically equate this desire to terminate with a loss of confidence confuses what is really happening. *Hill* v. *Parsons* can be explained as a case where the employer did not desire to terminate the relationship but was compelled to do so because of pressure from a third party. Left to himself, the employer would not have dismissed the worker at all. In the absence of a positive desire to terminate, the dismissal did not automatically terminate the contract.[26]

The elective theory and its implications

The automatic termination theory then has to be justified on the basis that the continuing existence of the personal relationship is crucial to the continuation of the contract: the maintenance of the social relationship is the essential core of the contract.

In contrast, the elective theory of termination assumes a different contractual structure.[27] According to this theory a repudiation does not automatically terminate the contract even where it terminates the employment relationship, but must be accepted by the innocent party. The continuation of the relationship is not, on this analysis, a condition of the contract continuing to subsist. However, the policy assumptions of no wages if no work, coupled with the duty to mitigate, are held no less firmly by the proponents of this theory than by those supporting the view of automatic termination. Broadly they distinguish between the first tier of the contractual obligations and the remainder of the contract. The dismissal terminates the wage-work bargain but leaves the rest of the terms intact, and the remainder is sufficient to keep the contract itself alive. To use the language of Lord Diplock in the celebrated *Photo-Productions* case,[28] the primary wage-work obligations are automatically converted into the secondary obligation to pay damages, but the innocent party may seek to continue to enforce the other primary obligations arising under the contract.

But why is the employee prevented from claiming wages? The usual justification, given for example by Salmon L.J. in *Denmark Productions* v. *Boscobel Productions*,[29] and more recently by Buckley L.J. in *Gunton* v. *Richmond-upon-Thames B.C.*,[30] is that there can be no wages without work. These obligations are said to be interdependent rather than independent so that enforcing one depends upon performance of the other. But the all-important underlying assumption in this analysis is that the consideration for wages is the actual performance of the work. No doubt this will sometimes be true, as with piece-rate workers for example. But is it universally so? Surely the consideration for most employees is not the actual doing of the work but being ready and willing to work. They are available to the employer and he can choose to utilise them or not as he wishes. They are at his disposal. Only exceptionally will he be contractually obliged to provide them with work—as Asquith J. pertinently commented in *Collier* v. *Sunday Referee Publishing Co. Ltd.*, "provided I pay my cook her wages regularly she cannot complain if I choose to take any or all of my meals out."[31] But why should his Lordship be so generous if the duty to pay arises only when the work is done? It suggests that they also serve who only stand and wait, but what is that if not being available for work?

Many other authorities support the view that being ready and willing to work defines the employee's obligation. In the important Australian High Court decision of *Automatic Fire Sprinklers* v. *Watson*[32] in 1946 the court anticipated the recent *Gunton* decision in the Court of Appeal in holding that a wrongful dismissal terminated the employment relationship but not the contract, and like *Gunton* they denied the right to wages on the grounds that no work had been done. However, they recognised—as the English courts have yet clearly to do in the context of repudiation—that ultimately the question of whether wages were due depended upon whether the consideration was work or being ready and willing to work.[33] They took the view that the latter would be exceptional. But the decision was 36 years ago, and in any event it is doubtful if it accurately stated the English position even then. By that time in England there had been a number of sick pay cases where a similar emphasis had been placed on the particular form which the consideration took, and the prevailing view was that at least for those who were paid a fixed sum by the week, rather than being paid by the hour, the right to payment continued during sickness because the consideration was the willingness to be available for work, if fit. To cite just one example, in *Petrie* v. *Macfisheries* Atkinson J. in the Court of Appeal commented:

> "Where there is nothing in the contract express or implied to the contrary, the consideration for wages is not the actual doing of the work contracted for but the readiness or willingness, if of ability, to do the work."[34]

The plaintiff in that case was denied his sick pay because there was indeed a term to the contrary. But it seems that he would have been entitled to full pay otherwise. Furthermore, he was employed as a smoker-packer in the defendant's fish-smoking department—hardly a high status job. So it is difficult to contend that only exceptionally will the consideration be being available and willing to work.

Other contract rules lead to a similar conclusion, such as the right—admittedly still not free from uncertainty—of workers to claim pay if laid off.[35] Of course, there are often express terms which will modify the contractual arrangements, and will detract from the rights which would be implied in their absence. But the structure of the contract, and the nature of the obligations it creates, is to be found by examining the general common law position, not any special rules the parties may adopt.

It may still be that only workers paid on a fixed system of remuneration rather than on a time-rate system, where the wage varies with the hours worked, will be treated as being under the obligation to be ready and willing to work rather than actually having to perform it. As Freedland has pointed out,[36] the time-rate worker is less fully integrated into the organisation and takes a greater share of the risk arising from variations in demand. But fewer workers are falling into this category now than once did, and as unions obtain greater job security for their members and achieve staff status for their manual members, so the number is diminishing. At any rate, it is clear that a high proportion of employees will be under no duty to actually work before they earn their remuneration.

The consequence of this is that an employee whose obligation is to be willing and ready to work can perform his side of the bargain—as opposed to merely promising to perform—without the need for the employer to provide him with any work at all. And under the contract doctrine of *White and Carter* v. *McGregor*[37] there would then be no reason why he should not continue to claim his wages for the duration of the contract. Furthermore, since he is then claiming a debt and not merely damages, there is no duty to mitigate.[38]

So if the elective theory is to deny the right to wages then it is submitted that it must be on some other basis. One possibility is that the maintenance of the personal relationship is the condition of the wage-work bargain continuing, though not of the continuance of all the contractual terms. This is suggested by Brightman L.J. in the *Gunton* case, though admittedly in rather ambiguous terms. He commented that a wrongful dismissal terminated the status of the employee so that the contractual relationship was at an end, but it did not terminate the contract itself. The worker lost his status as an employee but remained a party to a subsisting contract. He added:

> "As the relationship of master and servant is gone, the servant cannot claim wages for services no longer rendered. But it does not follow that every right and obligation under the contract is extinguished. An obligation which is not of necessity dependent on the existence of the relationship of master and servant may well survive."[39]

This may be interpreted to mean that the maintenance of the personal relationship is fundamental to the wage work bargain. This analysis would, of course, apply whether the consideration is work or being ready and willing to work, so it at least had the merit of explaining why no worker could claim his wages following a wrongful dismissal.

The elective theory and the point of termination

How long can the contract continue to stand once the first tier obligations have collapsed? When does the contract end under the elective theory? The matter was considered by Buckley L.J. in *Gunton's* case. He held that the employee was obliged to mitigate his damages and that the contract would end at least as soon as he found and entered into other employment, since that then put it out of his power to perform any duties for his employer.[40] This is an unsatisfactory analysis for a number of reasons. First, the rule about mitigation—an aspect of the law of remedies—is determining when the contract will be deemed to have ended. Second, its consequences are wholly arbitrary. This can be illustrated by taking one of the supposed benefits of the elective theory. It is said that an employee might under this theory be able to keep his contract alive and build up his period of continuous employment so as to render him eligible to claim for various statutory rights in circumstances where he would be precluded from so doing if the automatic theory applied.[41] This argument is in fact probably misconceived since, as the Employment Appeal Tribunal has recently pointed out,[42] the statutory concept of the effective date of termination, which defines the end of the continuity period, seems to be premised on the automatic termination theory. But even if this is not so, the operation of the elective theory as suggested by Buckley L.J. can lead to some very odd results. Take a person who is unlawfully summarily dismissed after 48 weeks and is entitled to three months' notice. If he finds a job after two weeks he remains ineligible to claim for unfair dismissal because he lacks the necessary 52 weeks' employment. But if he finds a job after four weeks, he can claim. Consequently the state of the labour market dictates the right to enforce the statutory claim—hardly a logical or satisfactory approach. A better solution has been suggested by the Employment Appeal Tribunal, namely that the contract is indeed terminated, at least for statutory purposes, after 48 weeks, but that the employee will be able to assert as a head of damage in a wrongful dismissal action the lost opportunity to claim for unfair dismissal.[43]

Finally, basing the termination on the obligation to mitigate benefits employers far more than workers. This at least seems to be the case when *Gunton* is contrasted with the decision in *Thomas Marshall Exports Ltd.* v. *Guinle*[44] where Megarry J. unequivocally adopted the elective theory. The employee in *Guinle* was a managing director who had terminated the employment relationship by resigning his job in the middle of a ten-year fixed-term contract. He then set up in competition to his employers. The latter sought to prevent him disclosing confidential information or soliciting orders from their customers or suppliers, and an injunction was issued on both counts. The no-soliciting order was made on the grounds that a duty of good faith and fidelity existed for the duration of the contract and that since the employer had never accepted the employee's repudiation, the contract continued in force. But there was no suggestion that once the employer had appointed another managing director the contract would be terminated on the grounds that the company would then have disabled itself from performing its part of the bargain. Yet unless the doctrine operates in this way, it would seem to operate inequitably against employees. They will be bound for the full period anticipated in the original contract whereas, the employer will be bound only until the employee successfully obtains another job.

It is submitted therefore, that the elective theory ought not to treat termination as depending upon mitigation. A better solution would be to permit the parties to retain the right to enforce their contractual rights—at least other than those which depend upon the continuing existence of the personal relationship—until the contract has been lawfully terminated; or to accept that the automatic termination theory is correct and that the contract ends with the relationship, whilst recognising that certain terms might continue in force beyond the contract itself.

The personal relationship

Whether the automatic or the elective theories are accepted it is evident that the fact that the contract of employment also creates a personal relationship has fundamentally affected the way in which the judges perceive that contract. On the automatic termination theory, maintenance of the relationship is the condition which underpins the contract itself, whilst on the elective theory it underlies the main element in the contract, the wage-work bargain. And of course it has been one of the principal reasons why the courts have refused to enforce specific relief of the contract of employment.

Is this overriding emphasis on the personal nature of the relationship justified? It is submitted that it is not. If we take the wage-work bargain, why should it be considered so "clear beyond argument," as Brightman L.J. described it in *Gunton*,[45] that the employee should not be able to claim his wages if the employer refuses to give him work to do, at least where the consideration for the wage is being ready and willing to work? Historically it has been done. In the nineteenth century employees sometimes sued for wages following a wrongful dismissal, and even though the courts seem to have assumed that the work had to be performed before wages were due, they were prepared to develop a notion of constructive service and treat the work which the employee was willing to do as having been done.[46] This doctrine of constructive service was simply a fiction, and it is not surprising that subsequent courts were unwilling to adopt it.[47] But the rejection of this doctrine does not preclude an employee claiming remuneration where the consideration is willingness to work. This involves no fiction at all. He is then actually doing what he is employed to do by making himself available for work even if no actual work is done.[48] Furthermore, compelling the employer to pay the wages does not inevitably force him into a personal relationship, though of course it will tempt him to do so. But as Lord Denning pointed out in *Hill* v. *C.A. Parsons & Co. Ltd.*,[49] a case in which he expressed the view that an order requiring the payment of wages might exceptionally be made, this is not very different from granting injunctions which prevent an employee from breaking his contract and working for a competitor in defiance of an express term forbidding it.[50] Admittedly such an injunction will not be issued if its effect is to leave the employee with no real option but to return to his original employer,[51] but it will be granted if it merely encourages, rather than compels, that result. And the fact that the employee may be financially worse off if he chooses not to perform his original contract is not of itself considered to amount to compulsion to perform. Similarly for an employer required to pay wages: he is thereby encouraged to give the employee work to do, but not forced to do so.

Finally the employer will have to pay wages only until he lawfully terminates the contract. Large sums will be at stake only where long fixed-term contracts are involved, and this will be very exceptional. Even then the result is unlikely to be that the employee will "sit in the sun" for the duration of the contract. Admittedly if this were to happen on a large scale it would involve a waste of general economic resources. But in practice it is inconceivable that this would occur to any significant extent, for if the employer is simply not prepared to give the employee work at all, he will want to agree a settlement to terminate the contract on acceptable terms. It will be cheaper to do this than to continue paying wages. This will then release the employee to work elsewhere. His skills will not be lost to the public. Of course, the right of the employee to claim wages, rather than damages subject to mitigation, will considerably strengthen his hand in the negotiations, but the only real objection to this can be if it is thought that on principle no innocent contracting party ought to be entitled to compensation for more than his unavoidable loss.

For similar reasons there should be no automatic denial of the right to specific performance, particularly since usually the only obligation on the employer will be to pay wages rather than to provide work. In any event, the contention that it is inevitably impossible for the law to successfully reinstate employees because of the element of personal relationship involved simply cannot be sustained. Both in Britain and elsewhere statute has provided such remedies and the evidence suggests that where such an order is made, there is every chance that a normal employment relationship will be re-established.[52] This is partly because where large companies are involved the maintenance of any particular personal relationship is less significant. This is not because the employer is an impersonal organisation—corporations have to operate through human agencies, and relationships can be just as important there as elsewhere—but because such an employer will often have the flexibility to reorganise work relationships should personal conflicts become particularly bitter.

Trends in the common law

Furthermore, it is sometimes forgotten that the common law has already accepted a class of employment situations where an unlawful dismissal will be treated as void, and in these cases the contract will continue despite the wish of the employer to terminate the relationship. These are where the employee is an office holder, or has some special status by virtue of being employed under statutory provisions. Here an injunction may be issued to prevent the employer from treating the dismissal as effective, or—and in practice this will be just as valuable—a declaration will be issued that the purported dismissal is void.[53] In these circumstances it appears that the employee remains entitled to claim his remuneration until his employment is lawfully terminated, even in respect of any period during which he has done no work.[54] Admittedly the law is not entirely clear on this point; the right to claim wages seems to have been assumed rather than directly argued in the cases, and indeed some judges have carefully refrained from holding that the right to wages necessarily continues following an invalid dismissal.[55] But the right to wages would appear to be the logical consequence of treating the dismissal as a nullity. Furthermore, if the employee cannot claim wages but even after an invalid dismissal has to claim damages and mitigate, the special protection which these groups of workers are supposed to have been afforded by these particular remedies will prove illusory. They will be in the same position as any other employee who had been wrongfully dismissed, at least if the elective theory of termination is applied.

It is possible that in this area we may be witnessing a change in direction in the common law approach. In two relatively recent cases the courts have been willing to treat as invalid dismissals in breach of contract. In *Stevenson* v. *U.R.T.U.*[56] the Court of Appeal was willing to declare that the dismissal of a trade union official for misconduct was invalid because by implication the contract required that the rules of natural justice should be complied with before such a dismissal could be carried out, and they were not. Again in *Jones* v. *Lee*[57] an interlocutory injunction was issued by another division of that court to restrain school managers from dismissing a teacher in breach of procedures established in the contract. It is true that these cases are not pure private employment cases: *Stevenson* might be seen as an extension of the office holder rules, and in *Jones* v. *Lee* statutory provisions were certainly in the background. But neither case emphasised these aspects. Indeed, in both the judges were keen to emphasise that they were concerned with the contractual situation.

These two cases may suggest a way forward for the common law. It may be that the courts are moving towards a position where they will treat a dismissal as invalid either if it is in breach of any substantive contractual limitation on the employer's power to dismiss, or if it is in breach of any procedural requirements, whether expressly or impliedly incorporated. Further and powerful support for this approach can be found in the House of Lords decision in *McLelland* v. *Northern Ireland General Health Services Board*,[58] decided a quarter of a century ago. In that case the employer explicitly provided in the appellant's contract of service that her contract could be terminated on certain specified grounds only, and as a matter of construction it was held that there could be no lawful dismissal for any other reason. An attempt to dismiss her on a non-specified ground was held to be not merely unlawful but also invalid and the employee obtained a declaration to that effect. This case is frequently explained on the basis that it concerned employment in the public sector and statutory provisions were in the background. But one will not find any significant emphasis of this in the judgments of their lordships. They dealt with the issue as being a question of contract only. Fitting this case into the status mould simply reveals the academic's desire to attempt to rationalise an apparently erratic decision on traditional grounds. Perhaps in the light of the other two cases mentioned above it may now come to be accepted that the decision is based on a different but still very sound principle: that where the employer has accepted limitations on his power to dismiss, be they procedural or substantive, the courts will hold him to his undertaking by treating any dismissal in breach of such limitations as invalid. It is surely not unreasonable for the courts to say that damages would be an inadequate substitute for breach of this promise to provide a greater job security than employers have traditionally been willing to grant, though of course this will be important only if the employee can continue to claim wages. As yet one can only speculate whether the courts will be prepared to take this step. But the raw materials for developing such a doctrine are available, should the judges wish to use them. If they do, it will be a step of great significance, for it will finally exorcise the ghost that has so long haunted this aspect of labour law—the notion that contracts of personal service cannot be enforced at common law. And this will in turn involve a shift away from the market assumptions which, albeit implicitly rather than explicitly, have largely determined judicial responses to the employment relationship.

Special features of the employment contract

To argue that the severance of the personal relationship should not automatically destroy the contract is not to diminish the importance of that relationship: it is simply to contend that the law is frequently capable of re-establishing it on a workable basis. Obviously the fact that the contract creates a set of both social and economic relationships is of profound importance and distinguishes the employment contract from, say, a consumer or commercial transaction. Yet curiously, although the courts have traditionally seen the element of personal relationship as fundamental, they have emphasised its importance only when the contract has been broken in order to justify not rebuilding it. Indeed, it is perhaps the supreme irony in this area that this emphasis on the social and psychological factors which make up the personal relationship should have operated to deny the employee job security, and should have enabled the contract doctrines to reflect economic market assumptions. Until recently the judges had not begun to work out the implications of this need to maintain the employment relationship for the day to day running of the employment contract. But following the advent of unfair dismissal there is now a growing volume of case law which has emphasised the obligation on the employer not to undermine the trust and confidence in the employment relationship.[59] This has been defined in various ways—to treat the employee with due respect,[60] not to behave towards employees in a way which is intolerable[61] not to behave so unreasonably that the conduct goes beyond the limits of the contract,[62] and not to victimise the employee by treating him in an arbitrary, capricious or inequitable way.[63] This development is achieving a quiet revolution in the perception of the contract of employment and is beginning to differentiate it quite markedly from the traditional contract model. The usual contractual rule is that if a contract gives a party a clear and express power, he is under no obligation to consider the interests of the other party when exercising it. But it now appears that the managerial prerogative arising under the contract of employment cannot be exercised in total disregard of the employee's interests. Although the Employment Appeal Tribunal has refused to accept explicitly that the employer must exercise his powers reasonably,[64] it has come very close to this position by holding that he must not exercise them in a way which undermines trust and confidence. It is beginning to exercise a profound effect upon the operation of the contract.

This notion of imposing judicial limits on the exercise of apparently unfettered legal rights is not a wholly new departure. Partnership law has accepted for over a century, since the leading case of *Blisset* v. *Daniel*,[65] that the notion of good faith underlies relations within the partnership, and that powers granted by the partnership deed cannot be exercised so as to unfairly prejudice any particular partner. More recently in *Ebrahimi* v. *Westbourne Galleries*[66] the House of Lords has extended a similar principle to small companies which operate as quasi-partnerships. They held that the powers granted by the Companies Act cannot be used unfairly against a particular member so as to undermine the underlying assumption of good faith which governs the relationship between all the members. Admittedly such conduct would not in this context constitute a breach of contract, but it would enable the minority shareholder to have the company wound up. In Lord Wilberforce's succinct phrase, "legal rights must give way to equitable considerations" in these circumstances. Of course, it is necessary to be cautious about extending principles applicable to business partners into the employment sphere since the community of interest is clearly stronger in the former context. But this caution should not preclude the recognition of the fact that the employment contract creates a psychological as well as an economic nexus, and that making it psychologically impossible for the employee to perform the contract can reasonably be equated with making it physically impossible for him to perform. Such an analysis does not involve adopting a unitary view of industrial relations, which sees unions and management striving to achieve a common objective.[67] But it does accept that the range of workers' interests extend beyond the purely economic.

The element of personal relationship is not the only distinctive feature of the employment contract. There are other facets which, if not quite unique to the contract of employment, certainly differentiate it from the archetype commercial transaction which has so dominated traditional contractual thinking. These, too, should be reflected in the legal principles which govern the employment relationship. To some extent they already are, though not, perhaps, as fully as they should be. Three aspects may be taken by way of illustration. First the fact that the contract is a continuing rather than a static one has left its mark upon the rules applicable to the contract, notably in the area of variation of contract where, as Dr. Freedland convincingly shows, the traditional importance given to the doctrine of consideration in general contract theory has had to be ignored.[68] Again, most contract questions now arise in a statutory context and this had also not passed unrecognised in the courts. For example, the Employment Appeal Tribunal has suggested that the doctrine of frustration should be applied very sparingly to employment contracts.[69] This is because if it is adopted too readily it could prevent the fairness of a dismissal being tested in an unfair dismissal case—because frustration is not a dismissal within the meaning of the statute—and not only the contract but also the policy of the statute itself would then be frustrated! This recognition that adopting a traditional contract approach might be inconsistent with the intentions of Parliament is sensible and justified.

In contrast there is one feature of the contract to which the judges continue to turn a blind eye. In most employment relationships—at least in non-unionised workforces—there is an inequality of bargaining power between the parties. The realities of the employment relationship are concealed behind the fiction that the parties to the contract are free agents with equal responsibility for the arrangements they make. This has had disastrous consequences in those cases where an employee has been deprived of a right to claim for unfair dismissal because the contract has been illegally performed. Usually this involves the employer paying the employee from the till and thereby evading his tax liabilities. The courts have refused to look at the relative blame which can be allotted to each party and to permit the employee to enforce his rights if he is not *in pari delicto* with the employer.[70] The consequence is that the employer, who is invariably the instigator of the scheme and may alone profit from it, escapes his statutory obligations altogether. It has been intimated that the employee should refuse to go along with the arrangement and perhaps even notify the Inland Revenue.[71] The reality is that he risks dismissal by so notifying and will certainly sour his relationship with the employer. No doubt, as the E.A.T. has pointed out, any such dismissal would be unfair,[72] but this will often provide cold comfort to the employee since the arrangement will frequently be made soon after the employment begins and he will be ineligible to claim in any event because of insufficient continuity of employment. Here in particular there should be a fuller recognition of the reality lying behind the employment relationship, and also of the conflicting public interests involved.[73]

CONCLUSION

So the employment contract, under pressure from statutory rights, is in a state of flux. The overriding importance given to the personal relationship at the point of termination may be waning, and with it the market assumptions which have so dominated judicial thinking in this area. At the same time there is a greater awareness of the significance of the personal relationship, of the psychological element, in the contract in the context of the daily operation of the contract. The legal recognition of this aspect has provided a device which is enabling the courts to regulate managerial prerogatives in a new and very important way. This development has involved accepting that the traditional contract rules cannot automatically be applied to the employment contract. But this is surely correct: rules conceal policies and should not be arbitrarily applied in diverse situations where policy objectives differ. There is evidence that the courts are becoming increasingly aware of this. In the long term this can only improve the foundations of the law regulating the employment contract.

Notes

[1] See his essay "Legal Framework" in the *System of Industrial Relations in Great Britain* (A. Flanders and H.A. Clegg eds. 1954), p.45.

[2] "The Contract of Employment" (1966) 19 C.L.P. 111.

[3] However, since the employment contract depends in the last resort upon the wishes of the parties, this is not using the concept of status in its traditional sense, where it means the totality of powers and disabilities imposed by law on an individual irrespective of his own volition. For a fuller development of this point, see O. Kahn-Freund, "Note on Status and Contract in British Labour Law" (1967) 30 M.L.R. 635.

[4] Equal Pay Act 1970, s.1(3). Sometimes the courts will treat a statutory right as founded in contract even where the Act creating the right is silent on the point: see, *e.g. Gutsell* v. *Reeve* [1936] 1 K.B. 272, C.A.

[5] M.R. Freedland, *The Contract of Employment* (1976), pp.19–21.

[6] *Hivac Ltd.* v. *Park Royal Scientific Instruments Ltd.* [1946] Ch. 169. A narrow interpretation of this case was adopted in *Electrolux Ltd.* v. *Hudson* [1977] F.S.R. 312.

[7] *e.g. Bents Brewery Co. Ltd.* v. *Hogan* [1945] 2 All E.R. 570.

[8] The ex-employee cannot be restrained from using the skill and "know-how" which he acquired in the course of his employment and it is often difficult to distinguish this from confidential information. For an attempt to draw this distinction see Megarry J. in *Thomas Marshall (Exports) Ltd.* v. *Guinle* [1978] 3 All E.R. 193.

[9] Restraint of trade clauses are prima facie void but are permitted provided they are reasonable in the interests of the respective parties and not contrary to the public interest. The courts no longer view such clauses with the hostility they once did: see *The Littlewoods Organisation Ltd.* v. *Harris* [1978] 1 All E.R. 1026, C.A. and *Greer* v. *Sketchley Ltd.* [1979] I.R.L.R. 445, C.A.

[10] *e.g. Thomas Marshall (Exports) Ltd.* v. *Guinle* [1979] Ch. 227. Though query whether it is necessary in that case to treat the contract as still subsisting in order to hold the employee to contractually agreed terms: see Elias, Napier and Wallington *Cases and Materials in Labour Law* (1980) p.491.

[11] See Employment Protection (Consolidation) Act 1978, ss.55(2) and 83(2).

[12] In unfair dismissal this is the "effective date of termination" defined in E.P.(C.)A. 1978 s.55(4), and in redundancy the "relevant date" defined in E.P.(C.)A. 1978 s.90.

[13] *White and Carter (Councils) Ltd.* v. *McGregor* [1962] A.C. 413.

[14] See Richard Posner, *An Economic Analysis of Law* (2nd ed., 1977) Chap. 3. for a further discussion of the ecomomic significance of contract remedies.

[15] For an interesting discussion of the policy considerations influencing the award of specific performance, see Robert J. Sharpe, "Specific Relief for Contract Breach," Chap. 5 in *Studies in Contract Law* (Reiter and Swan, 1980).

[16] The refusal to grant these remedies in the employment context has traditionally been justified on a variety of grounds: see Freedland, *op. cit.* pp.273–277.

[17] See Posner, *op. cit.*

[18] For a particularly forceful condemnation of the law's failings in this respect see David M. Beatty, "Labour is not a Commodity," Chap. 9 in *Studies in Contract Law* (Reiter and Swan, 1980).

[19] For discussions of the effect of a wrongful dismissal on the contract of employment, see Freedland, *op. cit.* pp.292–309; Elias, "Unravelling the Concept of Dismissal" (1978) 7 I.L.J. 16, 102; and the valuable recent analysis by J. McMullen, "A Synthesis of the Mode of Termination of Contracts of Employment" (1982) C.L.J. 110. There is also much useful discussion of this subject in the more general article by F.D. Rose, "The Effects of Repudiatory Breaches of Contract" (1981) 34 C.L.P. 235.

[20] *e.g.* Donaldson J. in *Sanders* v. *Ernest A. Neale Ltd.* [1974] I.C.R. 565 and Shaw L.J. in his dissenting judgment in *Gunton* v. *Richmond-upon-Thames London Borough Council* [1980] I.C.R. 755.

[21] [1962] A.C. 413, 445. Lord Tucker expressly concurred in his judgment.

[22] See, *e.g. Hill* v. *C.A. Parsons Ltd.* [1972] Ch. 305 where Lord Denning gave this as the reason why contracts of employment are usually automatically terminated on dismissal (p.314). See too *Johnson* v. *Shrewsbury and Birmingham Rly. Co.* (1853) De G.M. & G. 914 and *Pickering* v. *Bishop of Ely* (1843) 2 Y. & C. Ch. Cas 249.

[23] [1917] 1 K.B. 946.

[24] See too *Boston Deep Sea Fishing and Ice Co.* v. *Ansell* (1888) 39 Ch. D. 339. This, of course, is merely an application of the general principle that a repudiation falling short of an actual dismissal does not of itself terminate the contract but requires acceptance. For a further discussion of this still somewhat controversial point, see Elias, *op. cit.* pp.17–24, and McMullen, *op. cit.* pp.112–118.

[25] [1972] I.C.R. 305. This case was subsequently explained on the grounds that trust and confidence was maintained despite the dismissal: *e.g. G.K.N. (Cwmbran) Ltd.* v. *Lloyd* [1972] I.C.R. 214, 221; and *Sanders* v. *Ernest Neale* [1974] I.C.R. 565.

[26] This is not to say that motive is relevant in determining whether there has been a repudiation of the contract. That would be inconsistent with traditional contract theory. Rather its significance lies in determining whether the repudiation automatically terminates the contract or not.

[27] For a detailed analysis of the authorities supporting this approach, see McMullen, *op. cit.*

[28] *Photo-Productions Ltd.* v. *Securicor Transport Ltd.* [1980] A.C. 827.

[29] [1969] 1 Q.B. 699.

[30] [1980] I.C.R. 755. See, too, Francis Dawson, "Metaphors and Anticipatory Breach of Contract" (1981) C.L.J. 83, pp.95–96.

[31] [1940] 2 K.B. 647, 650.

[32] (1946) 72 C.L.R. 435.

[33] See the discussion by Dixon J., pp.463–465.

[34] [1940] 1 K.B. 259, 270. This comment was expressly relied on by the Court of Appeal in *O'Grady* v. *M. Saper Ltd.* [1940] 2 K.B. 469. See too, *Hancock* v. *B.S.A. Tools* [1939] 4 All E.R. 538, and the note by Lord Denning (as he is now) on the decision in *Marrison* v. *Bell* [1939] 2 K.B. 187 in (1939) 55 L.Q.R. 353.

[35] See the discussion by Freedland, *op. cit.* pp.86–92, and *McKenzie* v. *Smith* [1976] I.R.L.R. 345.

[36] See M.R. Freedland, "The Obligation to Work and to Pay for Work" (1977) 30 C.L.P. 175 which examines different methods of wage payments and their contractual significance.

[37] See note 13 above.

[38] Lord Reid did suggest that the innocent party would not be able to keep the contract alive if he had no legitimate interest in seeking to perform the contract, and damages would be an adequate remedy. But an employee would appear to have such an interest, namely in seeking to maintain the job itself. Certainly the employee's interest seems greater than that of the appellants in the *White and Carter* case. However, Lord Denning has suggested otherwise: see *Attica Sea Carriers Corpn.* v. *Ferrostaal Poseidon Bulk Reederei GmbH* [1976] 1 Lloyd's Rep. 250, 255. But see Neinaber, "The Effect of Anticipatory Repudiation: Principle and Policy" (1962) C.L.J. 213, who supports the view that in principle wages can be claimed.

[39] [1980] I.C.R. 755, 778.

[40] *Ibid.* p.772.

[41] The point is discussed more fully by McMullen, *op. cit.*

[42] *Robert Cort & Son Ltd.* v. *Charman* [1981] I.R.L.R. 437.

[43] *Ibid.*

[44] See note 10 above.

[45] [1980] I.C.R. 755, 778.

[46] The relevant authorities are well considered in *Smith's Leading Cases* (13th ed., 1929) Vol. 2, pp.51–54.

[47] *e.g. Fewings* v. *Tisdal* 1 Exch. 295, and *Goodman* v. *Pocock* 15 Q.B. 576.

[48] In *Denmark Productions Ltd.* v. *Boscobel Productions Ltd.* [1969] 1 Q.B. 699 Salmon L.J. seemed to think that the cases rejecting the constructive service doctrine established that a wrongfully dismissed worker could claim only damages (p.726). It submitted that this view is mistaken and ignores the fact that in the nineteenth century the consideration for wages would typically be work whereas now it will often be being willing and available for work. See too *Decro-Wall International S.A.* v. *Practitioners in Marketing Ltd.* [1971] 1 W.L.R. 361.

[49] [1972] 1 Ch. 305.

[50] The leading case is *Warner Bros. Pictures Inc.* v. *Nelson* [1937] 1 K.B. 209.

[51] *Page One Records Ltd.* v. *Britton* [1968] 1 W.L.R. 157.

[52] Recent research indicates that the success of reinstatement and re-engagement orders in unfair dismissal cases has been encouraging: see Kevin Williams and David Lewis, *The Aftermath of Tribunal Reinstatement and Re-engagement* (Dept. of Employment Research Paper No. 23, June 1981).

[53] See generally Freedland, *op. cit.* pp.272–292.

[54] *Ibid.* pp.290–292.

[55] See for example the cautious comments of Buckley L.J. in *Stevenson* v. *U.R.T.U.* [1977] I.C.R. 893, and also the fact that in one of the leading cases, *Vine* v. *National Dock Labour Board* [1957] A.C. 488, the House of Lords awarded damages rather than wages.

[56] [1977] I.C.R. 893.

[57] [1980] I.C.R. 310.

[58] [1957] 1 W.L.R. 594.

[59] There is much recent case law in this area: see, *e.g.* the discussion in *Harvey on Industrial Relations and Employment Law*, Div. 2, Ch. D. part 3.

[60] *Garner* v. *Grange Furnishing Ltd.* [1977] I.R.L.R. 206.

[61] *British Aircraft Corpn.* v. *Austin* [1978] I.R.L.R. 332.

[62] *Palmanor Ltd.* v. *Cedron* [1978] I.L.R. 1008.

[63] *F.C. Gardner Ltd.* v. *Beresford* [1978] I.R.L.R. 63.

[64] *Post Office* v. *Roberts* [1980] I.R.L.R. 347.

[65] (1853) 10 Hare 493.

[66] [1973] A.C. 360. See too *Clemens* v. *Clemens Bros.* [1976] 2 All E.R. 268, though *cf. Bentley Stevens* v. *Jones* [1974] 1 W.L.R. 638.

[67] For a fuller discussion of these different perceptions of industrial relations see Alan Fox, *Beyond Contract: Work, Power and Trust Relations* (1974) esp. Chap. 6.

[68] Freedland *op. cit.* pp.55–66.

[69] *Harman* v. *Flexible Lamps Ltd.* [1980] I.R.L.R. 418.

[70] *Tomlinson* v. *Dick Evans "U" Drive Ltd.* [1978] I.C.R. 639; *Newland* v. *Simons and Willer (Hairdressers) Ltd.* [1981] I.C.R. 521.

[71] See the *Newland* case, *ibid.*

[72] In *Brodie* v. *First Shaw Ltd.* (E.A.T., unreported, but referred to in the *Newland* decision).

[73] For a fuller argument along these lines see Christine Mogridge, "Illegal Employment Contracts: Loss of Statutory Protection" (1981) 10 I.L.J. 23.

* The writer is grateful to Dr. L. S. Sealy of Gonville and Caius College, Cambridge for valuable discussions on aspects of this article.

The Legal Battlefield of Care

M.D.A. FREEMAN

> "This is the world of social administration, not a legal battlefield. It is intended to provide for social casework to relieve a child's distress and danger: it is not concerned to vindicate rights or to set a scene for litigation" (Lord Scarman)[1]

THERE are over 100,000 children in the care of local authorities and voluntary organisations. Many of these children have been continuously in care for long periods. 27,500 have been in care for five years or more, nearly 19,000 for between three and five years and another 31,400 for more than one year but less than three. 7.7 *per* 1,000 of the child population are in care. Two-thirds of children in care live in residential homes: the remainder are boarded-out with foster parents.[2]

Children in care pose a large number of current legal problems. For too long, however, little interest has been shown either by legal academics or judges in these problems. The area has remained a veritable legal Alsatia into which the King's writ rarely intrudes.[3] It is less than a decade since the first real textbook on child law was published.[4] Interest in child law has expanded with the establishment of local legal centres. Social workers are now being taught the law relating to children which certainly was not the case until relatively recently.[5] There are journals, the *Journal of Social Welfare Law, Family Law, the Justice of the Peace* which devote considerable space to the treatment of legal issues relating to children in care. I.Y.C.[6] may have given all this some impetus: it certainly helped to father the first children's legal centre in Britain.

There has been an enormous expansion in litigation relating to children in the last decade. There has also been one recent Act, the Children Act 1975.[7] Much of this remains unimplemented seven years after its enactment. A consolidating measure, the Child Care Act of 1980,[8] has put together much of the statutory law relating to children in care. The 1980 Act consolidates statutes which are themselves not always united in ideology or design. The result is a patchwork quilt, the pieces of which do not always readily fit together. Much too remains outside the framework of the 1980 Act, in earlier Acts and in the common law.

Most of the current legislation relating to children in care is then found in one statute. But inconsistencies and gaps remain. Many questions remain unanswered. This is not an area in which the judiciary has excelled itself. The judges have shown little understanding of the realities of child care. They do not seem to understand how corporately managed bureaucracies operate. There seems to be a general assumption that local authorities act with the best interests of children uppermost in their collective mind. There is now considerable evidence that they do not.[9] As a result attention has been turned to ways of protecting children in care.[10] The accountability of local authority social services departments is a problem of immense concern to lawyers working in the area, to pressure groups like Justice For Children, the Family Rights Group,[11] the Voice of the Child in Care, the National Association of Young People in Care (NAYPIC), and the Children's Legal Centre, as well as to thoughtful and concerned social workers. I have written of accountability elsewhere.[12] My main concern in this article is with legal concepts. In it I present a framework for analysis of the concepts involved, point to the gaps and inconsistencies in the law and draw some conclusions as to possible directions the law might take. It will be apparent from what I argue that I deplore the position taken by Lord Scarman.[13] The world of social administration is also a legal battlefield.

COMING INTO CARE

Part of the complexity arises from the fact that children can come into care in a large number of different ways under different pieces of legislation passed at different times. There are eleven legal routes into care. For convenience I list them here:

(i) Child Care Act 1980, s.2: reception into care.

(ii) Child Care Act 1980, s.3: resolution assuming parental rights of a parent whose child is in care under section 2.

(iii) Children and Young Persons Act 1969, s.1 and s.2: care order (also under s.7(7) of the 1969 Act).

(iv) Family Law Reform Act 1969, s.7(2): Committal to care of ward of court.

(v) Matrimonial Causes Act 1973, s.43: committal to care by a divorce court.

(vi) Domestic Proceedings and Magistrates' Courts Act 1978, s.10: committal to the care of the local authority in the course of domestic proceedings.

(vii) Guardianship of Minors Act 1971, s.9, as amended by the Guardianship Act 1973, s.2(2)(*b*) and s.4: committal to care in the course of a custody hearing.

(viii) Children Act 1975, s.17: on refusal of adoption order.
(ix) Child Care Act 1980, s.57(6): removal of child on closure of a voluntary home.
(x) Foster Children Act 1980, s.12(5): removal by juvenile court of privately-fostered child kept in unsuitable surroundings.
(xi) Adoption Act 1958, s.43(3): removal of a protected child from unsuitable surroundings in adoption proceedings.

If and when custodianship (Children Act 1975, s.33) is brought into effect,[14] there will be an additional basis of care: *viz.* committal to care on the refusal of a custodianship order under section 36 of the Children Act 1975.

A number of these statutory provisions are couched in broadly similar terms: (iv), (v), (vi), (vii) and (viii) and the custodianship provisions all give the court power "in exceptional circumstances making it impracticable or undesirable for the child to be committed to either parent or any other person to commit the child into local authority care." In each case the statute states that the local authority must treat the child "as if" he had been received into care under section 2 of the 1980 Act, subject to the rule that the parent or any other person cannot remove the child from care. The scheme set up by section 2, as we shall see, envisages a system of voluntary care. We are thus introduced to the first of many inconsistencies: the legal effect of a committal to care being tantamount, with exceptions, to a reception into care. It is clear that the problems have not been thought through by those who draft the legislation or pass it. I look at each of the types of legal care in turn, though the committal provisions form a bloc and, wardship excepted, can be, and are, considered together.

A. *Receptions Into Care*

The Child Care Act 1980, s.2 derives principally from the Children Act 1948, s.1. It provides for receptions into care of orphans, deserted children and other children whose parents temporarily or permanently are not in a position to provide proper accommodation, maintenance and upbringing. There are about 45,000 children in care under section 2 (or its predecessor). Nearly two-thirds of the children in care for five years or more entered care under the "voluntary" care procedures of section 2. It is accepted that far too many children are in care and that better preventive work,[15] in part provided for by section 1,[16] could reduce the number of children who are separated from their parents. In particular it is recognised that many children are in care because their parents are homeless[17] or have inadequate accommodation. Preventive work makes economic sense[18] (it costs £107 a week to keep a child in a community home). It is also often conducive to the child's welfare. The longer a child stays in care the less likely he is to return to his parents and far too many children just drift in care with no positive planning for their future.[19]

1. *What is "care"?*

What is the legal status of children in care? Section 2 of the 1980 Act envisages that the child is in voluntary care. Lord Scarman has described this as "a not wholly accurate term, but in common use."[20] Certainly, the local authority has no power under this section to force a parent to place a child in care. Although judges will sometimes refer to a child being "taken" into care, this is not correct.[21] The Lord Chancellor of the day, Lord Jowitt, referring to, what became, section 1 of the 1948 Act (section 2 of the 1980 Act) said: "local authorities are not entitled under [s].1 to remove the child from the parents against their wishes."[22] This was re-iterated by Lord Scarman in his speech in the *Lewisham* case.[23] A local authority clearly, however, may receive a child into care without consent, where the child is abandoned (that is, left to its fate[24]), lost or where the parent's infirmity is such that he cannot express his consent.

The Act does not define what "care" means. The Curtis report, the source of the 1948 Act, stated that there was "no relation of legal guardianship between the authority and the child."[25] It suggested that the authority "should stand as a parent to the child."[26] in other words, that it was *in loco parentis*. This is not very precise, and Lord Scarman was right to note in the *Lewisham* case that the section was "silent" as to the local authority's powers.[27] It is clear that the authority has certain duties towards the child: it must "safeguard and promote the welfare of the child throughout his childhood."[28]; it must provide for his accommodation and maintenance,[29] among sundry other duties. But what rights does it have? It may be, as Susan Maidment indicates,[30] that Curtis envisaged that care would be rather like, what we now call, "actual custody."[31] As she rightly concedes, actual custody or possession is not defined by statute as a "right" to actual custody: the Children Act 1975 states "a person *has* actual custody of a child if he *has* actual possession of his person" (my emphasis).[32] Further, the 1975 Act actually states that a person with actual custody has the same duties as a person with legal custody. Legal custody is defined in terms of parental rights. But Maidment goes on to argue that because the local authority has some rights it cannot be accurate to describe its status vis-à-vis the child as actual custody simpliciter. She argues that the local authority has a right of possession. This cannot be a right against the parent for, as we shall see, the parent may remove his child from the local authority's care,[33] at least where the child has been in care for less than six months.[34] The local authority certainly has rights against foster parents to whom it has delegated the care of the child. But this is surely because foster parents are merely agents of the local authority.[35] The local authority's right to repossess the child is provided for the boarding-out agreement. The right arises from contract and not status.

The most interesting test-bed for the theory that a local authority has a "right" of possession occurs when a third party unlawfully removes the child from the local authority's control: a kidnap or something less dramatic takes place. Whether the local authority has a right[36] depends on whether others are under a duty not to remove the child from it and to restore the child if the possession is disturbed. The tort of harbouring a child has been abolished.[37] There are limited "remedies" in criminal law but they do not appear to protect a right as such. The offence of child-stealing is committed if a person by fraud or force takes or detains a child under 14 "with intent to deprive any parent, guardian or other person having the lawful care or charge of such a child, of the possession of such a child."[38] The requirement of fraud or force and the protection of all persons in lawful possession of the child (it would surely extend as far as a baby-sitter) indicates that the provision does not protect a right as such. The offence is clearly directed at keeping the peace.[39] The section (of the Offences Against the Person Act 1861) goes on to provide[40] that a mother or father (if the child is illegitimate) or anyone claiming "any right to the possession of such child" is exempt from prosecution.[41] Despite the language used this does not establish the existence of a right: it merely assumes its existence. It is an offence[42] also to take an unmarried girl under 16 out of the possession of her parent or guardian (defined as including "any person having the lawful charge or care of the girl"). As Eekelaar writes,[43] this "provision . . . merely illustrates the legislative view that a girl under 16 should remain under the supervision of a parent or adult acting as such, so long as they are willing to supervise her." He says it supports "no uniquely parental right": we may add "or right of anyone else." It is also clear that a wardship application brought against a person in possession of the child would be decided not in terms of rights at all but on the basis that the child's welfare is the "first and paramount consideration."[44] These words, Lord MacDermott has indicated, "connote a process whereby, when all the relevant facts, relationships, claims and wishes of parents, risks, choices and other circumstances are taken into account and weighed, the course to be followed will be that which is most in the interests of the child's welfare . . . That is the first consideration because it is of first importance and the paramount consideration because it rules upon or determines the course to be followed."[45]

Susan Maidment's premise thus appears to be inaccurate. A local authority clearly has some powers without which it would not be able to carry out its duties. It clearly also has privileges[46] (liberties, freedoms). It has discretion vested in it to choose how to exercise its powers. It may board a child out or place it in a secure unit. It may, if grounds exist, pass a resolution assuming parental rights. Its possession of the child is lawful: so it has a right in the strict sense not to be fraudulently or forcibly deprived of possession. But its rights may go no further than this, for once the child is out of its possession the welfare consideration rather than rights will be the guiding factor. I would accordingly suggest that the most accurate way of characterising a local authority's relationship with a child in section 2 care is in terms of actual custody. If this is correct, then it must be the case that legal custody (that is, the bundle of parental rights) remains with the parents. That is why they can remove their child at will[47] (subject to the statutory restriction imposed where the child is in care for six months). They also retain duties: maintenance of the child is the most obvious example. There are elaborate provisions in the 1980 Act dealing with this.[48] For obvious reasons parents are expected to delegate some of their authority to the local authority. For example, parents transfer their rights to determine medical treatment and to consent to operations to the local authority. That these are recognised as parental rights is indicated by the fact that the local authority requires parents to agree to a transfer of these rights and powers when they consent to the child being received into care.

2. *Access*

The question which currently causes greatest concern is whether a local authority may deny parents access to their child. In my opinion a whole shift of emphasis is required. The question should be not how to terminate parental contact[49] but how to start it and keep it going. The importance of contact between a parent and his child is such that in most cases it ought to assume the greatest priority in social casework. Even Albert Solnit has written of some contact being desirable for most children.[50] Yet the 1955 Boarding Out Regulations require social workers to visit foster parents but not natural parents. Parents are often discouraged from visiting their children initially. The excuse is that children need time to settle. The danger is that parents and children then drift apart.[51] The longer a child is in care the less likely it is for parental contact to be retained. The Harvie report on residential care for mentally subnormal children reminded us that a child is more likely to be abandoned in care by his parents "where the parents are effectively abandoned by the placing authority."[52] This lesson can be generalised.

In *Caring for Separated Children* the point is made that "unless they are specifically prohibited by a court order, parental meetings with their child, visits or correspondence cannot actually be prevented. Nor is there any way, short of arrest or imprisonment, in which parents can be stopped from intervening illegally to re-establish or maintain their sphere of parental influence."[53] But local authorities do commonly deny access.[54] It is not uncommon for a local authority to refuse to tell parents of their child's whereabouts. In law there can, in my opinion, be no doubt that a local authority may not deny parents access. I state this despite tenuous judicial authority to the contrary. Those[55] who argue that a local authority may deny parents access to a child in section 2 care usually rely on remarks of Ormrod L.J. in *Re Y*.[56] He held that section 21(2) of the 1980 Act included the power to grant access, even though the word is not specifically used in the sub-section. The sub-section provides: "a local authority may allow a child in their care either for a fixed period or until the local authority otherwise determine, to be under the charge or control of a parent, guardian, relative or friend." This statutory provision was not passed with access in mind. It was passed to facilitate the local authority's duty in section 2(3) to "endeavour to secure that the care of the child is taken over either—(a) by a parent or guardian or (b) by a relative or friend of his . . . " It assists, further, in promoting "home on trial" policies,[57] which would not be legal without it. Section 21(2) must be seen as permitting what would otherwise be a breach of duty by the local authority.[58] But section 21(2) should not be construed as giving the local authority the power to deny access. Ormrod L.J.'s remarks, as regards a section 2 case, were anyway strictly *obiter* since the issue in *Re Y* was whether, in exercising its power in wardship proceedings in committing the ward to the care of a local authority under section 7(2) of the Family Law Reform Act 1969, the court was also empowered to make specific directions as to access. Having decided that such an order lay within the court's jurisdiction, he added: "I certainly would not wish anyone to think because of anything I have said that I have cast any doubt whatever on the power of local authorities in ordinary cases under [s.2 of the 1980 Act] to control access as part of their responsibility."[59] He clearly had heard no argument on this: nor had he given the matter any serious thought. Far too much has been read into this gratuitous statement.

Two other authorities are commonly referred to. The first is *R.* v. *Oxford City Justices ex p. H*[60] in which it was held that a putative father's application for custody under section 9 of the Guardianship of Minors Act 1971[61] ought to be heard even though the child was in care under section 3 (the parental rights of the mother had been assumed by the local authority). It was said, *obiter*, that had the application been one for access, as in *Re K*[62] it may have been that it should not have been heard since access was "a matter which must necessarily be under the day to day control and discretion of the local authority."[63] Bagnall J. does not give any reason why this should be so. Lowe and White[64] also refer to *Re O*,[65] an unreported decision of Balcombe J. A putative father warded his two children who were in care by virtue of a care order, when foster parents with whom they had been placed applied to adopt them. Balcombe J. held that he should not make any order as to access since that was within the discretion of the local authority. In the absence of a report of his reasoning, it is difficult to place too much reliance on his decision. But it was anyway in the context of a compulsory measure of care and not a voluntary reception. The question of access under a care order is considered later in this article.[66]

Let us, however, return to first principles in search of an answer to our question. Section 10(2) states that a local authority "shall . . . have the same powers and duties with respect to a person in their care . . . as his parent or guardian would have apart from the order." The context is, of course, children committed to a local authority's care by a care order. But *a fortiori* what applies to a care order must apply to a voluntary reception since in the latter case a parent denied access could merely remove his child. What powers do parents have? There can be no doubt that one parent cannot deny the other access to their child. Goldstein *et al*[67] have argued that parents should have such a power and their views were greeted with some consternation.[68] A parent retains the right to contact with his child even where he is deprived of legal custody (if that is possible).[69] Just as a custodial parent has no right to deprive the non-custodial parent of access, so a local authority with the "same powers and duties" as a parent is in no better position. There is another way of looking at access: this is to see it, as Wrangham J. and Latey J. saw it in *M* v. *M*,[70] as a right of the child. On this view, as Thomson has argued,[71] only a court can deprive a child of his right of access in the interests of his own welfare. Whichever way one looks at it, a local authority has no right to deny a parent access in the context of s.2 care or a care order. One consequence of this conclusion is that a denial of access must constitute an impropriety so that, however *A* v. *Liverpool City Council*[72] is interpreted, review by means of a wardship application becomes legitimate.

3. *When Does Care End?*

The other principal problem raised by receptions into care is the point at which such care comes to an end. The statute is badly drafted. As already noted, "care" is not defined. Section 2(2) lays down a duty on local authorities "to keep the child in their care so long as the welfare of the child appears to them to require it." Section 2(3) is in two limbs. The first contains the peremptory statement: "Nothing in this section shall authorise a local authority to keep a child in their care under this section if any parent or guardian desires to take over the care of the child." The second limb indicates that the "local authority shall, in all cases where it appears to them consistent with the welfare of the child so to do, endeavour to secure that the care of the child is taken over" by a parent, guardian, relative or friend. The relationship of these three provisions in two sub-sections has long bemused courts and commentators alike. The problem was accentuated by the requirement, inserted by the Children Act 1975, that 28 days' notice is required of intention to remove a child who has been in care for a period of six months.[73] The language of the new provision creates a new criminal offence but its relationship to section 2 has provoked a difference of opinion amongst the judiciary[74] and has also divided legal commentators.

The issue had been raised before the *Lewisham* case. In *Re S* in 1965 Pearson L.J. said: "if the power of the local authority to keep a child in their care ceases under [s.2(3)], it is at least arguable that there is no power to make an order (*sic*) under [s.3]'.[75] Pearson L.J. prefaced his remarks by 'if' but section 2(3) makes it quite clear that the power does so cease. Goff. J. in *Krishnan* v. *L.B. of*

Sutton thought that "in practice, the local authority would probably make an order (sic) under [s.3] and, with respect, I do not share the difficulty which Pearson L.J. felt in *Re S*, as to the power to make such an order (*sic*)."[76] In *Krishnan* it was emphasised that there was no "mandatory" duty to return a child on parental request.[77] In *Halvorsen* v. *Hertfordshire C.C.*[78] Widgery L.C.J. ventured the remarks that it would be "quite astonishing if, notwithstanding that the child had been taken (*sic*) into the care of the local authority, the parent could immediately demand its return." He interpreted section 2(3) to refer to a parent "not disqualified" from being fit to take care of he child. In the Scottish case of *Cheetham* v. *Glasgow Corporation* Lord Dunpark read section 2(3) subject to the "overriding duty" in section 2(2).[79]

The law was thus in doubt, and in a mess. I commented on this in an article in 1976.[80] John Eekelaar made similar comments in an article of his about the same time.[81] The Children Act 1975 did not take the opportunity to clarify difficult points of practice on which there was judicial conflict and misunderstanding. Subsequently, the Court of Appeal in *Bawden* v. *Bawden*[82] and *Johns* v. *Jones*[83] were to hold that the right of a local authority to keep a child in care under section 2 ceased when a parent desired the child's return. It was three years before *Bawden* v. *Bawden* got into the law reports but when it and *Johns* v. *Jones* did, the decisions caused disquiet in social services departments. On the arguments held by Eekelaar and myself *Bawden* v. *Bawden* and *Johns* v. *Jones* were correctly decided.[84] The Children Act 1975 defined what being in the care of a voluntary organisation meant. It equated care with actual custody.[85] The Act remained silent as to the scope of a local authority's care. I have argued earlier in this article that the relationship between a local authority and a child in section 2 care is actual custody.[86] But this does not mean that an authority which has actual custody, that is actual possession, by that alone can be said to have a child in its care. An authority which takes a child unlawfully does not have the child in its "care." "Care" entails more than bare possession. Back in 1976 I suggested that this additional element was "authority."[87] I still think that a local authority only has a child in its care when it has the authority to retain the child. But when may a local authority refuse to hand over a child when a parent has requested his return? If a parent demands his child back, is that child in local authority care and, if so, what terminates that care? The questions are crucial if for no other reason than that a local authority's powers to assume parental rights apply to a child "in their care under section 2.[88]

These questions should have been conclusively answered by the House of Lords in the *Lewisham* case. But the four speeches are so full of ambiguities that the law is permeated with doubt. On the question when care ends we get the following answers: not "directly" a parent desires to take care of the child (Viscount Dilhorne),[89] "until delivered up" (Lord Keith of Kinkel)[90]; "until the parent in fact removes the child" (Lord Scarman)[91] and "automatically," "once a parent presents herself to the authority and demands the immediate return of her child" (Lord Salmon).[92] Lord Wilberforce was in agreement with all four speeches. What is one to make of the speeches and the tests? Susan Maidment thinks it "quite clear"[93] that the House of Lords decided that a child remains in care as long as he is not actually removed or delivered up by the local authority: a parental demand or request does not, in other words, automatically or directly terminate section 2 care. But when she discusses the ability of the local authority to delay delivering up the child long enough to take out a wardship summons, a step which Lord Salmon thought might well be considered a local authority's "moral duty,"[94] she admits: "this without doubt must be strictly improper."[95] She does not say why. Propriety can only be judged by some standard. I would suggest that the steps to which she refers are legally improper and that they are legally improper because "care" ceases upon demand even though care must obviously continue for so long as the child remains in the local authority's possession. This distinction is even clearer if the steps the authority takes are procrastination with a view to passing a parental rights resolution. Obviously, this would take longer. But that is not the point. It is that the child would not be in its "care" under section 2 and that is a pre-requisite of a section 3 resolution. The distinction between "the 'right' to actual custody which terminates on the parental request and the 'fact' of actual custody which terminates on the parental removal of the child" is not "meaningless," as Maidment suggests it is.[96] Her reasons for so characterising the distinction are dependent on her understanding of the concept of care, on which I have thrown doubt earlier in this article.[97]

I am ready to concede that my interpretation runs up against difficulties where there is a substantial time-lag between a request or demand for a child's return and actually collecting the child to take him home. It is undesirable that a parent could give notice of intention to remove and then fail to collect the child for months or longer. I think there is a simple answer to this: legislation should provide that a request for a child's return should only be operative for some fixed period (say seven days). After the efflux of the specified time the child would go back into section 2 care as if no request had ever been made. But during the period the child would not be in "care." As I argued in an earlier article,[98] "even if care under [s.2] ceases someone must have rights and responsibilities in relation to the child in the interim period between demand and repossession. The child is not in (s.2) care but the authority remains *in loco parentis*. At the very least it is in charge or control of the child and some responsibilities flow from this." I suggested then that legislation should provide what the legal status of the local authority and the child is during the period. It is clear from this article that a legislative framework is urgently required. The question raised here is not the only one in need of a solution.

Thus far I have avoided introducing the additional complication of section 13(2). It is drafted clumsily[99] and appears to do nothing more than create a criminal offence (removing a child from care without the consent of the local authority or without first giving 28 days' notice). The offence only applies where the child has been in care for more than six months. Why was section 56 of the 1975 Act (what is now section 13(2)) passed? The answer is to be found in the Houghton report which recognised that "a sudden move, without preparation, can be damaging to the child and may have long-term repercussions."[1] But if the interpretations of at least three of the Lords (Dilhorne, Keith and Scarman) are right, there need be no "sudden move," for, despite the clear language of section 2(3), a local authority has power to keep a child in care even though a parent or guardian has requested his return. I believe that section 56 (now section 13(2)) was only passed because the legislature's understanding of section 2(3) was that "care" terminated upon parental demand. What then is the effect of the 28 days' provision? Two of the Lords (Dilhorne and Keith) repudiate the idea that it creates a "breathing space" in which the local authority can take the steps that it regards as appropriate. They reach this conclusion by highly formalistic reasoning[2] (only where a section is ambiguous may one call in aid a later statute as an aid to the construction of an earlier provision). The other two Lords (Salmon and Scarman)[3] and Waterhouse J. in *Wheatley* v. *L.B. of Waltham Forest*[4] see the 28 days' provision as a "breathing space." The section, on this interpretation, does not only create a criminal offence but also provides that a child remains in the care of the local authority for the 28 days' period. It gives time to prepare the child for a change, if he is to be returned, and time to pass a section 3 resolution or seek wardship, if the authority considers that it is in the child's best interests that he be not returned. It recognises that children who have been in care for six months are in a different legal position from those more temporarily in care.[5] There is no magic in six months but there is a case for distinguishing short-term and long-term care.

The courts have yet to consider the status of a child unlawfully removed by parents who have failed to give appropriate notice. The parents have committed a criminal offence. But the criminal law will not protect the child.[6] What steps can the local authority take? Much depends upon whether the child is still in "care," even though not in the local authority's physical possession. If he is, then, if grounds exist, a resolution assuming parental rights could be passed. If not, such a course of action is not open. A local authority cannot use place of safety powers or care proceedings to retain a child in care[7] but there seems no reason why a place of safety warrant or order under section 40 of the Children and Young Persons Act 1933 or section 28 of the Children and Young Persons Act 1969 should not be sought. As Susan Maidment writes: "it is a nice point, whether a child who is legally in section 2 care but physically in the unlawful possession of its parent(s) can be the subject of care proceedings."[8] Certainly, as she says, it is no abuse of place of safety powers to use them to protect a child lawfully removed by parents: *a fortiori*, there should be no objection to the use of section 28 of the 1969 Act or section 40 of the 1933 Act where the removal is unlawful.

B. *Assumptions of Parental Rights*

Under section 3 of the 1980 Act a local authority may by resolution passed by the social services committee assume the parental rights and duties of the parent or parents of any child "in their care under section 2" of the Act. A resolution may only be passed if at least one of eight specified grounds is satisfied. It has been said that the conduct of the parent must be "culpable, and culpable to a high degree."[9] There are detailed procedures for notice to parents; parents may object, in which case the local authority must take the matter to the juvenile court for confirmation of its resolution. Appeals lie to the High Court.[10]

Parental rights resolutions raise a large number of legal[11] questions. Some of these have been considered already in this article. It seems from the *Lewisham* case that a child in the physical possession of the local authority is in "care" even though his parents have requested his return. A local authority has, however, no "general residual discretion as to whether or not the child should be returned."[12] Lord Scarman indicated in *Lewisham* that "care" after a parent informs the local authority that he desires to resume care of his child is, pending the child's actual removal, a continuation of care under section 2.[13] I believe this to be wrong in law but, in the absence of legislation or the Lords invoking the 1966 Practice Direction,[14] it must be taken to represent the existing legal situation. Where the child has been in care for six months, the local authority has 28 days to pass a section 3 resolution. I believe that a resolution passed after the expiry of the breathing space of 28 days is invalid since the child is no longer in "care." In *Lewisham* the resolution was passed within the 28 days' period, as it was in *Wheatley*. But this was not the case in *Johns* v. *Jones*.[15] Although I have been taken to task[16] for arguing this, I still maintain that *Johns* v. *Jones* is still good authority for the invalidity of resolutions which purport to assume parental rights after the expiry of the 28 days' period. The decision to divest a parent of parental rights and duties is "a very serious one"[17] and local authorities should comply with statutory procedures. Comments in *Lewisham* on resolutions passed after 28 days are *obiter* and, given that on a proper analysis of the concept of "care" they are wrong, should have no persuasive force. I should like to see a court courageous enough to adopt this approach.

The pre-requisite of "care under section 2" raises another important question. Under a number of statutory provisions (see iv–viii and the custodianship provision)[18] the court may commit a child to the care of the local authority. The custodianship provision is defective in that it does not state the legal effect of such a committal.[19] The other provisions indicate that the child is to be treated "as if" received by the local authority into its care under section 2 of the 1980 Act. The enactments demonstrate that a committal to care is not equivalent to a section 2 reception for they state: "while an order made under this section is in force with respect to a child, the child shall continue in the care of the local authority notwithstanding any claim by a parent or other person."[20] Lowe and White see a committal as having a "similar effect"[21] to a section 3 resolution in so far as the parent cannot require the child to be returned but it is clear that the order does not vest parental rights and duties in the local authority. This may not matter where the child is a ward of court for the local authority can, indeed must, go back to the court for directions as to what it should do, at least insofar as major decisions are concerned.[22] But what is a local authority to do when a child has been committed to its care in matrimonial proceedings? The local authority does not have parental rights; nor does the court; the parent presumably still has legal custody,[23] though cannot exercise it because he cannot remove the child from the local authority. The law is in an unholy mess.

It would not be surprising if a local authority were, in appropriate circumstances, to think that the solution might lie in passing a parental rights resolution. But can it do this? Section 3 states that the child must be "in their care under section 2 of this Act." Is a child committed to care by (say) section 10 of the Domestic Proceedings and Magistrates' Courts Act 1978 in care under section 2 of the 1980 Act? Section 10(4) of the 1978 Act states that part II of the 1948 Children Act (that is part III of the 1980 Act) applies, with some exceptions, "as if the child has been received by the local authority into their care under section [2 of the 1980] Act." Since section 3 is in part I of the Act, it must follow that a local authority is not empowered to assume parental rights. Susan Maidment is not so certain. She says "probably not"[24] and adds that a resolution may be permissible where the child has been committed to care by a juvenile court. I am puzzled by this comment. I can find no authority for the distinction whatsoever. I think the better view must be that a local authority cannot assume parental rights and duties of children committed to its care.

One might be pardoned for thinking that the effect of a parental rights resolution would be crystal clear. Nothing could be further from the truth. Of course, dispute still rages on the scope of parental rights and duties themselves.[25] They are defined (if we can call this a definition) in section 85 of the Children Act 1975. They mean "as respects a particular child (whether legitimate or not), all the rights and duties which by law the mother and father have in relation to a legitimate child and his property; and reference to a parental right or duty shall be construed accordingly and shall include a right of access and any other element included in a right or duty." Section 2(11) of the 1948 Act, inserted by section 57 of the Children Act 1975, states that for the purpose of, what is now, section 3 parental rights and duties "in relation to a particular child means all rights and duties which by law the mother and father have in relation to a legitimate child and his property." From parental rights and duties are excluded specifically the right to consent to adoption applications and agree to adoption orders.[26] Further, parents (and step-parents[27]) are not relieved from any liability to maintain or contribute to maintenance[28] and a resolution does not authorise a local authority to cause a child to be brought up in any religious creed other than that in which he would have been brought up but for the resolution.[29] Legislation also provides that section 2(3) of the 1980 Act does not apply whilst a resolution is in force.

The original legislation (the Children Act 1948) referred to "all rights and duties of the person on whose account the resolution was passed" vesting in the local authority. "All" cannot have been correct: this is borne out by the limits to which reference has already been made. Parental duties to maintain (called then, as now, "liabilities") were retained by the 1948 Act s.3(6). The duty on the local authority not to cause the child to be brought up in any religious creed other than that in which he would have been brought up but for the resolution was also imposed by the 1948 Act (s.3(7)). The parents' right to consent to adoption was preserved in the adoption legislation.[29] So it seems that the 1948 Act cannot have meant what it said. The 1975 Act changed "all rights and powers" to "rights and duties,"[30] and inserted the definition of parental rights and duties to which reference has been made.

The question then is: adoption and religion apart, are all parental rights assumed by a section 3 resolution? Thomson,[31] writing before the 1975 Act, argued that the legislator could not really intend all rights to pass to the local authority. As he noted, this would mean, for example, that the local authority would have rights on intestacy, rights to appoint a testamentary guardian, possibly even to change a child's name.[32] He also argued that the parents' rights of access was not a matter for the local authority, but one for a court. If the draftsmen of the 1975 Act had read Thomson they appeared to take no notice of what he wrote. If anything, the 1975 Act makes it clearer just how wide the scope of a parental rights resolution is. The draftsmen could have conferred "legal custody" on the local authority. The effect of this would have been, in the language of section 86 of the 1975 Act, to have given the authority "so much of the parental rights and duties as relate to the person of the child (including the place and manner in which his time is spent)." But, by conferring parental rights, they have included rights relating to the child's property.

How far does this right extend? It seems to be generally assumed that it gives the local authority rights to succeed on the child's intestacy. Bevan and Parry certainly think this to be the case. They are critical of the injustice of this. Indeed, they ask: "will such injustice persuade the courts to hold that rights of succession do not pass to a local authority, notwithstanding the explicit terms of s.2(11) [of the 1975 Act]?"[33] I do wonder, however, whether the local authority would actually be legally entitled to the child's estate. The Administration of Estates Act 1925 in section 46 provides rules for the distribution of the residuary estate of an intestate. The relevant rule (s.46 (i) (iii), as amended), states: "if the intestate leaves no husband or wife and no issue but both parents then . . . the residuary estate of the intestate shall be held in trust for the father and mother in equal shares absolutely."[34] I do not recognise the local authority in the character of "both parents" or as "father and mother" nor do I think that on a strict interpretation courts would hold these named individuals to include a local authority with parental rights vested in it. The matter is, however, far from clear and statute should clarify that a local authority is not entitled to take the child's property on his death. A surprisingly high number of children do die in care.[35] Few have any property. But that is not the point: what is at stake is the principle. It is certainly wrong where parental rights have been assumed because of disability and not through culpability. It is equally wrong where the parents have paid for their child's maintenance. It is less objectionable where parental behaviour has been culpable. But whatever the surrounding circumstances, the point remains that no court order except adoption[36] has this total effect and a local authority's assumption of parental rights is an administrative act and not the result of a judicial hearing.[37]

A second problem area is the question whether a local authority may consent to the marriage of a child in its care. According to Lowe and White: "in practice registrars require the consent of the local authority if a child is in care under the 1980 Act and parental rights have been assumed under section 3 or if he is in care under the 1969 Act."[38] Bevan and Parry think that the right to consent to marriage passes to the local authority.[39] Bromley[40] and Cretney[41] disagree. Maidment comes to no conclusion. Though the matter is not beyond doubt the fact that the 1975 Children Act did not amend the Marriage Act 1949 to take account of this when the 1949 Act was amended to take account of custodianship is weak support for the view that the consents provided for in the Marriage Act are still required.

Neither succession nor marriage are major problems: access is. Two situations must be distinguished: where the parental rights of both parents have been assumed and where the resolution only extended to the rights of one parent. In the first case it would seem that the local authority may deny access. Whether or not access to a child is a parental right within the meaning of section 2(11) of the 1948 Act (the provision is not in the 1980 Act) is not beyond doubt. It is expressly included as a parental right in section 85 of the 1975 Act (and in the Interpretation Act 1978) but section 2(11) is silent about it. Bevan and Parry think "the courts may be willing to extend the philosophy of the 1975 Act to section 2."[42] Where something as crucial as the control of parental contact, or as drastic as its termination, is in issue strict interpretation of statutory provisions rather than expansive extrapolation is called for. But the evidence, flimsy though it is, suggests courts adopt the approach indicated by Bevan and Parry. Thomson, writing before the 1975 Act, was in no doubt that access, being a basic right of the child rather than a right in the parent,[43] was not taken over by the local authority.[44] I think that Maidment dismisses these arguments too readily.[45] The 1975 Act has not, as she says, "completely negated Thomson's earlier arguments." It would have done this without doubt had section 2(11) been formulated more carefully. I agree that courts will interpret section 2(11) as giving local authorities the power to deny access. I do not, however, think the power is clearly provided for.

Whether or not access is (and remains) a parental right may be more important where the parental rights of only one parent have been assumed. The other parent then shares parental rights and duties with the local authority. He is entitled to retain contact with his child. If the local authority refuses him access, he may apply to the court by virtue of section 9 of the Guardianship of Minors Act 1971. The court may then make such order as it "thinks fit having regard to the welfare of the minor and to the conduct and wishes of the mother and father."

The position of the putative father in such circumstances is more difficult to establish. In *Re K*[46] Payne J said: "bearing in mind the existence of the order (*sic*) under section 2 of the Children Act 1948 it seems to me that the justices in the circumstances of this case had no alternative but to decline the application of the father, and to leave discretion with regard to access to the local authority." He did not decide whether the court had the power to make an order. But in *S.* v. *Huddersfield Borough Council*,[47] Buckley L.J. regarded *Re K* as authority for the proposition that magistrates had no alternative but to decline a putative father's application under the 1971 Act for access to his illegitimate child in respect of whom a local authority had passed a section 3 resolution. Buckley L.J.'s remarks are *obiter*. *Re K* has, however, to be read in the light of *R* v. *Oxford City Justices ex parte H*,[48] where the Divisional Court relying on *Re K* held that magistrates could entertain an application for custody by the father of an illegitimate child, though it conceded that the existence of a section 3 resolution was a most important consideration in deciding whether, on the paramountcy principle, the father should succeed. Bagnall J. suggested that there might be a difference between asking for custody and asking for access since access was "a matter which must necessarily be under the day to day control and discretion of the local authority."[49] *Re K* and *Oxford City Justices* are not easily reconciled.[50] The pity is that the Court of

Appeal in *S.* v. *Huddersfield B.C.* did not grasp the matter and consider whether the earlier cases were correctly decided. Whatever the position of the putative father, there is no doubt that the "other parent" is in a stronger position. The putative father only has a procedural right to apply for access: the "other parent" has a substantive right to access.[51] As Bevan and Parry put it, "the question is whether he shall be allowed to exercise it. The answer must depend on the strength to be given to the right in applying the principle that the child's welfare is paramount—the discretion about access is not automatically to be left to the local authority."[52]

C. *Care Orders*

Most children in care are there as the result of a care order made under the Children and Young Persons Act 1969: in March 1979 just under 48,000 were in care as a result of such an order.[53] Care orders may be made in criminal or care proceedings. The differences do not concern us here. In terms of the law there is nothing to distinguish different types of "care order children." The effect of a juvenile court care order is laid down now by the Child Care Act 1980 s.10. This imposes a duty on the local authority to whose care a child is committed by a care order (or a warrant under section 23(1) of the Children and Young Persons Act 1969) to receive the child into its care and "notwithstanding any claim by his parent or guardian" to keep him in care while the order (or warrant) is in force.[54]

The local authority has the "same powers and duties" with respect to a person in its care by virtue of a care order (or warrant) "as his parent or guardian would have apart from the order (or warrant)" (s.10(2) of the 1980 Act). The language used is different from that in section 3 dealing with an assumption of parental rights: here it is "powers and duties"; there "rights and duties."[55] In itself I do not think this variation of language makes any difference. But the effects of a care order are not identical to an assumption of parental rights.

Statute excepts certain powers from the local authority's control. It cannot change a child's religion (see section 10(3)). This veto is expressed in identical language in section 4(3) on parental rights resolutions. It cannot agree to the child's adoption. Observers as astute as Bevan and Parry missed this[56] and may be forgiven for so doing. The parental veto is preserved by the Commencement Order which brought section 8(1) and Schedule 4, Part 4 of the 1975 Children Act into operation: section 4(3)(a) of the Adoption Act 1958 was preserved in this way.[57] It is not clear whether the right to consent to the marriage of a child under 18 subject to a care order vests in the local authority and, if it does so, whether it is to the exclusion of the parent or in addition. Registrars apparently require the consent of the local authority.[58] I agree with Lowe and White that it would be "bad local authority practice not to consult the parent, unless the welfare of the child required otherwise."[59] There would, accordingly, be grounds for challenging the decision by means of wardship. Since no reference is made to the child's property, a care order does not vest this in any way in the local authority. Whatever doubt there is in relation to parental rights resolutions,[60] there can be none as regards care orders.[61] A local authority is not entitled to succeed on the child's intestacy. This limitation suggests that a care order confers something akin to legal custody on the local authority: a parental rights resolution may be closer in conception to guardianship.

The legislation expressly states that the local authority has the right to restrict the liberty of a child subject to a care order (see s.10(2)). It can accordingly place him in a secure unit[62] and may do this, to protect the public, even though it is contrary to the child's welfare.[63] There is no appeal against decisions to "lock up" children,[64] a matter on which there is disquiet which has now reached official bodies.[65] Parents cannot restrict their child's liberty in this way, at least once they reach the "age of discretion" (14 for boys and 16 for girls).[66] Brenda Hoggett, I note, thinks these powers "obviously necessary."[67] But most children "locked up" have committed no criminal offence. The majority are absconders and their running away is thought to be more a reflection on the homes from which they run than on the children themselves.[68] A local authority may also apply to the court for a child over 15 who is disrupting life in a community home to be transferred to borstal.[69]

Parents retain some duties. They must keep the local authority informed of their address.[70] They have certain duties to contribute to the maintenance of their child.[71] These duties apply equally to parents whose child is in care under s.2 and under a care order.[72]

The main problem area once again is access.[73] The question arose in *Re W* in 1979[74] and in *A* v. *Liverpool City Council*[75] in 1981. In *Re W* the Court of Appeal held that a natural parent does not have an inalienable right of access to her child. In *A* v. *Liverpool City Council* Lord Wilberforce said that access was "undoubtedly a matter within the discretionary power of the local authority."[76] Of course, the right of access is not inalienable. But the question must be: who can take it from a parent? Can this be done by a local authority with a care order or does it require a court to terminate or regulate parental contact? Lord Wilberforce's statement has gone relatively unchallenged. But is he right? I doubt it. If we look at the statute we find, in section 10(2), that a local authority "shall . . . have the same powers and duties with respect to a person in their care . . . as his parent or guardian would have apart from the order . . . " Does one parent have the "power" to refuse the other access?

There are two ways of looking at access. If it is a right of the child,[77] then neither a local authority nor a parent can deprive a child of his right. On this view, as Thomson has argued,[78] only a court of law can deprive a child of his right of access in the interests of his own welfare. If access to his child is a parental right, as is probably the better view,[79] a parent retains that right even when he is deprived of custody of his child, as, for example, on divorce. Just as a custodial parent has no right to deprive the non-custodial parent of access; so a local authority with the "same powers and duties" as a parent would have apart from the care order is in no better position. The argument that in law local authorities may not control access has to counter one other supposedly major authority that is commonly referred to in support of the local authority's right to deny access.

This is the case of *Re Y*.[80] Ormrod L.J. held that section 21(2) of the 1980 Act included a power to grant access, even though the word is not specifically used in the sub-section. This states: "a local authority may allow a child in their care, either for a fixed period or until the local authority otherwise determine, to be under the charge and control of a parent, guardian, relative or friend." It is quite clear that Parliament did not pass this provision with access in mind. It was passed to facilitate the local authority's duty in section 2(3) to "endeavour to secure that the case of the child is taken over either—(*a*) by a parent or guardian or (*b*) by a relative or friend of his . . . " It assists, further, in promoting "home on trial" policies, which would not be legal without it. Accordingly, section 21(2) is to be seen as permitting what would otherwise be a breach of duty by the local authority. It should not be construed as giving the local authority the power to deny access. Ormrod L.J.'s remarks in *Re Y*, insofar as they refer to cases of section 2 care, were anyway strictly *obiter* since the issue in *Re Y* was whether, in exercising its power in wardship proceedings in committing the ward to a local authority's care, the court was also empowered to make specific directions as to access. Having decided that it was, he added: "I certainly would not wish anyone to think because of anything I have said that I have cast any doubt whatever on the powers of local authorities in ordinary cases under [s.2 of the 1980 Act] to control access as part of their responsibility."[81] Other cases referred to are *R* v. *Oxford City Justices ex p. H*[82] and *Re O*[83] discussed earlier in this article. Remarks about access in the *Oxford* case are *obiter*, as are those in *Re O*.

Re W in 1979 is thus the first case in which the issue of access to a child subject to a care order was raised directly. The court held that a decision as to access lay within the discretion of the local authority. *A* v. *Liverpool City Council* affirmed this. But neither case contains any real argument. Not only is there no statutory basis for denying access but, if my interpretation of section 10(2) is right, there is an express negation of the local authority's right to deny access. The local authority only has the powers and duties of a parent, except as statute adds to[84] or subtracts from them,[85] and one parent cannot deny the other access to his child. Are *Re W* and *A* v. *Liverpool City Council* therefore decisions *per incuriam*[86] a binding statute? There is certainly an arguable case for so holding.

D. *Wardship and Committal to Care*

Wardship is a growth industry. Its character has undergone a remarkable transformation in the last decade.[87] Concomitant with its rapid growth and development has come increased reliance on powers in section 7(2) of the Family Law Reform Act 1969.[88] *Inter alia* this provides: "where it appears to the court that there are exceptional circumstances[89] making it impracticable or undesirable for a ward of court to be, or continue to be, under the care of either of his parents or any other individual the court may, if it thinks fit, make an order committing the care of the ward to a local authority." The effect of an order is that Part III of the Child Care Act 1980 applies "as if" the child had been received into care under section 2 of that Act. This is subject to the following qualification: section 2(3) of the 1980 Act does not apply and the ward accordingly continues in the local authority's care "notwithstanding any claim by a parent or other person." If a parent wishes to have the committal[90] terminated he may apply to the High Court to have the order discharged.[91]

The consequences of a committal in wardship proceedings are far from clear. It has a similar effect to section 3 resolution in that a parent cannot require the child to be returned. But the local authority is not vested with parental rights and duties with respect to the ward. Custody, in the wide meaning of that term, what we should now call "legal custody" is retained by the court. What the local authority is given can amount to nothing more than care and control or actual custody.[92] Part III of the 1980 Act applies. It is provided, however, that the exercise by the local authority of its powers under sections 18, 21, and 22 of the 1980 Act are subject to "any directions by the court."[93] It is also provided that the local authority's powers to arrange for emigration of children do not apply.[94]

The court has to be consulted about major decisions, such as whether an attempt should be made to rehabilitate the child with his parents; whether there should be long-term fostering with or without a view to adoption[95]; and whether a child can be transferred from one foster parent to another.[96] "No important step in the child's life can be taken without the court's consent."[97] The court may also give directions as to access. *Re Y*[98] is clear authority for that and I agree Lowe and White[99] are correct as far as their interpretation of section 7(2) is concerned. They have criticised my questioning of *Re Y* but what I questioned[1] was Ormrod L.J.'s statement that access could be denied a section 2 parent. I agree that, as regards a ward committed to a local authority's care, section 43(5)(*a*) of the Matrimonial Causes Act 1973 is conclusive.[2] In a recent case the Court of Appeal has said that it is "unwise" for a court to try to direct the future of wards "except in a broad way."[3] It held that a judge was wrong to direct that the local authority should take all practical steps and means to return the child to its 16-year-old mother (she was also in care) and to see that the child was brought up by her. This decision may herald the courts' willingness to delegate more decision-making power to local authorities.

Uncertainties and doubts remain. What, for example, is a "major decision?"[4] Division of responsibilities between the court and local authority is in urgent need of clarification. The very status of care exercised by local authorities over wards is, to say the least, ambiguous. Children who come into care through a court committal order are not in section 2 care though the powers and duties of the local auhority under part II of the 1980 Act are to operate "as if the local authority had taken (*sic*) the child into care under [s.2]—no more."[5] But if they are not in section 2 care and they are certainly not in section 3 care, they must be in care by virtue of the court order. But this tells us very little about the local authority's powers and duties. Parents cannot remove their children; directions may be given by the court; major decisions, whatever they are, may not be taken without the court being consulted. But more than this we do not know. As already indicated, a parental rights resolution cannot be made. There are two reasons for this: first, the child is not in section 2 care and secondly, parental rights are vested in the court and not the parents. It would be strange if an agent, for that is what the authority is, were able by administrative act to divest the principal of its rights.

E. *Committals To Care Under Other Legislation*

There are five other legislative sources for committal to care. No two of them are identical.

(i) *Divorce court committals*

The powers of a divorce court[6] to commit a child to care are close in conception to those of wardship jurisdiction. Part III of the Child Care Act 1980 applies "as if" the child had been received by the local authority into its care under section 2 of that Act.[7] The local authority may not arrange for the child's emigration.[8] It is subject to "any directions given by the court" as regards matters governed by sections 18, 21 and 22 of the 1980 Act.[9] The child remains in care "notwithstanding any claim by a parent or other person,"[10] for example, a step-parent.[11] A parent, or presumably any other person, who wants custody of the child may apply to the court to vary or discharge the committal.[12] A divorce court has power to make a custody order superseding a care order made by a juvenile court.[13]

(ii) *Committals in magisterial domestic proceedings*

The magistrates' court seised of a custody application may, within its domestic jurisdiction, commit a child to care.[14] The jurisdiction is expressed in similar terms to section 43 of the 1973 Matrimonial Causes Act. Thus, Part III of the 1980 Act applies to children so committed; it is "as if" the local authority had received the child into care under section 2 of that Act; parental claims to the child are excluded. There are, however, differences. The court is not empowered to make directions to the local authority. The court cannot make an order as to access.[15] There is no power to apply for a variation or discharge of the order. The justification for using wardship to challenge the local authority's powers are thus substantial. It is doubtful whether a magistrates' court could do what the Court of Appeal held the divorce court had power to do in *Ellard* v. *Ellard*.[16] Can a local authority deny access to a parent or party to the marriage? It is not subject to direction on section 21 (which has been interpreted, wrongly I have suggested, to cover access). The court itself cannot make an access order. Since the local authority does not have parental rights, it is clear that it cannot deny access.

(iii) *Committals in guardianship*

Committals to care in guardianship proceedings are governed by section 9 of the Guardianship of Minors Act 1971, as amended by the Guardianship Act 1973, s.2(2)(*b*), (3) and section 4. It is provided that part III of the 1980 Act (and other sections in the Act including some originally found in the 1963 Children and Young Persons Act) apply "as if" the minor had been received into care under section 2 of the 1980 Act. Once again, but only where the order is made by the High Court,[17] the exercise by the local authority of its powers relating to welfare and accommodation and maintenance are subject to any directions given by the court. The local authority may not arrange emigration. The minor continues in care notwithstanding any claim by a parent or other person.[18] Once again it is clear that the local authority cannot deny access.

(iv) *Care on refusal of adoption order*

Section 17(1)(*b*) of the Children Act 1975, as amended by section 89 of and Scheaule 3 to the Domestic Proceedings and Magistrates' Courts Act 1978,[19] empowers a court on the refusal to make an adoption order to commit the child to the care of a specified local authority. This is a little strange since the parent, having placed the child for adoption, will have wished to sever links with the child. The parent is unlikely to want access but clearly would be within his rights in requesting it. The local authority has no power to gainsay access. Statute does not provide for the court to make any directions to the local authority. There is no power for the parents to apply for variation or discharge. The local authority's powers are expressed to be identical to those vested in it by a committal in guardianship proceedings.[20–21] The child is in care "as if" received into care under section 2 of the 1980 Act but is not in section 2 care.

(v) *Care on revocation of custodianship*

The Children Act 1975, s.36(2) directs the court that, when it revokes a custodianship order,[22] if the child would not then be in legal custody[23] of any person, it should commit the child to the care of a specified local authority. The provision is different from all others. They refer to "exceptional circumstances making it impracticable or undesirable for the child to be entrusted" to a parent, etc. (depending on the circumstances): section 36 refers to a particular case. The other provisions give the courts power to commit to care if they think fit: section 36 is mandatory ("the court shall . . ."). The standard form of the other provisions states that on committal to care it is "as if" the child had been received into care under section 2 of the 1980 Act. Inexplicably, the custodianship revocation provision is silent as to the effect of a committal. It would be idle to speculate as to the consequences of an order under section 36(2). Custodianship is not yet in operation so that Parliament has still got time to fill in this strange and inexcusable gap.

F. *Reception Into Care of Children In Unsuitable Surroundings*

A child may come into care in three other ways. The aim of each of the provisions is common, so that they may be treated together. The Child Care Act 1980, s.57(6), the Foster Children Act 1980, s.12 and the Adoption Act 1958, s.43(3) all provide for the removal of children from unsuitable surroundings and their reception into care under section 2 of the Child Care Act 1980.

The Foster Children Act and Adoption Act are expressed in similar terms. They state that if a juvenile court is satisfied that a child (within the terms of the relevant Acts) is kept or is about to be received by an unfit person or in contravention of a prohibition or in premises or environment detrimental or likely to be detrimental to him "the court may make an order for his removal to a place of safety until he can be restored to a parent, relative or guardian of his or until other arrangements can be made with respect to him." The court, it will be noted, has a discretion. The place of safety order is no ordinary place of safety order. It is governed by section 23 of the Children and Young Persons Act 1963. Where a child is removed in this way the local authority shall "if practicable" inform a parent or guardian or "any person who acts as his guardian." It is provided that a local authority "may" receive into their care under section 2 of the Child Care Act 1980 any child removed under this section. It is not under a specific duty to do so. Should it do so, the child will be in section 2 care. The conditions in section 2(1) need not exist and the child may be over 17. But despite these jurisdictional differences, the reception is a section 2 reception and the same law must apply as applies to ordinary section 2 receptions. So, for example, a resolution assuming parental rights under section 3 is permissible, provided grounds exist. On the other hand, it must also follow that section

2(3) of the Child Care Act 1980 applies, so that parents may remove their children from care. These provisions are thus different from the committal powers which give the local authority the power to retain a child in care notwithstanding the claim of any parent. In normal circumstances a section 2 reception requires parental consent but these are not normal circumstances and it is thought a reception may take place in the absence of parental consent, though not where a parent specifically objects to a reception. Presumably, in such a case care proceedings might be brought if appropriate.

The Child Care Act 1980, s.57(6) is couched in slightly different language. The Secretary of State may "require" the local authority "forthwith" to remove a child from a voluntary home and receive him into care under section 2 of the same Act. This it must do irrespective of whether the usual conditions in section 2(1) exist or the child is over 17. This looks more like a committal but is expressed as a section 2 reception. Nothing is said about informing the parent or guardian or about his consent. The provision is puzzling. Can it be that section 2(3) applies so that a parent may remove the child at will? In the absence of evidence to the contrary I am inclined to think that this is so. It is after all a section 2 reception. If this is right it must also follow that a local authority may assume parental rights under section 3 of the 1980 Act where grounds exist.

The three provisions considered here are in many ways typical of the provisions considered in this article: badly-phrased, ambiguous, using concepts loosely and full of gaps.

CONCLUSION

This article has demonstrated the inadequacy of the conceptual framework of our child care law. It has shown that the law is riddled with doubt; that it suffers from loose drafting and imprecise language; that there is accordingly a lack of clarity that would be tolerable in few other areas. There are gaping holes in the fabric of the law on matters as crucial as access, property, succession and marriage. Despite the attempt at consolidation in 1980 the law is still not contained in a single enactment. But worse still, there is so much legislation by cross-reference that even experts stumble as they grope for answers. We can blame history for the fortuitous growth of different bases of care. History too can be blamed for the overlap in jurisdictions in family law. Such reification is convenient but it does not exonerate those responsible for the current mess. Because for too long child care law has been regarded, as Lord Scarman put it, as the "world of social administration,"[24] responsibility for legislation has fallen to the Department of Health and Social Security. Its officials may understand social welfare but they do not appear to be as concerned about rights. Too much is currently going by default. This is not assisted by the courts which have taken a non-interventionist line.[25] A major debate today is about the accountability of local government. A pre-requisite of this is a framework of rules governing relationships. Local authorities can get away with bad practices when their powers are curbed as loosely and policed as inadequately as they are in relation to child care decisions. In this article I have deliberately steered clear of discussing ways of controlling local authorities. I have written elsewhere about that.[26] This article undertook what is essentially a preliminary task, that of clearing a path through a tangled thicket of concepts.

Notes

[1] *Lewisham L.B.C.* v. *Lewisham Juvenile Court* [1979] 2 All E.R. 289, 318.

[2] These statistics are drawn from *Children In Care In England and Wales, March 1979*, DHSS, 1981.

[3] *Cf. Czarnikow* v. *Roth, Schmidt & Co.* [1922] 2 K.B. 478, 488 *per* Scrutton L.J.

[4] H.K. Bevan, *The Law Relating to Children* (Butterworths, 1973).

[5] The move resulted from a C.C.E.T.S.W. Paper, *Legal Studies In Social Work Education*, 1974. On the reverse, teaching lawyers about social work, see M.D.A. Freeman, *Adoption and Fostering* no. 94 (1978), p.36.

[6] See M.D.A. Freeman, "The Rights of Children in the International Year of the Child," (1980) 33 C.L.P. 1.

[7] On which see H.K. Bevan and M. Parry, *Children Act 1975*, (Butterworths, 1979) and M.D.A. Freeman, *The Children Act 1975* (Sweet & Maxwell, 1976).

[8] See M.D.A. Freeman, *The Child Care Act and Foster Children Act 1980*, (Sweet & Maxwell, 1980).

[9] This comes to the public's attention when a scandal, a death like Maria Colwell or allegations of sexual abuse, as in the Kincora boys' home occurs. But it is the everyday bad practices which are not exposed which should cause concern.

[10] A good discussion of the issues of K. Fitzherbert, "Protecting Children in Care" *New Society*, February 4, 1982, pp.180–181.

[11] See *Social Work Today*, Vol. 13, no. 25, March 2, 1982, p.5.

[12] "Controlling Local Authorities in Child Care Cases—*A* v. *Liverpool City Council* Revisited," *Justice of The Peace*, Vol. 146, pp.188, 202 (1982).

[13] His attitude is rather typical of the judicial approach to "welfare" matters. For another, perhaps better known example, see the Court of Appeal's reasoning in *R.* v. *Preston Appeal Tribunal ex p. Moore and Shine* [1975] 2 All E.R. 807.

[14] There is no indication that its introduction is imminent. See the critical comments of Ormrod L.J. in *Re F.* [1982] 1 W.L.R. 102, 105.

[15] See R.A. Parker, *Caring For Separated Children* (Macmillan, 1980) and M. Kellmer-Pringle (ed.), *A Fairer Future for Children* (Macmillan, 1980). See also B. Jordan, "Prevention," *Adoption and Fostering* no. 105, p.20 (1981).

[16] See J. Heywood and B. Allen, *Financial Help in Social Work* (Manchester U.P., 1971); M. Jackson and B. Valencia, *Financial Aid Through Social Work* (Routledge & Kegan Paul, 1979); M.D.A. Freeman, "Rules and Discretion In Local Authority Social Services Departments" (1979) J.S.W.L. 84.

[17] See *Children In Care in England and Wales March 1978*, H.C. 542 (1980), App. A, Table A1, p.20.

[18] A point made strongly in research carried out by the London Borough of Barnet. See *Community Care*, September 17, 1981, p.5.

[19] See G. Kelly, "The Lost Cord," *Social Work Today*, Vol. 13, no. 12, November 24, 1981, pp.7–9 for his incisive analysis of the issues involved. See also D. Fanshel and E.B. Shinn, *Children in Foster Care—A Longitudinal Investigation* (Columbia U.P., 1978) and Jane Aldgate, "Identification of Factors Influencing Children's Length of Stay in Care" in J. Triseliotis (ed.), *New Developments In Foster Care and Adoption* (Routledge & Kegan Paul, 1980), pp.22–40.

[20] *Op. cit.* note 1, p.537.

[21] See, *e.g.* Widgery L.C.J. in *Halvorsen* v. *Hertfordshire C.C.* (1975) 5 Fam. Law 79.

[22] H.L. Vol. 153, col. 918.

[23] *Op. cit.* note 1, p.319.

[24] See *Wheatley* v. *London Borough of Waltham Forest* [1979] 2 All E.R. 289; *R.* v. *Whibley* [1938] 3 All E.R. 777; *R.* v. *Boulden* (1957) 41 Cr. App. R. 105; *Watson* v. *Nikolaisen* [1955] 2 Q.B. 286; *Mitchell* v. *Wright* (1905) 7 F. (Ct. of Sess.) 568.

[25] *Care of Children*, Cmd. 6922, para. 425 (ii).

[26] *Summary of the Main Provisions of The Children Bill*, Cmd. 7306, para. 5.

[27] *Op. cit.* note 1, p.318. See also Viscount Dilhorne at p.300.

[28] See Child Care Act 1980, s.18.

[29] *Ibid.* ss.21, 22.

[30] "The Fragmentation of Parental Rights and Children In Care" (1981) J.S.W.L. 21, 24.

[31] See Children Act 1975, s.87.

[32] Children Act 1975, s.87(1).

[33] See Child Care Act 1980, s.2(3). See *post*, p.125.

[34] See Child Care Act 1980, s.13(2) (the derivation of this is s.56 of the Children Act 1975).

[35] The foster parent derives his authority to care for the child from the local authority. He has no independent right.

[36] That is in the Hohfeldian sense. There is no denying that it has privileges.

[37] See the Law Reform (Miscellaneous Provisions) Act 1970, s.5.

[38] See the Offences Against the Person Act 1861, s.56.

[39] It does not protect any right as such.

[40] *Op. cit.* note 38.

[41] For a recent interpretation of this see *R.* v. *Austin* [1981] 1 All E.R. 374, commented upon by M.D.A. Freeman, "Child-Snatching and the Inquiry Agent—A Comment on *R.* v. *Austin*," *Justice of the Peace*, Vol. 145, pp.474–475 (1981).

[42] Sexual Offences Act 1956, s.20.

[43] "What Are Parental Rights?" (1973) 89 L.Q.R. 210, 215.

[44] Guardianship of Minors Act 1971, s.1.

[45] *J.* v. *C.* [1970] A.C. 668, 710.

[46] In the Hohfeldian sense. See his *Fundamental Legal Conceptions As Applied in Judicial Reasoning*, Yale U.P. 1919.

[47] See Child Care Act 1980, s.2(3).

[48] See Pt. V of the 1980 Act. The liability section is not assisted by the fact that the Queen's Printers' copy contains an error! (s.45(1)(i) "or" should read "and").

[49] For characteristic emphasis of B.A.A.F. see the A.B.A.F.A. Discussion Paper, *Terminating Parental Contact* (ed. M. Adcock and R. White, 1980).

[50] See also DHSS, *Foster Care: A Guide To Practice* (HMSO, 1976).

[51] One of the lessons of J. Rowe and L. Lambert, *Children Who Wait* (A.B.A.A., 1973).

[52] DHSS, *Mentally Handicapped Children In Residential Care* (1974), p.7.

[53] Edited by R.A. Parker (Macmillan, 1980), p.73.

[54] The case for their doing so put by Margaret Adcock, "Parental Contact" (1979) *Adoption and Fostering* no. 97, p.19. See also Eva Holmes, "Assessing Parental Relationships" (1980) *Adoption and Fostering* no. 102, p.23.

[55] See, *e.g.* N. Lowe and R. White, *Wards of Court* (Butterworths, 1979).

[56] [1975] 3 All E.R. 348.

[57] On which see J. Thoburn, *Captive Clients*, (Routledge & Kegan Paul, 1980).

[58] See s.2(2) and 10(1) of the 1980 Act.

[59] *Op. cit.* note 56, p.354.

[60] [1974] 2 All E.R. 356.

[61] See s.14.

[62] [1972] 3 All E.R. 769. The distinction between the two cases is not convincing but a critical discussion is not relevant here.

[63] *Op. cit.* note 60, p.360.

[64] *Op. cit.* note 55, pp.310–312.

[65] *Adoption and Fostering* no. 91, p.57 (1978).

[66] *Post*, p.136.

[67] *Beyond The Best Interests of The Child* (Burnett, 1980 (revised ed.)), pp.38 and 116–133.

[68] See S. Maidment, (1975) 2 Br. J. of Law and Society 182.

[69] See *Dipper* v. *Dipper* [1980] 2 All E.R. 722; discussed by M.D.A. Freeman "Custody Confused: An Analysis of *Dipper* v. *Dipper*" (1981) 145 *Justice of The Peace* 391.

[70] [1973] 2 All E.R. 81. See also remarks of Dame E. Butler-Sloss "Parental Contact" *Adoption and Fostering* no. 102, p.29 (1980); "We are considering the right of the child to contact with the parent in preference to the rights of the parent."

[71] "Local Authorities and Parental Rights" (1974) 90 L.Q.R. 310 and (1975) 91 L.Q.R. 14.

[72] [1981] 2 All E.R. 385.

[73] See Child Care Act 1980, s.13(2).

[74] *Cf.* the speeches of Viscount Dilhorne and Lord Keith of Kinkel with those of Lords Salmon and Scarman in the *Lewisham* case, *op. cit.* note 1.

[75] [1965] 1 All E.R. 865, 871.

[76] [1970] Ch. 181, 185–186.

[77] The case may be explained on its own facts. The child in question was almost 18 and did not want to return to her parents.

[78] *Op. cit.* note 21.

[79] (1972) Scots. L.J. 50. (Interpreting identical Scots provisions).

[80] "Children In Care: The Impact of the Children Act 1975" (1976) 6 Fam. Law 136.

[81] "Children In Care and the Children Act 1975" (1976) 40 M.L.R. 121. Bevan and Parry, *op. cit.* note 7, are in general agreement with the interpretations of Eekelaar and myself.

[82] [1978] 3 All E.R. 1216 (decided in 1975).

[83] [1978] 3 All E.R. 1222.

[84] "Retaining A Child In Care" (1979) 129 N.L.J. 223.

[85] See s.88.

[86] *Ante*, p.120.
[87] *Op. cit.* note 80, p.138. See also Eekelaar, *op. cit.* note 81, p.125 for agreement.
[88] See s.3 of the 1980 Act.
[89] *Op. cit.* note 1, p.301.
[90] *Ibid.* p.316.
[91] *Ibid.* p.320.
[92] *Ibid.* p.306.
[93] *Op. cit.* note 30, p.28.
[94] *Op. cit.* note 1, p.306.
[95] *Op. cit.* note 30, p.29. Later in her article she says "somewhat improper."
[96] *Ibid.* p.28, n.38.
[97] *Ante*, p.120–121.
[98] "Who Cares? Some Comments On The Lewisham Case" (1979) 129 N.L.J. 648, 650.
[99] A point recognised by Lord Scarman in *Lewisham*, p.319.
[1] *Report of the Departmental Committee on the Adoption of Children*, Cmnd. 5107, 1972, para. 152.
[2] *Op. cit.* note 1 (1st series), pp.299, 316.
[3] *Ibid.* pp.307, 319.
[4] *Op. cit.* note 24 (1st series), p.293.
[5] In the Houghton report, the suggested period was one year. This period was in the Children Bill 1975 but was amended to six months.
[6] The offence cannot be thought to have any real deterrent effect.
[7] See *Essex C.C.* v. *T.L.R.* (1979) 9 Fam. Law 15.
[8] *Op. cit.* note 30 (1st series), p.30.
[9] *Per* Waterhouse J. in *op. cit.* note 14 (1st series), p.294.
[10] Child Care Act 1980, s.6. It is rare that a parental rights resolution is opposed formally. The Strathclyde Social Work Depatment study, *Strathclyde's Children* (1980) found that this happened in only 15 cases out of 111.
[11] I do not consider the policy issues here. An attempt, which I support, has recently been made to transfer jurisdiction to the juvenile court. See *The Times*, March 11, 1982, and *Hansard* H.C. Vol. 17, cols. 866–70.
[12] *Op. cit.* note 1 (1st series), p.3156, *per* Lord Keith of Kinkel. [13] *Ibid.*
[14] [1966] 3 All E.R. 77.
[15] [1978] 3 All E.R. 1223.
[16] By Nigel Lowe in the Society of Public Teachers of Law Newsletter in a review of my *The Child Care and Foster Children Act 1980*. It is true of course, that three of the lords in *Lewisham* did expressly state that *Johns* v. *Jones* should be overruled (Dilhorne at p.303, Keith at p.317, Scarman at p.320).
[17] *Per* Waterhouse J. in *Wheatley* v. *London Borough of Waltham Forest* [1979] 2 All E.R. 289, 294.
[18] *Ante*, p.118–119.
[19] A point also noted by H.K. Bevan and Martin Parry, *op. cit.* note 7 (1st series), p.156.
[20] See, *e.g.* s.10(5) of the Domestic Proceedings and Magistrates' Courts Acts 1978.
[21] *Op. cit.* note 55 (1st series), p.90.
[22] See *post*, p.139.
[23] See S. Maidment, "The Fragmentation of Parental Rights" (1981) 40 C.L.J. 135–158.
[24] *Op. cit.* note 30 (1st series), p.30.
[25] See Eekelaar, *op. cit.* note 43 (1st series). See also Justice Report (the Godfrey report), *Parental Rights and Duties and Custody Suits* (Justice, 1975).

[26] See the Child Care Act 1980, s.3(1).
[27] If they have "treated" the child as a child of the family.
[28] See Child Care Act 1980, s.4(2) which refers to the liability of "any person."
[29] *Ibid*. s.4(3).
[30] See Children Act 1975, s.57.
[31] *Op. cit*. note 71 (1st series).
[32] See Enrolment of Deeds (Change of Name)(Amendment) Regulations 1969.
[33] *Op. cit*. note 7 (1st series), p.155.
[34] See, for agreement, P. Bromley, *Family Law* (Butterworths, 6th ed., 1981), p.399, n. 1.
[35] See *op. cit*. note 17 (1st series), Table A4, p.25, suggesting about 100 in 1978. It was 150 in 1975 and 132 in 1976. These figures are higher than might be expected. Concern was expressed by Parket *et al* in *Caring for Separated Children* (Macmillan, 1980), p.129.
[36] See Children Act 1975, Sched. 1, Pt.II, paras. 5/6.
[37] The Child Care Bill 1982 would have transferred jurisdiction to the juvenile court.
[38] *Op. cit*. note 55 (1st series), p.276, n. 5 and 307.
[39] *Op. cit*. note 7 (1st series), p.156.
[40] *Op. cit*. note 34 (1st series), p.399, n. 1.
[41] *Principles of Family Law* (Sweet & Maxwell, 3rd ed., 1979), p.513.
[42] *Op. cit*. note 7 (1st series), p.156.
[43] *Op. cit*. note 71 (1st series), p.314.
[44] But only by a court.
[45] *Op. cit*. note 30 (1st series), p.33.
[46] [1972] 3 All E.R. 769.
[47] [1974] 3 All E.R. 296.
[48] [1974] 2 All E.R. 356.
[49] *Ibid*. p.360.
[50] See Maidment 125 N.L.J. 726 (1975).
[51] See *Re O*. [1965] Ch. 23.
[52] *Op. cit*. note 7 (1st series), p.157
[53] *Op. cit*. note 2 (1st series).
[54] It is a compulsory measure of care. *Cf*. s.2(3) of the 1980 Act on receptions into care.
[55] Formerly "rights and powers." See Children Act 1948, s.2. See *ante*, p.131–2.
[56] See *op. cit*. note 7 (1st series), p.34.
[57] For agreement see Maidment, *op. cit*. note 30 (1st series), p.34 n. 62.
[58] See Lowe and White, *op. cit*. note 55 (1st series), p.276, 307.
[59] *Ibid*. pp.307–308.
[60] *Ante*, pp.132–133.
[61] Maidment is less certain of the distinction. *Op. cit*. note 30 (1st series), p.35.
[62] As to which see S. Millham *et al, Locking Up Children* (Saxon House, 1978).
[63] See Child Care Act 1980, s.18(3).
[64] See N. Shepherd "No Appeal For Children Behind Bars?" (1977) 127 N.L.J. 80. See also *The Guardian*, August 25, 1979 and M. Hoghughi, *Troubled and Troublesome* (Burnett, 1978).
[65] DHSS, *Legal and Professional Aspects of The Use of Secure Accommodation For Children In Care* (DHSS, 1981), paras. 46–49. See also now Children's Legal Centre, *Locked Up In Care* (1982) and H.L. vol. 432, cols. 72–96.
[66] See P.H. Pettitt in R. Graveson and F.R. Crane, *A Century of Family Law* (Stevens, 1957), p.62.
[67] *Parents and Children* (Sweet & Maxwell, 1982).
[68] See S. Millham, *op. cit*. note 62 (2nd series).

[69] See Children and Young Persons Act 1969, s.31. The consent of the Secretary of State is required.
[70] Child Care Act 1980, s.12(1).
[71] Child Care Act 1980, s.45. There is a printing error in the Queen's Printer's copy in s.45(1)(i): "or" should read "and."
[72] Child Care Act 1980, s.9(1) and s.45. Where the child is in care under s.3 parents have a duty to maintain (s.4(2)) but not a duty to inform the authority of any change of address.
[73] It is never out of the news for long. See *The Times*, March 10 and 11, 1982 and H.C. Vol. 17, col. 866 raising the Pritchard case. See also *Social Work Today*, Vol. 13, no. 27, March 16, 1982, p.3 and *Community Care*, July 22, 1982, p.2.
[74] [1980] Fam. 60.
[75] [1981] 2 All E.R. 385.
[76] *Ibid.* p.388.
[77] See *M.* v. *M.* [1973] 2 All E.R. 81.
[78] "Local Authorities and Parental Rights" (1974) 90 L.Q.R. 310, 314.
[79] See *S.* v. *S.* [1962] 2 All E.R. 1, 3, *per* Willmer L.J. See also J. Eekelaar (1973) 89 L.Q.R. 210, 218–219.
[80] [1975] 3 All E.R. 348.
[81] *Ibid.* p.354.
[82] [1974] 2 All E.R. 356.
[83] *Adoption and Fostering* no. 91, p.57 (1978).
[84] *e.g.* giving the authority power to deprive the child of his liberty.
[85] *e.g.* denying the authority right to cause the child to be brought up in a different religion.
[86] On the doctrine of *per incuriam* see *Morelle* v. *Wakeling* [1955] 2 Q.B. 379, 406 *per* Lord Evershed M.R.; *Farrell* v. *Alexander* [1976] Q.B. 345 and *Dixon* v. *B.B.C.* [1979] 2 All E.R. 112.
[87] There were 74 originating summonses in 1951; 258 in 1961; 622 in 1971 and 1962 in 1980.
[88] About 100 children a year are committed to care in wardship proceedings.
[89] On exceptional circumstances, see Bevan, *op. cit.* note 4 (1st series), p.155 and Lowe and White, *op cit.* pp.87–89. *Cf.* where the local authority has initiated wardship. See *Re C.B.* [1981] 1 All E.R. 16.
[90] Lowe and White wrongly call it a "care order," *op. cit.* note 55 (1st series), p.89.
[91] See Family Law Reform Act 1969, s.7(5).
[92] See *per* Ormerod L.J. in *Re W.* [1964] Ch. 202, 210.
[93] See Matrimonial Causes Act 1973, s.43(5) which applies by virtue of s.7(3) of the Family Law Reform Act 1969.
[94] *Ibid.*
[95] *F.* v. *S.* [1973] Fam. 203.
[96] *Re C.B.* [1981] 1 All E.R. 16, 24.
[97] *Per* Cross J. in *Re S.* [1967] 1 All E.R. 202, 209. See also *B.(M.)* v. *B.(R.)* [1968] 3 All E.R. 170, 174 (psychiatric examination), and *Re D.* [1976] Fam. 185 (sterilisation). See, further, Lowe and White, *op. cit.* note 55 (1st series), pp.73–77.
[98] [1975] 3 All E.R. 348. See also *L.B. of Lewisham* v. *M.* [1981] 3 All E.R. 307, 320.
[99] *Op. cit.* note 55, p.90.
[1] (1976) 6 *Fam. Law* 136, 139.
[2] See their note 3 on p.91. I am unhappy with the way they link as a single sentence their discussion of s.21(2) of the 1980 Act and s.43(5)(*a*) of the 1973 Act (see pp.90–91). The two powers are totally unrelated and putting them together only confuses the issues.

[3] See *Surrey C.C.* v. *W.* (1982) 126 S.J. 155.

[4] Returning the ward to a parent is surely a major decision but Lowe and White suggest, surely wrongly, that a local authority may do this. See *op. cit.* note 55 (1st series), pp.80–81.

[5] *Per* Ormrod L.J. in *Re Y.* [1975] 3 All E.R. 348, 352.

[6] See s.43 of the Matrimonial Causes Act 1973.

[7] *Ibid.* s.43(1).

[8] *Ibid.* s.43(5)(*b*).

[9] *Ibid.* s.43(5)(*a*).

[10] *Ibid.* s.43(3).

[11] Step-parents do not have parental rights. See *Re N.* [1974] Fam. 40.

[12] See s.43(7).

[13] See *Ellard* v. *Ellard* (1980) 1 F.L.R. 42, 73.

[14] See Domestic Proceedings and Magistrates' Courts Act 1978, s.10.

[15] *Ibid.* s.10(9).

[16] *Op. cit.* note 13 (3rd series).

[17] See the Guardianship Act 1973, s.4(4)(*a*).

[18] *Ibid.* s.4(5). A recent example is *Cooke* v. *Cooke* (1982) 12 Fam. Law 61.

[19] The original provision was limited to children under 16.

[20–21] See Children Act 1975, s.17(3).

[22] On custodianship see M.D.A. Freeman (1976) 6 Fam. Law 57.

[23] As to which see the Children Act 1975, s.86.

[24] *Op. cit.* note 1 (1st series), p.318.

[25] See *A.* v. *Liverpool City Council* [1981] 2 All E.R. 385, and the earlier cases of *M.* v. *Humberside C.C.* [1979] 2 All E.R. 744 and *Re W.* [1980] Fam. 60.

[26] See my "Is Care Without Wardship, Wardship Without Care?" (1981) 145 *Justice of The Peace* 333 and "Controlling Local Authorities In Child Care Cases—*A.* v. *Liverpool City Council* Revisited" (1982) 146 *Justice of The Peace* 188, 202. A more orthodox interpretation of the *Liverpool* case is N. Lowe "To Review Or Not To Review?" 45 M.L.R. 96 (1982).

Conditional Contracts for the Sale of Land

A.J. OAKLEY*

CONDITIONAL contracts for the sale of land have been increasingly before the courts in recent years, largely because many of the conditional clauses which have been employed in such contracts have failed to make sufficiently clear the category of conditional contract into which the parties intended their own particular contract to fall. The purpose of this paper is to consider the various different ways in which conditional contracts are capable of being construed and to highlight the factors which need to be taken into account by those responsible for the drafting of such contracts.

Certainty

The initial requirement that must be satisfied by any express term of a contract is the requirement of certainty and this is as true of the clause in a contract that makes it conditional as of its other provisions. In accordance with the maxim *certum est quod certum reddi potest*, the law regards as certain any provision which is capable of being rendered certain. Nevertheless the issue of certainty of terms in contracts for the sale of land has been before the courts repeatedly in recent years, most commonly in connection with certainty of price. Indeed the law governing this latter question has recently been reviewed by the Court of Appeal in *Sudbrook Trading Estate* v. *Eggleton*.[1] However, the issue of certainty has been raised surprisingly infrequently in relation to conditional contracts for the sale of land. Many potentially vulnerable conditional clauses have escaped challenge on the issue of certainty—for example, in *Re Longlands Farm*,[2] a contract for the purchase of land "subject to my company obtaining Planning Permission to its entire satisfaction" was not challenged on the grounds of uncertainty (perhaps because on any view the condition had not been satisfied). However, such challenges have occasionally been made. In *Lee-Parker* v. *Izzet* (*No.*2),[3] the validity of a contract which was expressed to be "subject to the purchaser obtaining a satisfactory mortgage" was successfully challenged on the grounds of uncertainty, Goulding J. holding that "the concept of a satisfactory mortgage [was] too indefinite for the court to give it a practical meaning" since "[e]verything [was] at large, not only matters like rate of interest and ancillary obligations on which evidence might establish what would be usual or reasonable, but also those two most essential points—the amount of the loan and the terms of repayment."[4] This decision was consistent with *Re Rich's Will Trusts*[5] (which Goulding J. expressly followed) but is far from easy to reconcile with the immediately preceding decision in *Lee-Parker* v. *Izzet* (*No.*1),[6] where Goff J. upheld the validity of somewhat similar contracts (made between different parties in respect of different properties) on the grounds that 'a satisfactory mortgage' meant a mortgage to the satisfaction of the purchaser acting reasonably"[7]—an attitude which was also adopted in the most recent decision, *Janmohamed* v. *Hassan*.[8] Whatever the merits of these decisions, however, it is at the very least clear that one of the easiest grounds of escaping from a conditional contract may often be a challenge on the issue of certainty. Certainly this possibility should not be overlooked by those advising parties to such contracts in the event of a dispute or a change of mind as to the desirability of the transaction.

Time

Assuming that the initial requirement of certainty has been satisfied, the next question that normally arises for consideration is within what period of time the condition has to be fulfilled. This important issue was considered by the Privy Council in *Aberfoyle Plantations* v. *Cheng*.[9] The Board stated the following general rules:[10]

> "The answer . . . must plainly depend on the true construction of the agreement, or in other words on the intention of the parties as expressed in, or to be implied from, the language they have used. But, subject to this overriding consideration their lordships would adopt, as warranted by authority and manifestly reasonable in themselves, the following general principles: (i) Where a conditional contract of sale fixes a date for the completion of the sale, then the condition must be fulfilled by that date; (ii) where a conditional contract of sale fixes no date for completion of the sale, then the condition must be fulfilled within a reasonable time; (iii) where a conditional contract of sale fixes (whether specifically or by reference to the date fixed for completion) the date by which the condition is to be fulfilled, then the date

> so fixed must be strictly adhered to, and the time allowed is not to be extended by reference to equitable principles."

Thus any time limit specified in the contract for satisfaction of the condition obviously applies. In the absence of any such express time limit, then the condition must be fulfilled by the contractual completion date (unless the fulfilment of the condition in question is merely a part of the vendor's duty to show title, in which case it appears from certain remarks made by Ungoed-Thomas J. in *Property and Bloodstock* v. *Emerton*[11] that the crucial date is "the date by which title has to be established"). In all the cases so far mentioned, compliance with the deadline is, contrary to the general rule in contracts for the sale of land,[12] of the essence of the contract. In the absence of any such express or implied time limit, the condition has to be fulfilled within a reasonable time which, as Cross J. held in *Re Longlands Farm*,[13] has to be "determined as at the date of contract . . . by an objective test applicable to both parties" (thus in that case a period of more than three and a half years, during which the vendor had waited for the purchaser to obtain planning permission, was held to be far more than reasonable).

The rules thus laid down by the Privy Council certainly apply whenever any disagreement arises between the parties to a contract for the sale of land as to the fulfilment of conditions therein. However, it was held by the Court of Appeal in *Property and Bloodstock* v. *Emerton*[14] that the operation of the rules is confined to the situation where vendor and purchaser are not in accord and so the rules were not applied in that case where the vendor and purchaser had agreed to extend the time limit more or less indefinitely and the person not in accord was the vendor's mortgagor. A similar distinction of *Aberfoyle Plantations* v. *Cheng* appears to have been made by Russell L.J. in *Hargreaves Transport* v. *Lynch*.[15] Presumably it will only rarely be possible for someone other than the vendor or purchaser to make any valid objection to the non-fulfilment of a condition. Consequently it is apparent that the rules laid down by the Privy Council in *Aberfoyle Plantations* v. *Cheng*[16] will apply in the vast majority of cases. Where so applicable, the rules seem to operate no matter which of the various possible constructions of the condition as to the rights and duties of the parties is adopted.

The rights and duties of the parties

The major difficulty associated with conditional contracts for the sale of land is to determine the rights and duties of the parties to the contract. This is basically a question of construction of the wording of the conditional clause in question so as to establish into which of the various categories of conditional contract the particular contract falls. The result of this process of construction has considerable significance; not only does it determine whether any of the parties is under any obligation to seek fulfilment of the condition, it also affects the question of whether performance of the condition can be waived, the passing of the risk of accidental destruction of the subject matter and the fiscal liabilities of the parties. It has generallly been accepted that conditional contracts may be construed in four different ways—this was stated by Goff J. in *Wood Preservation* v. *Prior*.[17] This case concerned a contract for the sale and purchase of the entire issued share capital of an English company subject to a condition that within one month a letter should be produced from a certain German company confirming the continuation of an agreement giving the English company the exclusive right to import and distribute the products of the German company. Performance of this condition was subsequently waived. The question later arose as to whether the vendors had divested themselves of the beneficial interest in the share capital on the date of the contract or on the date when performance of the condition was waived. Goff J. construed the condition in the fourth way mentioned below and consequently held that the beneficial interest in the shares had passed to the purchasers on the date of the contract. In the course of his judgment, his lordship approved a submission by counsel (H.H. Monroe Q.C.) classifying[18] conditional contracts under the following four heads (which classification he held to be "justified by the most careful and detailed analysis which was undertaken by Diplock L.J. in *United Dominions Trust (Commercial)* v. *Eagle Aircraft Services*)":[19]

> "The first is where the arrangement between the parties, which would otherwise be a contract, is subject to a condition precedent to the making of any agreement at all.
>
> The second class of case is where there is a contract under which one party assumes a unilateral obligation to purchase from another in a certain event, and there is no obligation on the other to bring that event about. In that class of case there is a contract from the start imposing a unilateral obligation, but no bilateral obligation arises and no contract of sale until the condition has been discharged. That type of case covers options and analogous agreements.
>
> His third class is where you have a bilateral contract of sale

> subject to a condition precedent with an immediate obligation on one of the parties to perform the condition or to use his best endeavours to perform it. There he says there is an immediate obligation, but the bilateral obligations of the contract of sale are nonetheless subject to a condition precedent, and there is no sale until the condition is performed.
>
> His fourth class is where you have an immediate contract of sale but on the basis or term that one of the parties, say the vendors, would obtain some particular information or assurance or something of that sort. In such a case the contract of sale is immediate—it is not subject to a condition precedent—but if the vendor fails to discharge his obligation he will not be liable in damages for the breach, and if the breach goes to the root of the contract, then the purchaser may be discharged from further performance, but the contract of sale is nonetheless immediate and not subject to any condition precedent."

These four possible constructions will hereafter be denoted by the following brief respective descriptions (admittedly imprecise and arguably technically inaccurate but adopted purely for the purpose of facilitating exposition): the agreement to agree construction, the unilateral contract construction, the condition precedent construction, and the condition subsequent construction. Each possibility must now be examined in detail.

1. *The agreement to agree construction*

This possible construction was expounded by Goff J. as follows:

> ". . . where the arrangement between the parties, which would otherwise be a contract, is subject to a condition precedent to the making of any agreement at all."

Thus the vendor and purchaser have merely expressed their intention to make a contract of sale if the condition is fulfilled; in other words, they have merely agreed to agree in that event. When such a construction is adopted, no contract of any sort exists between the parties and their freedom of action is not in any way circumscribed. Thus even if the condition is subsequently satisfied, neither party is under any legally enforceable obligation whatsoever. This sort of construction is rarely adopted save in the case of agreements which are expressed to be "subject to contract" or some analogous expression.

It is now beyond argument that the use of the expression "subject to contract" indicates that the agreement in question, whether written or oral, does not constitute a binding contract. This was stated particularly clearly by the Court of Appeal in *Eccles* v. *Bryant and Pollock*[20] and reiterated more recently by the same court in *Munton* v. *Greater London Council*[21] (the latter decision in effect putting to rest any doubts that may have lingered following *Law* v. *Jones*[22] and *Tiverton Estates* v. *Wearwell*).[23] It is also clear from the decision of the Court of Appeal in *Sherbrooke* v. *Dipple*[24] that, once the expression "subject to contract" has been used, all subsequent negotiations are also "subject to contract" so that any consensus reached therein will not be binding on either party unless both agree expressly or by necessary implication that the "subject to contract" should be expunged.

The immunity from liability thus conferred on agreements which are expressed to be "subject to contract" is also enjoyed by agreements which contain equivalent phrases. In *Lockett* v. *Norman-Wright*,[25] the phrase "subject to suitable agreements being arranged between your solicitors and mine" was held to be indistinguishable from "subject to contract." However it has been held that to describe an agreement as "provisional" does not deprive it of binding force. This was in *Branca* v. *Cabarro*[26] where the parties had reduced an agreement for the sale of certain mushroom farms to writing, which concluded: "This is a provisional agreement until a fully legalised agreement, drawn up by a solicitor and embodying all the conditions herewith stated, is signed." The Court of Appeal held that these words were not expressive of a condition or stipulation so that the writing constituted a binding contract. Rather more uncertainty surrounds the effect of contracting "subject to survey." In *Marks* v. *Board*[27] Rowlatt J. held that a formal document expressed to be "subject to surveyor's report" was of no legal effect whatsoever. This decision was subsequently followed by Megaw J. in *Astra Trust* v. *Adams*[28] and in an intervening case, *Batten* v. *White*,[29] Russell J. stated that "such a phrase is properly regarded as a badge of no contract" (this was admittedly only a dictum since the condition in that case related to the obtaining of planning permission). These authorities all clearly indicated that the use of "subject to survey" conferred the same immunity as the use of "subject to contract." However, in the most recent case, *Ee* v. *Kakar*,[30] Walton J. refused to follow these earlier authorities and held that an agreement "subject to survey of the property" constituted a binding conditional contract—as will be seen in due course,[31] it is rather uncertain whether his lordship construed the agreement in accordance with the condition precedent construction or the condition subsequent construction but he undoubtedly held that the agreement had binding force. This decision is somewhat unsatisfactory for a number of reasons. Walton J. stated that *Marks* v. *Board* had been decided on the basis that such a contract lacked consideration in that, while the vendor was bound to keep his offer open pending the survey, there was no corresponding detriment to the purchaser. His lordship held that this argument was not sound since such a purchaser was clearly bound to obtain and consequently pay for the necessary survey, something which was undoubtedly detrimental to him; therefore there was no good reason why the words "subject to survey" should negate the existence of a binding contract. This argument is of course sound if such a phrase is construed as imposing such an obligation on the purchaser, as is the case under both the condition precedent construction and the condition subsequent construction. But if such a phrase is construed in accordance with either the agreement to agree construction or the unilateral contract construction, no such obligation arises and it is scarcely satisfactory to use as a justification for departing from the "agreement to agree" construction something which is a consequence of adopting an alternative construction. It is also less than desirable that parties who had entered into a contract at a time when the authorities unanimously indicated that "subject to survey" was equivalent to "subject to contract" should subsequently discover that they had unwittingly entered into a binding conditional contract. No doubt the conflict of authority produced by the decision in *Ee* v. *Kakar* will ultimately have to be resolved by the Court of Appeal. There is in fact much to be said for construing agreements "subject to survey" as binding conditional contracts rather than as agreements to agree. Such agreements seem more analogous to agreements conditional on the obtaining of planning permission or mortgage finance (which have never been construed as agreements to agree) than to agreements "subject to contract." However any clear decision, either way, would be preferable to the present confusion which renders impracticable and dangerous any attempt to enter into an agreement "subject to survey."

Whatever the final outcome of this issue, however, the basic rule that agreements "subject to contract" have no binding force appears to be subject to one exception: according to *Michael Richards Properties* v. *Corporation of Wardens of St. Saviour's Southwark*,[32] the phrase can be disregarded if it is "meaningless." In that case, the defendants advertised property for sale by tender. The tender documents contained full particulars of the property and the terms of the contract and provided that whoever submitted the tender which was accepted would be the purchaser and would be notified by registered post. The plaintiffs duly submitted a tender on a form which incorporated the tender documents; the defendants accepted this tender and despatched the appropriate letter to the plaintiffs. Due to a clerical error, the words "subject to contract" were typed at the end of this letter immediately under the signature. Both parties subsequently proceeded on the basis that there was a binding contract. The plaintiffs now sought to withdraw from the contract and recover their deposit on the basis that the defendants' acceptance had been "subject to contract." Goff J. held that, since the tender documents set out all the terms of the contract, nothing remained to be negotiated and so there was no need or scope for a further formal contract. Accordingly he held[33] that the words "subject to contract" were, in the context of a written acceptance of a written tender, meaningless and so could be ignored. This decision engendered some criticism[34] and in the subsequent case of *Munton* v. *Greater London Council*[35] (where, as has already been seen, the immunity conferred by the phrase "subject to contract" was upheld by the Court of Appeal) the same judge (by then Goff L.J.) accepted that the facts of *Michael Richards Properties* v. *Corporation of Wardens of St. Saviour's Southwark* had been "very strong and exceptional," if not virtually unique, and had not been intended to cast any doubt on what his lordship described as "the well established and well settled sanctity of the words 'subject to contract.' "[36] It is therefore highly likely that nothing more will be heard of this apparent exception to the immunity from liability conferred on agreements which are expressed to be "subject to contract."

While the agreement to agree construction will thus clearly be adopted in respect of agreements which are expressed to be "subject to contract" or contain some equivalent phrase, it is obviously highly unlikely that this construction will be adopted in other cases. It is clearly improbable that a court will decide, in the absence of some phrase such as "subject to contract," that parties who have formally entered into an agreement subject to a condition did not in fact intend to be bound. For this reason in such circumstances it will only be in extremely rare cases that the agreement to agree construction is likely to be adopted.

2. *The unilateral contract construction*

This possible construction was expounded by Goff J. as follows:

> ". . . where there is a contract under which one party assumes a unilateral obligation to purchase from another in a certain event, and there is no obligation on the other to bring

> that event about. In that class of case there is a contract from the start imposing a unilateral obligation, but no bilateral obligation arises and no contract of sale until the condition has been discharged. That type of case covers options and analogous agreements."

Thus the vendor and purchaser have agreed to become bound respectively to sell and to purchase upon the occurrence of a specified event with the appropriate time limit but neither is under any obligation to try to bring about the occurrence of that event. The only obligation of the parties is therefore to keep their offers open for that time and, if the event occurs within that time, to sell and purchase the subject matter under the concluded contract of sale that then arises. Obviously the vast majority of cases falling within this category of contracts are grants of options and rights of pre-emption. Each of these types of contracts is governed by a number of special rules which will be discussed later. However occasionally the unilateral contract construction has been adopted in the case of contracts which are not, in any normal sense, either options or rights of pre-emption. Such a case was the decision of the Court of Appeal in *Daulia* v. *Four Millbank Nominees*.[37]

The plaintiffs and the defendants had agreed "subject to contract" to buy and sell, under the terms of draft contracts as amended orally, certain properties of which the defendants were mortgagees. The plaintiffs alleged that an agent of the defendants had orally undertaken that the defendants would enter into a contract of sale if the plaintiffs, before a specified time, brought to the defendants' offices a banker's draft for the agreed deposit and a duly executed contract in the terms already agreed. The plaintiffs duly complied with these conditions but the defendants refused to exchange contracts (apparently because their mortgagor had in the interim found a purchaser who was prepared to pay a higher price). The plaintiffs now sought damages for breach of contract and the defendants sought by way of motion to have the action struck out as disclosing no cause of action. Thus the matter had to be decided on the assumption that all the facts pleaded by the plaintiffs were capable of being proved. The Court of Appeal held that the facts pleaded disclosed a concluded unilateral contract, under which the defendants had contracted to sell the properties to the plaintiffs if the latter satisfied certain pre-conditions. Since the plaintiffs had fully performed the conditions before the defendants had purported to revoke their offer, the defendants, by refusing to exchange contracts, had clearly breached a valid unilateral contract. (The decision that the plaintiffs had fully performed the conditions meant that the court did not actually have to decide the controversial question as to whether the offeror becomes bound as soon as the offeree starts to perform the condition or only when it has been fully performed—it has of course always been clear that the offeror is free to revoke his offer at least until the offeree commences performance. However, the Court of Appeal expressed the view that, while "the offeror is entitled to require full performance of the condition which he has imposed and short of that he is not bound, that must be subject to one important qualification, which stems from the fact that there must be an implied obligation on the part of the offeror not to prevent the condition becoming satisfied, which obligation . . . must arise as soon as the offeree starts to perform. Until then the offeror can revoke the whole thing, but once the offeree has embarked on performance, it is too late for the offeror to revoke his offer."[38] This is the first occasion on which this proposition has been enunciated by an English court and this straightforward dictum of the Court of Appeal must presumably supersede the rather more ambiguous dicta in *Offord* v. *Davies*[39] and *Errington* v. *Errington and Woods*).[40] The court then went on to hold that, nevertheless, the unilateral contract was unenforceable by reason of Section 40 of the Law of Property Act 1925 (the performance of the conditions not constituting a valid act of part performance) and so affirmed the decision of Brightman J. to strike out the action.[41]

Thus where such a contract is construed in accordance with the unilateral contract construction, the offeror will be bound, if the offeree satisfies the condition within the appropriate time, to enter into a contract to buy or sell the land in question. Until the offeree commences performance of the condition, the offeror is clearly free to revoke his offer at any time on the grounds that at that stage no consideration will have moved from the offeree.[42] However, once the offeree has commenced performance of the condition, the offeror will be under an implied obligation not to revoke his offer until the appropriate time has passed—any such revocation will amount to a breach of contract actionable when and if the offeree fully performs the condition. Not until the condition has been fully performed will there be a binding contract for the sale of land so that, subject to the availability of specific performance, at that stage the purchaser will acquire an equitable interest in the property and assume the risk of accidental destruction of the subject matter. Further, if the unilateral contract is itself specifically enforceable (which would apparently have been the case in *Daulia* v. *Four Millbank Nominees* had the contract not been caught by Section 40),[43] the unilateral contract will itself give rise to an equitable interest in the property but not of course until the condition has been fully performed. In such circumstances, the question may arise as to whether the unilateral contract is capable of protection as an estate contract. At present, it seems that neither the registration of a Class CIV Land Charge under Section 2(4) of the Land Charges Act 1972 nor the registration of a notice under Section 49(1)(*c*) of the Land Registration Act 1925 is possible since each is restricted to contracts "to create or convey a legal estate" and it was held in *Thomas* v. *Rose*[44] that this does not include a contract to enter into such a contract. It is however arguable that the purchaser will be sufficiently "interested . . . in . . . land" to register a caution under Section 54 of the Land Registration Act 1925, in which case yet another anomalous difference between registered and unregistered conveyancing has emerged. However, since the situation under discussion can only arise where such a unilateral contract is capable of immediate specific performance (because all the conditions must have been fully performed), the purchaser will in any event be able to solve this difficulty by issuing a writ for specific performance and registering that as a *lis pendens*—this should protect his interest both in registered and unregistered conveyancing.[45]

The facts of *Daulia* v. *Four Millbank Nominees* pointed fairly clearly towards the adoption of the unilateral contract construction. However on at least one occasion this construction has been adopted in a much less clear cut case. This was in *Tesco Stores* v. *William Gibson & Son*,[46] where the parties agreed to buy and sell land "on the footing that the purchasers obtain planning permission . . . and . . . subject to such consent being obtained." Contracts of this type are normally construed according to either the condition precedent construction or the condition subsequent construction but on this occasion Buckley J. rather unexpectedly construed the contract according to the unilateral contract construction and consequently held that the purchasers, who had decided that the premises were not capable of economic use and so had not bothered to apply for planning permission, were perfectly entitled to decline to fulfil the condition and, once the time limit for fulfilment of the condition had expired, were entitled to recover their deposit. The very fact that a deposit had been paid at all indicates a high probability that the parties imagined that they were entering into a binding contract for the sale of land. Consequently they are unlikely to have anticipated the adoption of the unilateral contract construction in such circumstances. Nevertheless, given that this construction was adopted, there can be no doubt whatsoever that the purchasers were rightly permitted to recover their deposit. However, it is not particularly likely that many contracts of this type will be construed in this way.

Thus far attention has been concentrated upon the more unusual types of unilateral contracts. Consideration must now be given to what are by far the most common categories of unilateral contracts, grants of options and rights of pre-emption.[47]

An option contract confers upon the grantee the right, usually exercisable only for a period of fixed duration, to call for a conveyance of the subject matter of the grant for a consideration that is either predetermined or capable of being determined with certainty at the appropriate time.[48] Thus an option constitutes a unilateral contract conditional upon exercise by the grantee in the manner and within the time stipulated. Option contracts are subject to the following special rules.

The procedure laid down in the contract for the exercise of the option must be complied with in every detail. Thus in *Holwell Securities* v. *Hughes*,[49] where the contract provided that the option should "be exercisable by notice in writing to the intending vendor at any time within six months from the date hereof," the Court of Appeal held that the option had not been validly exercised by the posting of a letter which was never delivered, the normal posting rule having been ousted by the words "notice in writing to the intending vendor" and also by Section 196 of the Law of Property Act 1925 (which provides that a notice shall be sufficiently served if sent by registered letter or by recorded delivery). Similarly in *Wheatley* v. *Burrell Enterprises*,[50] where the contract provided for three months' notice and provided for the payment of rent until the expiry of that period, it was held that notice one month before the end of the term was too late.

Option contracts will only be valid if they satisfy the rule against perpetuities. Options created by instruments taking effect after 16th July 1964 are governed by the provisions of the Perpetuities and Accumulations Act 1964 (options created by instruments taking effect before that date will be void if there is any possibility, however remote, of its exercise outside the perpetuity period—the duration of a life or lives in being plus twenty-one years).[51] The effect of the Act is to distinguish options in leases from all other options. Section 9 of the Act provides that:

> "(1) The rule against perpetuities shall not apply to a disposition consisting of the conferring of an option to acquire for valuable consideration an interest reversionary (whether directly or indirectly) on the term of a lease if—

(a) the option is exercisable only by the lessee or his successors in title, and
(b) it ceases to be exercisable at or before the expiration of one year following the determination of the lease.

(2) In the case of a disposition consisting of the conferring of an option to acquire for valuable consideration any interest in land, the perpetuity period under the rule against perpetuities shall be twenty-one years and section 1 of this Act shall not apply . . ."

Thus options to purchase leasehold or freehold reversions, whether or not contained in the lease itself, are exempt from the rule against perpetuities and thus may be exercised at any time in the future, provided that the option is exercisable only by the lessee or his successors in title no later than one year after the end of the lease. All other options are exercisable only within a period of twenty-one years from their creation; options which on their face are capable of exercise outside this period remain valid for twenty-one years under the "wait and see" principle contained in Section 3 of the Act but if not exercised by that time become void for perpetuity and thereafter cannot be exercised either against the successors in title of the grantor or against the grantor himself—this latter proposition, which constitutes an amendment of the pre-existing law,[52] is contained in Section 10 of the Perpetuities and Accumulations Act 1964.

An option contract creates not simply contractual rights in that, unless exercisable only against the grantor and his estate, it vests in the grantee an immediate equitable interest in the land,[53] even before exercise of the option.[54] It is for this reason that such option contracts need to be protected in the manner described in the next paragraph. However, between the creation and exercise of the option, the grantor does not become a constructive trustee for the grantee so that the latter is not owner of the property in equity, nor assumes the risk of accidental destruction of the subject matter, nor can impeach the vendor for any failure to maintain the property in a reasonable state of preservation.[55] These consequences only arise upon exercise of the option and the formation of a specifically enforceable contract for the sale of land.[56]

Nevertheless option contracts, unless exercisable only against the grantor and his estate, clearly require immediate protection against successors in title of the grantor[57] (save in the case of options for the renewal of leases, which clearly touch and concern the land and so bind all successors in title of the grantor).[58] In unregistered conveyancing, options entitling the grantee to call for the conveyance of a legal estate must be registered as Class CIV Land Charges under Section 2(4) of the Land Charges Act 1972. Failure to register will render the option void against any subsequent purchaser of a legal estate for money or money's worth[59] even if he has taken the land expressly subject to the option[60] or has actual notice thereof.[61] However, the option will nevertheless remain enforceable against all other transferees.[62] In registered conveyancing, options entitling the grantee to call for the conveyance of a legal estate must be protected by the registration of a notice or restriction or caution under, respectively, Sections 49(1)(*c*), 58(1) and 54(1) of the Land Registration Act 1925. Failure to register will render the option void against any subsequent purchaser for value who takes under a registered disposition,[63] even if he has taken the land expressly subject to the option or has actual notice thereof,[64] unless the grantee is in actual occupation of the land or is in receipt of the rents and profits (in which case the option will be protected automatically as an overriding interest under Section 70(1)(*g*) of the Act).[65] As in the case of unregistered conveyancing, an unprotected option will nevertheless remain enforceable against all other transferees. Where an option does require protection, any extension of time requires a fresh registration, as does the contract of sale entered into on exercise of the option (which supersedes the option contract).[66]

In comparison with option contracts, grants of rights of pre-emption (which are also known as rights of first refusal) merely confer on the grantee the right, usually exercisable only for a period of fixed duration, to call for a conveyance of the subject matter if the grantor decides to sell within that period. As with an option, the consideration for the conveyance must be either predetermined or capable of being determined with certainty at the appropriate time.[67] The crucial difference is that, whereas the grantee of an option has an unassailable right to call for a conveyance at any time during the period, the grantee of a right of pre-emption has no right to do anything unless and until the grantor decides to sell; consequently if the period ends without him having taken any such decision, the right of pre-emption disappears. Thus while a right of pre-emption, like an option, is a unilateral contract, it is conditional first and foremost on the grantor deciding to sell and only secondarily conditional upon exercise by the grantee in the manner and within the time stipulated. It is of course a matter of construction whether an option or a right of pre-emption has been created; uncertainties have been caused by provisions in contracts for the sale of land by public or local authorities for repurchase in certain events (such as failure to develop the subject matter within a certain time or cesser of user for religious purposes). Parliament has described the latter right as a right of pre-emption but it is nevertheless submitted that, since the original vendor (the grantee[68] of the right) has an absolute right to repurchase if and when a particular event occurs, such rights should more properly be classified as options. This is an important point because of the differences between the special rules that govern options and rights of pre-emption.

The principal controversy surrounding rights of pre-emption concerns the question of whether such rights give rise to the creation of an interest in land. This question has traditionally been answered in the negative—principally because of the decision of the Court of Appeal in *Manchester Ship Canal Co.* v *Manchester Racecourse Co.*[69] which, as Goff L.J. stated in *Pritchard* v. *Briggs*[70] "though not absolutely binding authority, does strongly support the view that in general a right of pre-emption does not create an interest in land." Certainly that decision was relied on by Goulding J. in *Murray* v. *Two Strokes*[71] when holding that a right of pre-emption could not be protected by a caution under Section 54 of the Land Registration Act 1925 and also by Oliver J. in the unreported decision *Imperial Chemical Industries* v. *Sussman*.[72] On the other hand, a number of sections in the 1925 Property Legislation were clearly drafted on the assumption that a right of pre-emption does create an interest in land (this is particularly true of what is now Section 2 (4) of the Land Charges Act 1972[73] which includes a "right of pre-emption" among the categories of "charges on, or obligations affecting land" which may be protected by registration as Class CIV Land Charges). Consequently, it has been said[74] "to be a little difficult, in view of this wording,[75] to imagine that a right of pre-emption is not now, whatever may have been the position before 1925, an equitable interest." This was the background of authority which confronted the Court of Appeal in *Pritchard* v. *Briggs*.[76]

In 1944, Major and Mrs. Lockwood sold part of their land to the predecessor in title of the defendants and also granted him a right of pre-emption of the retained land for £3,000 during the joint lives of himself and the survivor of the Lockwoods. This right was duly registered as a Class CIV Land Charge. Subsequently, in 1963 the Lockwoods leased the retained land to the plaintiff and granted him an option to acquire the freehold, also for £3,000, exercisable only after the death of the survivor of the Lockwoods. This right was also duly registered as a Class CIV Land Charge.[77] After the death of Mrs. Lockwood, Major Lockwood became incapable of managing his affairs and his receiver sold and conveyed the retained land to the defendants, who were assignees of the benefit of the right of pre-emption, pursuant to that right but at the market value rather than for £3,000. After the death of Major Lockwood, the plaintiff sought to exercise his option against the defendants. The outcome of this claim depended on the nature of the right of pre-emption. If it had created an interest in land, then its protection by registration prior to the creation of the option clearly meant that the plaintiff had taken his option subject to the defendants' right of pre-emption so that his claim would fail (this was what Walton J. held at first instance).[78] If, on the other hand, the right of pre-emption had not created an interest in land, its protection by registration was obviously of no effect and the plaintiff would be able to enforce his duly protected option against the defendants who would have taken the land subject thereto (this was what was held by the Court of Appeal).

All three members of the Court of Appeal agreed that no interest in land is created by the grant of a right of pre-emption.[79] Goff L.J., after an elaborate review of the authorities, conceded that the drafters of the 1925 Property Legislation may well have been under a misapprehension as to the pre-existing law but "the beliefs or assumptions of those who frame Acts of Parliament cannot make the law."[80] On the other hand, their lordships accepted that, as soon as an offer to sell made by the grantor in accordance with the right of pre-emption is accepted by the grantee, an interest in land arises under the contract of sale thus formed.[81] Templeman and Stephenson L.JJ. also stated that, in the event of a sale by the grantor to a third party in breach of the right of pre-emption, that right then becomes an interest in land which, if already registered, will bind and be enforceable against the third party.[82] Goff L.J. however disagreed, stating that even in such circumstances no interest in land arises.[83] (Thus, according to Templeman and Stephenson L.JJ., had the Lockwoods sold the land to the plaintiff in 1963 instead of granting him an option to purchase it after their deaths, the defendants could have enforced their already registered right of pre-emption against him—on this view, of course, there is considerable point in considering to register rights of pre-emption). This latter point, which was obviously not directly in issue in *Pritchard* v. *Briggs*, is not without difficulties.[84] On the view taken by Goff L.J., a right of pre-emption becomes of relatively little worth. Admittedly if the grantee of the right discovers a proposed sale to a third party before that sale has been completed, he will be able to enjoin completion of the contract[85] and compel an offer to himself in accordance with the contract.[86] If, on the other hand, he discovers the sale only after it has been completed (which is obviously much more likely) he will have to be content with his actions for damages (against the grantor for breach of contract and, in appropriate circumstances, against the third party for inducing breach[87] of contract[88] and against both grantor and third party for conspiracy)[89] unless the court disapproves so strongly of the conduct of the third party that he is ordered to reconvey the land to the grantee.[90] On the other hand, the view adopted by Templeman and Stephenson L.JJ. raises a considerable number of unresolved issues. At what point does the right of pre-emption become an interest in land? This can hardly occur until the grantor has actually bound himself to sell in breach (it would be impossible to pinpoint the precise moment at which he first decided to sell) so the two possibilities must be at contract and at completion. In either case problems arise over priority—will not the estate contract or legal title acquired by the third party necessarily be prior in time to and consequently prevail over the interest in land belatedly created by the right of pre-emption? Further, what is the effect of a disposition of the land by the grantor other than for value? Presumably this must constitute a breach[91] (otherwise a donee would be in a better position than a purchaser for value) but if so why does this not also apply to a voluntary disposition on death under the will or intestacy of the grantor? None of these problems arose in *Pritchard* v. *Briggs* because of the fact that there the right of pre-emption determined before the option became exercisable. But these issues will have to be considered in any future case and it is only when this has occurred that it will become clear whether the view of Goff L.J. or the view of Templeman and Stephenson L.JJ. is preferable.

If the view expressed by Goff L.J. is correct and a right of pre-emption can thus never create an interest in land, obviously there will be no point in protecting such an interest by registration and any such registration will be totally ineffective. On the other hand, if the view expressed by Templeman and Stephenson L.JJ. is correct so that a right of pre-emption will become an interest in land in the event of a breach by the grantor, there obviously becomes considerable point in protecting such rights in the same manner as that in which options can be protected—by the registration of a Class CIV Land Charge in unregistered conveyancing and by the registration of a notice, restriction, or caution in registered conveyancing. (Presumably the judicial disagreement in *Pritchard* v. *Briggs* together with the advice in Ruoff and Roper[92] still to register will constitute sufficient "reasonable cause" to resist any attempt to impose liability under Section 56 (3) of the Land Registration Act 1925 for lodging a caution without reasonable cause). If it has been thought appropriate to protect the right of pre-emption by registration, then any extension of the right will, as in the case of options, require fresh protection. Further, whether or not the right of pre-emption has been protected, the contract of sale created by the acceptance by the grantee of any offer to sell by the grantor should certainly be protected by the appropriate registration. It should also be mentioned that certain statutory rights of pre-emption expressly bind successors in title quite independent of the general law[93]; such statutory rights clearly create interests in land from their commencement and are therefore certainly registrable in the appropriate manner.

When and if the grantor of a right of pre-emption decides to sell, he must comply in every detail with the procedure laid down in the contract for communication of this fact to the grantee (otherwise he will be unable to sell elsewhere without incurring liability in damages). In the absence of any express contractual provision to the contrary, his offer once made can be withdrawn at any time prior to acceptance provided that the reason is a genuine change of mind as to the intention to sell. On the other hand, any attempt to sell to a third party in breach of the right of pre-emption can be restrained[94] and it appears that in such circumstances the grantee can compel the grantor to make an offer in accordance with the right of pre-emption provided that there is clear evidence that the grantor desires to sell—this would presumably be provided by any advertisement of the property, any negotiations with a third party or any attempt to sell to the grantee other than in accordance with the contract. This all follows from *Banstead U.D.C.* v. *Wilkinson*,[95] where the grantor made an offer to the grantee to sell other than in accordance with the contract. The court held the grantee to be entitled to disregard this offer and compel the grantor to make an offer in accordance with the contract on the basis that this attempt to obtain better terms amounted to clear evidence that the grantor wished to sell. On the other hand, where the grantee discovers nothing until after the land has been sold and conveyed to a third party, his remedies will, as has already been mentioned, depend on whether or not his right at that point becomes an interest in land. If it does, then the grantee will be able to enforce his right against the third party unless the latter has taken free of his interest (which will presumably be the case if he has purchased a legal estate for value and the right has not been protected in the appropriate way—unless the land in question is registered and the grantee is in actual occupation).[96] If, on the other hand, the right of pre-emption does not at that point become an interest in land, then the grantee will be confined to his remedies in damages (against the grantor for breach of contract[97] and, in appropriate circumstances, against the third party for inducing breach of contract[98] and against both grantor and third party for conspiracy)[99] unless the court disapproves so strongly of the conduct of the third party that he is ordered to reconvey the land to the grantee.[1] Finally, it should be remembered that, if the grantee receives an offer to sell made in accordance with the terms of the contract and wishes to accept that offer, he must comply in every detail with the procedure laid down in the contract for the communication of his acceptance to the grantor. (Otherwise he will be taken to have rejected the offer and will have no remedies against anyone). Further, as has already been mentioned, the contract of sale created by such a valid conveyance must be protected by the appropriate means.

Finally, rights of pre-emption must clearly comply with the rule against perpetuities. It has already been seen[2] that options created by instruments taking effect after 16th July 1964 are governed by Section 9 of the Perpetuities and Accumulations Act 1964. It is unclear whether this provision also governs rights of pre-emption. Some support for this view can be drawn from the fact that Section 9(2) excludes from its operation certain statutory rights of pre-emption, thus implying that other rights of pre-emption may be within its ambit. If Section 9 does indeed also apply to rights of pre-emption, then such rights will be governed by exactly the same rules as have already been considered in relation to options.[2] On the other hand, it may be held that Section 9(2) is yet another instance of the type of misapprehension of the law referred to by Goff L.J. in *Pritchard* v. *Briggs*. If this is so and Section 9 does not therefore apply to rights of pre-emption, such rights will be governed by Section 10 which provides:

> "Where a disposition inter vivos would fall to be treated as void for remoteness if the rights and duties thereunder were capable of transmission to persons other than the original parties and had been so transmitted, it shall be treated as void as between the person by whom it was made and the person to whom or in whose favour it was made or any successor of his, and no remedy shall lie in contract or otherwise for giving effect to it or making restitution for its lack of effect."

If this Section applies to rights of pre-emption, such rights will be valid if exercised during a life or lives in being plus twenty-one years or, if the parties have expressly opted for the alternative eighty-year period provided by Section 1 of the Act, during that period. Rights which on their face are capable of exercise outside the appropriate period remain valid for that period under the wait and see principle contained in Section 3 of the Act but if not exercised by the end of the period become void for perpetuity. There seems no reason why options and rights of pre-emption should be subject to such very different requirements as to perpetuity. But unless Section 9 of the Act can be construed so as to include rights of pre-emption (which must be highly doubtful given the attitude of the Court of Appeal in *Pritchard* v. *Briggs*), there seems no other possible interpretation of the legislation.

This second possible construction of conditional contracts is, in numerical terms, principally adopted in relation to options and rights of pre-emption, although the small minority of cases outside these categories in which the construction is adopted must not be forgotten. By and large, the law is both sound and certain save for the rules governing rights of pre-emption, whose uncertainties cannot be resolved until it is finally decided whether and if so to what extent such rights create interests in land. Further clarification of this point is urgently needed.

3. *The condition precedent construction*

This possible construction was expounded by Goff J. as follows:

> ". . . where you have a bilateral contract of sale subject to a condition precedent with an immediate binding obligation on one of the parties to perform the condition or to use his best endeavours to perform it. There . . . there is an immediate obligation, but the bilateral obligations of the contract of sale are nonetheless subject to a condition precedent and there is no sale until the condition is performed."

Thus the vendor and purchaser have agreed that, in consideration of one of them seeking to bring about fulfilment of the condition within the appropriate time limit, the other will keep his offer open for that time; if the condition is fulfilled within the time limit, the parties will respectively sell and purchase the subject matter of the contract. (The wording of the condition will obviously determine which of the parties is obliged to seek fulfilment of the condition—a condition relating to the obtaining of the landlord's consent to an assignment will necessarily have to be fulfilled by the vendor, just as a condition relating to the obtaining of a mortgage or survey will necessarily have to be fulfilled by the purchaser, while a condition relating to the obtaining of planning permission could impose the duty to seek this permission on either party). Thus far, the condition precedent construction differs not at all from the condition subsequent construction. However, where the condition precedent construction is adopted, while there is an immediate binding contract between the parties which is capable of giving rise to an action for damages if no attempt is made to seek fulfilment of the condition within the time limit or if an offer is withdrawn before the time limit, there is no immediate contract for the sale of land. Such a contract does not arise unless and until the condition is fulfilled. Consequently no relationship of vendor and purchaser arises until that moment so that until then the vendor will not have disposed of any interest in land and does not become a constructive trustee of the subject matter for the purchaser; consequently the latter does not become owner of the property in equity nor assumes the risk of accidental destruction of the subject matter nor can impeach the vendor for any failure to maintain the property in a reasonable state of preservation. These consequences only ensue when and if the condition is fulfilled. It also seems that, as in the case of a contract construed in accordance with the unilateral contract construction,[3] the contract will not be capable of being protected either by the registration of a Class CIV Land Charge in respect of unregistered land or by the registration of a notice or restriction in respect of registered land (although it may be possible to register a caution in the latter case) unless and until the condition has been fulfilled. Further, any action for damages arising out of a breach of the contract before fulfilment of the condition will not be caught by the rule in *Bain* v. *Fothergill*[4]—consequently the purchaser will where appropriate always be able to obtain substantial damages for loss of bargain and will not be restricted by the rule to the recovery of his deposit, interest thereon and costs. (Such an action would arise if the vendor made no attempt to comply with an obligation imposed on him to seek fulfilment of the condition or withdrew his offer while the purchaser was in the process of complying with an obligation to seek fulfilment of the condition. Admittedly, even if the rule in *Bain* v. *Fothergill* did apply in principle to contracts construed in this way, it would not in fact operate in either of these situations due to the fact that the breach in question was due to the vendor's own fault. It is therefore probable that the inapplicability of the rule to conditional contracts of this type makes no difference in practice).

These rules may be illustrated by *Michael Richards Properties* v. *Corporation of Wardens of St. Saviour's Southwark.*[5] In this case the contract formed on acceptance by the vendors of the purchasers' tender was expressed to be "subject to the approval of the Charity Commissioners." Any absolute and unqualified contract entered into without the prior approval of the Charity Commissioners would have been void under the provisions of the Charities Act 1960. However, Goff J. construed this condition in accordance with the condition precedent construction[6]; consequently, the contract became an effective contract for the sale of land only when this consent had been obtained and so did not offend the Charities Act.

The condition precedent construction has, for no obvious reason, rarely been adopted in the reported decisions. It was, however, adopted in *Aberfoyle Plantations* v. *Cheng*,[7] where the Privy Council construed in this way a contract which was expressed to be subject to the vendor obtaining the renewal of seven leases[8] (this case, as has already been seen,[9] was primarily concerned with the question of how long the vendor had to fulfil the condition). This construction was also adopted, much more controversially, in *Myton* v. *Schwab-Morris.*[10] A contract for the grant of a sub-lease provided, in Clause 2, that "The Lessee shall on or before the signing hereof pay ten per centum of the premium of £70,000 due on the said Underlease as a deposit to the Lessor." The lessee duly gave the lessor a cheque for £7,000 but this bounced on both the occasions on which it was presented for payment. The lessor therefore purported to terminate the contract for this failure to comply with Clause 2; however, the lessee refused to accept this and registered a caution to protect her estate contract. The lessor now sought vacation of the register, contending that the obligation to pay the deposit was a condition precedent of the contract and that, in default of payment, there was no contract for the sale of land in respect of which the lessee could register a caution. This argument was upheld by Goulding J., who stated that, in a contract for the sale of land, "a deposit is demanded and paid on the signing of the contract as an earnest of the purchaser's ability and intention to complete the purchase in due course. The vendor, in the normal case never intends to be bound by the contract without having the deposit in his own or his stakeholder's possession as a protection against possible loss from default by the purchaser."[11] Consequently, despite the fact that the term for the payment of the deposit was not in any sense couched in conditional terms, he held that that term nevertheless constituted a condition precedent of the existence of the contract. His lordship then went on to accept an alternative submission by the lessor that the failure to pay the deposit was a breach sufficiently substantial to entitle him to terminate the contract.[12] This ground of the decision, although somewhat inconsistent with the condition precedent argument, is, it is submitted, much more satisfactory than the decision to accept the condition precedent argument which, superficially, seems somewhat surprising. It is inconsistent with the earlier (admittedly uncited) decision in *Beck* v. *Box*[13] where the judge refused to vacate a land charge because on the evidence he was not satisfied that the payment of a deposit was a condition precedent of the contract. Further, it seems inappropriate to construe as a condition precedent a clause of a contract which is in no sense framed in conditional terms. Indeed, if this construction of clauses relating to the payment of deposits is generally adopted (such clauses are invariably found in contracts for the sale of land since no deposit is payable under open contract),[14] it may well be possible for purchasers who have failed to pay a deposit to escape from liability by contending that, in such circumstances, no contract for the sale of land has come into existence at all (this will admittedly not be possible in the case of contracts subject to the current (1980) edition of The Law Society's General Conditions of Sale, Condition 9 of which seems to prevent either party from raising the condition precedent argument). It is therefore submitted that, unless a clause relating to the payment of a deposit is expressly framed in conditional terms—in which case it is obviously wholly appropriate to construe it in accordance with the conditon precedent construction, such clauses should not be construed in a way so diametrically opposed to the obvious intentions of the parties. However, it remains to be seen how the principle enunciated in *Myton* v. *Schwab-Morris* will be treated in subsequent decisions.

Thus, while the effects of the adoption of the condition precedent construction (albeit rarely seen in the reported decisions) are both clear and certain, it is submitted that the decision to adopt this construction in *Myton* v. *Schwab-Morris* cannot be supported.

4. *The condition subsequent construction*

This possible construction was expounded by Goff J. as follows:

> " . . . where you have an immediate contract of sale but on the basis or term that one of the parties, say the vendors, would obtain some particular information or assurance or something of that sort. In such a case, the contract of sale is

> immediate—it is not subject to a condition precedent—but if the vendor fails to discharge his obligation, he will not be liable in damages for the breach, and if the breach goes to the root of the contract, then the purchaser may be discharged from further performance, but the contract of sale is nonetheless immediate and not subject to any condition precedent."

Thus the vendor and purchaser have agreed that, in consideration of one of them seeking to bring about fulfilment of the condition within the appropriate time limit, the other will keep his offer open for that time; if the condition is fulfilled within the time limit, the parties will respectively sell and purchase the subject matter of the contract. (Thus far this construction differs not at all from the condition precedent construction and, as in contracts construed in that way, the wording of the condition will obviously determine which of the parties is obliged to seek fulfilment of the condition). However, in the case of a contract construed in accordance with the condition subsequent construction, the fulfilment of the condition is merely one of the terms of an immediately effective contract for the sale of land. An action for damages will be available (as under the condition precedent construction) if no attempt is made to seek fulfilment of the condition within the time limit or if an offer is withdrawn before the time limit, but any such action is capable of being caught by the rule in *Bain* v. *Fothergill*.[15] Consequently where the vendor is able to prove that his failure to secure fulfilment of the condition occurred other than by his own fault, the purchaser will not be able to obtain substantial damages for loss of bargain but will be limited to the recovery of his deposit, interest thereon and costs. (Most of the relevant authorities concern contracts where it has been necessary to obtain the consent of a landlord; in such circumstances the vendor will be able to rely on the rule in *Bain* v. *Fothergill* provided that he has made all reasonable attempts to obtain such consent[16] but not where he has failed to seek the consent or has actively dissuaded the landlord from giving it).[17] However, the relationship of vendor and purchaser arises immediately. Consequently the vendor has disposed of an interest in land—this emerges from *Property and Bloodstock* v. *Emerton*,[18] where a mortgagee contracted to sell leasehold property subject to the consent of the landlord and the condition was construed in accordance with the condition subsequent construction so that there was an immediately effective contract for the sale of land which deprived the mortgagor of his right to redeem. Further, subject to the availability of specific performance, the vendor will become a constructive trustee of the subject matter for the purchaser who will therefore become owner of the property in equity,[19] assume the risk of accidental destruction of the subject matter and become entitled to impeach the vendor for any failure to maintain the property in a reasonable state of preservation. Further, the contract will immediately become capable of being protected by registration (of a Class CIV Land Charge in respect of unregistered land and of a notice, restriction or caution in respect of registered land).

This type of construction has been adopted in the vast majority of reported decisions (other of course than those concerned with options or rights of pre-emption). The rules governing contracts construed in this way have thus received far greater judicial scrutiny than those governing contracts construed in any of the other three possible ways, in consequence the rules are for the most part entirely clear and certain.

Fulfilment of conditions

Whichever construction is adopted as to the rights and duties of the parties, it is possible for difficulties to arise in determining whether or not the condition has been fulfilled. In principle, such difficulties should be able to be resolved by the simple expedient of construing the contract but all too often situations arise for which the parties have not provided.

In *Richard West and Partners (Inverness)* v. *Dick*,[20] the contract was expressed to be "conditional upon planning permission being granted by the local authority." Was this condition satisfied by a grant of planning permission conditional upon the approval of any alterations by the building inspector and upon access improvements? The Court of Appeal, while conceding that in some circumstances a grant of conditional planning permission might amount to a refusal of permission, held that these conditions were not so onerous as to prevent fulfilment of the condition in the contract and so upheld the vendors' action for specific performance. On the other hand, in *Hargreaves Transport* v. *Lynch*,[21] the Court of Appeal held that a similar condition had not been satisfied by a grant of outline planning permission where detailed permission was subsequently refused, the court specifically holding that the purchasers were in the circumstances not obliged to appeal to the Minister against this refusal of permission on the grounds that a commercial firm could not be expected to wait for any such appeal to be decided. Problems can also arise where such appeals are pursued. In *Guiness* v. *Pearce*,[22] the contract provided for an abatement of the purchase price if planning permission was refused within six months. The local planning authority duly refused permission during this period but an appeal was allowed by the Minister after that time. Foster J. held that permission had not been refused by the relevent date so that the provision for abatement did not operate.

Obviously problems of this type can be avoided by careful drafting, although it is fair to say that considerable foresight is necessary to anticipate all the potential difficulties. It is interesting to note that in *Hargreaves Transport* v. *Lynch* the parties had made express provision for the difficulty that arose in *Richard West and Partners (Inverness)* v. *Dickro* (by providing that "planning permission shall not be deemed to be received if such planning permission is subject to a condition which the purchaser reasonably considers to be acceptable") but had not anticipated the possibility of a grant of outline planning permission being followed by a denial of detailed permission. However, even superb foresight in drafting cannot solve another problem also highlighted by this same provision in *Hargreaves Transport* v. *Lynch*: how expressions such as "reasonable" and "satisfactory" are to be interpreted. Such expressions are employed not infrequently and indeed occasionally have to be implied by the courts even where the parties have not expressly inserted them. In *Smith and Olley* v. *Townsend*,[23] the contract was "subject to answers to preliminary enquiries and subject to searches" and it was held that the answers to the enquiries and searches had to be satisfactory to a reasonable purchaser. Thus this type of difficulty can arise whether or not the parties have made express reference to such criteria.

The attitude of the courts has, in general, been to adopt an objective stance towards criteria of this sort. Both in *Lee-Parker* v. *Izzet* (*No.*1)[24] and *Janmohamed* v. *Hassan*,[25] "a satisfactory mortgage" was held to be a mortgage to the satisfaction of the purchaser acting reasonably. In *Aquis Estates* v. *Minton*,[26] the contract was subject to "property being found free from adverse entry on the purchaser's local land charge, land charge and land registry searches" and the Court of Appeal held that an objective test must be applied in deciding whether any entry was or was not adverse. In *Caney* v. *Leith*[27] a condition relating to the approval of the title by the purchaser's solicitors was held by Farwell J. to give the solicitors the right to reject even a good title provided they acted in good faith (his lordship did not adopt the view of Earl Cairns L.C. in *Hussey* v. *Horne-Payne*[28] that such conditions are meaningless on the grounds that all that is conferred is the right to reject a bad title, which would anyway be implied). On the other hand, on occasions a more subjective test has been adopted, as in *Marks* v. *Board*[29] where it was stated that an agreement to buy "subject to survey" gave the purchaser an "absolute and undisputed right to say whether he liked the report" (although this was only a dictum since, as has already been seen, the expression "subject to survey" was in that case construed as being analogous to "subject to contract"). However, this attitude was not followed in the subsequent "subject to survey" cases such as *Ee* v. *Kakar*[30] where the purchaser was held to be obliged to act bona fide if presented with a satisfactory report. It is of course clearly preferable that those responsible for drafting conditional clauses should avoid expressions such as "satisfactory" and "reasonable"—apart from anything else, such a practice will considerably reduce the risk of the clause being held to be void for uncertainty. It is even more preferable that the courts should not import such expressions into contracts where the parties have not themselves used them. Occasionally, however, it will clearly be necessary for such expressions to be given definition and in such circumstances it is submitted that the courts should, as seems to be the general practice, adopt an objective stance.

The question of whether or not a condition has been fulfilled (and indeed a clear cut decision that it has not been) often causes consideration to be given to the possibility of one or other of the parties waiving performance of the condition. There is obviously no difficulty where both parties wish to waive performance of a condition—they can simply agree to amend the contract accordingly. However, unilateral waiver of a condition poses rather more problems. As a matter of principle, this should only be possible where the contract in question has been construed in accordance with the condition subsequent construction. Where any of the other three constructions has been adopted, the conditional clause constitutes the entire basis of the contract; consequently in the event of its disappearance, the whole contract would necessarily also fail. There is in fact no English authority in support of this proposition although this conclusion was reached in New Zealand in *Daubney* v. *Kerr*.[31] However, with one possible exception, all the cases in which waiver has been permitted have been cases in which the condition subsequent construction has been adopted. The exception is *Ee* v. *Kakar*[32] where Walton J. permitted the waiver of a "subject to survey" condition which he had classified as a "condition precedent." However, *Wood Preservation* v. *Prior* had not been cited to his lordship and it is possible that he was therefore not using the expression "condition precedent" in its strict technical sense. In any event, principle is clearly in accord with the proposition upheld in New Zealand in *Daubney* v. *Kerr* and it is therefore submitted that waiver should only be possible where the condition subsequent construction is adopted. In such circumstances, a party to a contract will be able unilaterally to waive the performance of a condition if it is exclusively for his benefit. Conditions relating to the obtaining of a mortgage[33] or survey[34] and conditions relating to the title being approved by the purchaser's solicitors[35] or being free from adverse entries[36] are all clearly invariably for the exclusive benefit of the purchaser and so have been held capable of being waived unilaterally by him. At the other extreme, conditions relating to the obtaining of the consent of a landlord to an assignment or subletting clearly concern both parties and are thus incapable of unilateral waiver—apart from anything else, completion of the contract without the consent would in practice almost inevitably lead to re-entry and forfeiture of the lease in question. Sometimes, however, it is much more difficult to decide for whose benefit a condition has been inserted and this is particularly true of conditions relating to the obtaining of planning permission. In the normal case, such conditions are likely to be for the exclusive benefit of the purchaser—he is likely to be paying a price consistent with planning permission having been obtained so that it can hardly matter to the vendor if performance of the condition is waived. This indeed was held in *Batten* v. *White*.[37] However if fulfilment of the condition is interrelated with other provisions of the contract or if the vendor is retaining adjoining land, the obtaining of planning permission will clearly be of importance to him as well and so the condition will be incapable of unilateral waiver. This was held by Brightman J. in *Heron Garages Properties* v. *Moss*,[38] where the contract provided that completion should be one month after the grant of permission and the vendor was retaining adjoining land. A similar decision was reached in *Federated Homes* v. *Turner*[39] where the contract was expressed to be conditional on the obtaining of planning permission and of access both for the land being sold and for that being retained.

In conclusion, the question of whether or not a condition has been fulfilled is essentially a matter of construction of the wording of the contract, something which should be considered extremely carefully by those responsible for its drafting. In general, expressions such as "reasonable" and "satisfactory" should be avoided but where expressed or necessarily implied should be construed in an objective way. However, uncertainties may be able to be resolved by the doctrine of unilateral waiver, whose rules seem both clear and in accordance with principle.

Fiscal considerations

In addition to the very considerable differences in the rights and duties of the parties under each of the four possible constructions of conditional contracts, there are also important differences in the incidence of Development Land Tax and Capital Gains Tax.[40] Development Land Tax is payable upon any realisation of the development value of land, liability arising as a result of any disposal of an interest in land. Since the first £50,000 of realised development value in each financial year is exempt from taxation (which is otherwise levied at a rate of 60 per cent.), it is obviously important to ascertain with certainty in which year a disposal under a conditional contract occurs. Capital Gains Tax, levied at a rate of 30 per cent., is payable on any disposal of a chargeable asset giving rise to a chargeable gain by any person other than bodies which are subject to Corporation Tax (chargeable gains realised by the latter are charged to Corporation Tax but at a fraction such that the effective rate of tax paid is also 30 per cent.). The first £3,000 of chargeable gains in each year of assessment is exempt from taxation and this exemption, although much smaller than in the case of Development Land Tax, nevertheless makes it important to ascertain with certainty in which year a disposal under a conditional contract occurs. Further, both taxes are payable in full at a very early stage (three months after the disposal in the case of Development Land Tax and by 1st December following the year of assessment in the case of Capital Gains Tax) so that decisions on tax planning must inevitably be influenced by the year in which a disposal occurs.

The time at which a disposal occurs for the purposes of Development Land Tax is governed by Section 45 of the Development Land Tax Act 1976. In general a disposal occurs at the date of the contract but under Section 45(2)

> "where under a contract an interest in land is disposed of then—
> (a) if the contract is conditional (and in particular if it is conditional on the exercise of an option) the time at which the disposal and acquisition is made is the time at which the condition is fulfilled";

The equivalent provision for the purposes of Capital Gains Tax is Section 27(2) of the Capital Gains Tax Act 1979, which is couched in effectively identical terms. How do these provisions operate in relation to the four different ways in which conditional contracts can be construed?

Where a contract is construed in accordance with the agreement to agree construction, neither party is under any legally enforceable obligation whatsoever. Consequently it must inevitably follow that no disposal has taken place either for the purposes of Development Land Tax or for the purposes of Capital Gains Tax.

Where a contract is construed in accordance with the unilateral contract construction, it is quite clear that the contract falls directly within Section 45(2) of the Development Land Tax Act 1976 and Section 27(2) of the Capital Gains Tax Act 1979. Consequently no disposal will occur for the purposes of either tax until the condition has been fulfilled. Thus in the case of an option, the disposal of the subject matter occurs upon exercise (although it must be remembered that the grant of an option is itself treated as the creation and disposal of a separate interest in land[41]; in the event of abandonment or lapse of the option this is presumably deemed to occur at the moment of grant so that any consideration paid for that grant will become liable to tax as at that date[42]; in the event of exercise, the grant is regarded as part of and is deemed to occur at the same time as the disposal of the subject matter so that any consideration paid for that grant will become liable to tax at the same time and on the same basis as the consideration for the sale).[43] Given the decision in *Pritchard* v. *Briggs*,[44] it might be thought that these sections, which refer to contracts disposing of an interest in land, do not apply to rights of pre-emption. However, although no case seems yet to have arisen, the Inland Revenue seem to regard a right of pre-emption as "within the wide definition of 'interest in land' in section 46(1) of the DLT Act"[45] quite irrelevant of the general law. On this basis, unless and until this view is successfully challenged in the courts, rights of pre-emption must presumably be treated in exactly the same way as options.

Where a contract is construed in accordance with the condition precedent construction, it is also quite clear that the contract falls directly within Section 45(2) of the Development Land Tax Act and Section 27(2) of the Capital Gains Tax Act 1979. Consequently no disposal will occur for the purpose of either tax until the condition has been fulfilled. This is consistent with the general law, since it was held in *Michael Richards Properties* v. *Corporation of Wardens of St. Saviour's Southwark*[46] that no effective contract for the sale of land arose until such a condition had been fulfilled.

Where a contract is construed in accordance with the condition subsequent construction, however, fulfilment of the condition is merely one of the terms of an immediately effective contract for the sale of land and it was held in *Property and Bloodstock* v. *Emerton*[47] that under such a contract the vendor disposes of an interest in land at the date of the contract. This was admittedly a decision on the general law, not a decision on the interpretation of the taxation statutes, but it was expressly followed in *Eastham* v. *Leigh London and Provincial Properties*[48] in relation to the interpretation of the then Capital Gains Tax legislation.[49] From this decision, it must follow that, for the purposes both of the Development Land Tax Act 1976 and the Capital Gains Tax 1979, a contract construed in accordance with the condition subsequent construction is not treated as a conditional contract and so will be governed by the general rule that the disposal occurs at the date of the contract. This may be very much to the disadvantage of the vendor in that, if the period during which the condition is capable of being fulfilled is lengthy, he may become liable to pay Development Land Tax and Capital Gains Tax thereon before the contract has actually been completed.

These differing fiscal consequences of the various types of conditional contracts clearly need to be borne in mind by those responsible for drafting such contracts. If for any reason it is desirable to postpone the date of disposal in relation to either Development Land Tax or Capital Gains Tax, it will clearly be advisable to frame the contract in such a way that it will be construed in accordance with either the unilateral contract construction or the condition precedent construction. On the other hand, if it is desirable to advance the date of disposal (in order to use up the exemption from Development Land Tax in any particular financial year for example) then it will clearly be advisable to frame the contract in such a way that it will be construed in accordance with the condition subsequent construction.

CONCLUSION

It is clear that, apart from considerations of certainty and time which apply equally to all types of conditional contracts, much depends on the category of conditional contract into which any particular contract is construed to fall. This affects not only the rights and duties of the parties but also the question of what constitutes fulfilment of the condition (because waiver of performance is only possible in the case of contracts construed in accordance with the condition subsequent construction) and the fiscal liabilities of the parties. All these factors should therefore be taken into consideration by those responsible for drafting conditional contracts and, once a decision has been reached on which of the possible types of contract is most suitable, every effort should be made to draft a clause which deals clearly and explicitly with all the points in respect of which the types of contracts differ. In particular, reference should be made in the clause to the time limits appropriate for each stage of the proceedings, whether either party is to be under an obligation to secure fulfilment of the condition, what constitutes fulfilment of the condition and (where appropriate) whether performance of the condition can be waived and, lastly, whether the contract as formed disposes of an interest in the subject matter. If all these matters are dealt with explicitly, there should be little risk of the courts adopting a construction different from that intended by the parties. Last, and most important of all, all the provisions should be drafted with sufficient certainty to remove any risk of the conditional clause (and consequently the contract) being held to be void for uncertainty.

Notes

* The author would like to thank Mr. J.D.R. Adams and Mr. Charles Harpum for reading this paper in draft.

1 [1981] 3 W.L.R. 361.

2 [1968] 3 All E.R. 552.

3 [1972] 1 W.L.R. 775.

4 *Ibid*. p.779.

5 (1962) 106 S.J. 75 ("vendor's solicitors to be instructed to obtain and fix a suitable mortgage)."

6 [1971] 3 All E.R. 1099; [1971] 1 W.L.R. 1688.

7 [1971] 3 All E.R. 1099, 1105. This section of the judgment, which is in brackets, does not appear in the report of the case in [1971] 1 W.L.R. 1688.

8 (1977) 241 E.G. 609 ("mortgage satisfactory to purchaser)."

9 [1959] 3 W.L.R. 1011.

10 *Ibid*. pp.1015–1016.

11 [1967] 2 All E.R. 839, 848.

12 See *Seton* v. *Slade* (1802) 7 Ves. 265, Law of Property Act 1925 s.41, and *United Scientific Holdings* v. *Burnley Borough Council* [1977] 2 W.L.R. 806.

13 [1968] 3 All E.R. 552, 555–556.

14 [1967] 3 W.L.R. 973.

15 [1969] 1 W.L.R. 215, 220.

16 See n.9 above.

17 [1969] 1 W.L.R. 1077.

18 *Ibid*. p.1090.

19 [1968] 1 W.L.R. 74, 82.

20 [1948] Ch. 93.

21 [1976] 1 W.L.R. 649.

22 [1974] Ch. 112.

23 [1975] Ch. 146.

24 (1980) 225 E.G. 1203. The Court of Appeal cited with approval the remarks of

Brightman J. in *Tevanan* v. *Norman Brett (Builders)* (1972) 223 E.G. 1945 at p.1947.

[25] [1925] Ch. 56.

[26] [1947] K.B. 854.

[27] (1930) 46 T.L.R. 424.

[28] [1969] 1 Lloyd's Rep. 81.

[29] (1960) 12 P. & C.R. 66, 70–71.

[30] (1980) 225 E.G. 879.

[31] See pp.177–178.

[32] [1975] 3 All E.R. 416.

[33] *Ibid*. p.424, relying on *Nicolene* v. *Simmonds* [1953] 1 Q.B. 543.

[34] See C.T. Emery [1976] C.L.J. 28.

[35] [1976] 1 W.L.R. 649.

[36] *Ibid*. p.656.

[37] [1978] 2 W.L.R. 621 (see C. Harpum and D. Lloyd Jones [1979] C.L.J. 31).

[38] *Per* Goff L.J. at p.625. See also the judgment of Buckley L.J. at p.631. Orr L.J. agreed with both judgments.

[39] (1862) 12 C.B. (N.S.) 748.

[40] [1952] 1 K.B. 290.

[41] Questions of formality are outside the scope of this paper.

[42] Determined under the rules established by *Aberfoyle Plantations* v. *Cheng* [1960] A.C. 115 (see pp.152–153).

[43] [1978] 2 W.L.R. 649 *per* Goff L.J. at p.627, *per* Buckley L.J. at p.632.

[44] [1968] 1 W.L.R. 1797 (actually an authority on the Land Charges Act 1925).

[45] Under respectively Land Charges Act 1972, s.5(1) and Land Registration Act 1925, s.59(1).

[46] (1970) 214 E.G. 835.

[47] A full treatment of these rules may be found in D.G. Barnsley, *Land Options* (1978).

[48] Formulae for determining the price payable under an option contract have often been struck down on the grounds of uncertainty, as in *King's Motors (Oxford)* v. *Lax* [1970] 1 W.L.R. 426 "at such rental as may be agreed upon between the parties hereto in writing)."

[49] [1974] 1 W.L.R. 155.

[50] (1963) 186 E.G. 259.

[51] The detailed rules governing such options may be found in Barnsley: *op. cit.* pp.31–33.

[52] *Hutton* v. *Watling* [1948] Ch. 26.

[53] *London and South Western Rail Co.* v. *Gomm* (1882) 20 Ch.D. 562 *per* Jessel M.R. at p.581.

[54] *First National Securities* v. *Chiltern District Council* [1975] 1 W.L.R. 1075, 1079.

[55] *Edwards* v. *West* (1878) 7 Ch.D. 858.

[56] *Lysaght* v. *Edwards* (1876) 2 Ch. 499 *per* Jessel M.R. at pp.506–507.

[57] Such options apparently do not constitute a charge on or obligation affecting land and so are not properly capable of protection (*First National Securities* v. *Chiltern District Council* [1975] 1 W.L.R. 1075, 1079).

[58] This exception does not apply to options to purchase a freehold or leasehold reversion which do not touch and concern the land (*Woodall* v. *Clifton* [1905] 2 Ch. 257).

[59] Land Charges Act 1972, s.4(6). This applies even if the money or money's worth is grossly inadequate (*Midland Bank Trust Co.* v. *Green* [1981] 2 W.L.R. 28).

[60] *Wright* v. *Dean* [1948] Ch. 686; *Hollington Brothers* v. *Rhodes* [1951] 2 T.L.R. 691.

[61] *Midland Bank Trust Co.* v. *Green* [1981] 2 W.L.R. 28.

[62] *McCarthy & Stone* v. *Julian S. Hodge & Co.* [1971] 1 W.L.R. 1547 (subsequent equitable mortgagee bound by prior unregistered option).

[63] Land Registration Act 1925, s.20(1).

[64] *Ibid.* s.74 (the contrary decision in *Peffer* v. *Rigg* [1977] 1 W.L.R. 285 cannot stand with the decision of the House of Lords in *William & Glyn's Bank* v. *Boland* [1980] 3 W.L.R. 138.

[65] *Webb* v. *Pollmount* [1966] Ch. 584.

[66] See A.M. Pritchard, (1964) 38 *Conveyancer* 8.

[67] This causes as many problems as it does with options (see *Smith* v. *Morgan* [1971] 1 W.L.R. 803).

[68] In Perpetuities and Accumulations Act 1964, s.9(2) (see p.169) from whose effect this right is excluded.

[69] [1901] 2 Ch. 37.

[70] [1979] 3 W.L.R. 868, 886.

[71] [1973] 1 W.L.R. 823.

[72] (1976) discussed in *Pritchard* v. *Briggs* [1979] 3 W.L.R. 868.

[73] Formerly s.10(1) of the Land Charges Act 1925. The other sections include Law of Property Act 1925, ss.2(3), 186 and Settled Land Act 1925, ss.58(2), 61(2).

[74] By Walton J. in *Pritchard* v. *Briggs* [1978] 2 W.L.R. 317, 339.

[75] Referring specifically to Law of Property Act 1925, s.2(3).

[76] [1979] 3 W.L.R. 868 (see C. Harpum [1978] C.L.J. 213, [1979] C.L.J. 35, J. Martin [1980] *Conveyancer* 433).

[77] The Court of Appeal held that the apparent conflict between these two contracts should be resolved by inferring that the grant of the option to the plaintiff involved a decision by the Lockwoods not to sell during their lifetimes, thus ensuring breach of neither contract. On this inference, no sale would have occurred but for the subsequent receivership.

[78] [1978] 2 W.L.R. 317.

[79] [1979] 3 W.L.R. 868, *per* Goff L.J. at pp.887–891, *per* Templeman L.J. at p.909, *per* Stephenson L.J. at p.913.

[80] The words of Viscount Simonds in *Kirkness* v. *John Hudson & Co.* [1955] A.C. 696, 714, quoted by Goff L.J. at p.890.

[81] *Per* Goff L.J. at p.889. This proposition is implicit in the judgments of Templeman and Stephenson L.JJ.

[82] *Per* Templeman L.J. at p.911, *per* Stephenson L.J. at p.913.

[83] At p.889.

[84] See Harpum [1979] C.L.J. 35, 38, Martin [1980] *Conveyancer* 433.

[85] *Manchester Ship Canal Co.* v. *Manchester Racecourse Co.* [1901] 2 Ch. 37, applying *Lumley* v. *Gye* (1852) 1 De G.M. & G. 604.

[86] *Banstead U.D.C.* v. *Wilkinson* (1962) 182 E.G. 155.

[87] *Gardner* v. *Coutts & Co.* [1967] 1 W.L.R. 172.

[88] *Sefton* v. *Tophams* [1965] Ch. 1140, 1187, 1196.

[89] Such an action was brought (admittedly by the holder of the option rather than by the holder of the right of pre-emption) in *Pritchard* v. *Briggs*. Goff L.J. upheld the claim (at pp.901–908). Templeman and Stephenson L.JJ. held that there was no scope for such a claim in the light of the plaintiff's success (at pp.911, 914).

[90] As in *Esso Petroleum Co.* v. *Kingswood Motors (Addlestone)* [1973] 3 W.L.R. 780—the possibility was also mooted by Eveleigh L.J. in *Midland Bank Trust Co.* v. *Green* [1979] 3 W.L.R. 167, 178.

[91] This was held to be a breach in *Gardner* v. *Coutts & Co.* [1967] 1 W.L.R. 173 but only in relation to an action for damages.

[92] *The Law and Practice of Registered Conveyancing* (4th ed. 1979) (the authors are the present and immediately past Chief Land Registrars).
[93] *First National Securities* v. *Chiltern District Council* [1975] 1 W.L.R. 1075.
[94] See note 85 above.
[95] See note 86 above.
[96] Such occupation will constitute an overriding interest in registered land.
[97] See note 87 above.
[98] See note 88 above.
[99] See note 89 above.
[1] See note 90 above.
[2] On pp.162–163.
[3] See pp.162–163.
[4] (1874) L.R. 7 H.L. 158—the rule is discussed in detail in [1980] C.L.J. 58 at pp.67–70.
[5] [1975] 3 All E.R. 416. Another aspect of this decision was considered on pp.157–158.
[6] *Ibid*. p.421.
[7] [1960] A.C. 1150.
[8] See above n.7.
[9] See pp.152–153.
[10] [1974] 1 W.L.R. 331.
[11] *Ibid*. at p.336.
[12] *Ibid*. at p.337.
[13] (1973) 231 E.G. 1295.
[14] See above n.13.
[15] See pp.171–172.
[16] *Lehmann* v. *McArthur* (1868) L.R. 3 Ch. App. 496 (where the vendor was held able to rely on the rule even though he had not taken proceedings against the landlord for unreasonably withholding his consent under Landlord and Tenant Act 1927, s.19(1)).
[17] *Day* v. *Singleton* [1899] 2 Ch. 320.
[18] [1968] Ch. 94.
[19] *Gordon Hill Trust* v. *Segall* [1941] 2 All E.R. 379.
[20] [1969] 2 W.L.R. 1190.
[21] [1969] 1 W.L.R. 215.
[22] (1971) 220 E.G. 191.
[23] (1949) 1 P. & C.R. 26.
[24] [1971] 3 All E.R. 1099.
[25] (1977) 241 E.G. 609.
[26] [1975] 1 W.L.R. 1452.
[27] [1937] 2 All E.R. 1099.
[28] (1879) 4 App.Cas. 311.
[29] (1930) 46 T.L.R. 424.
[30] (1980) 255 E.G. 879.
[31] [1962] N.Z.L.R. 319.
[32] (1980) 255 E.G. 879.
[33] *Janmohamed* v. *Hassan* (1977) 241 E.G. 609.
[34] *Ee* v. *Kakar* (1980) 255 E.G. 879.
[35] *Bennett* v. *Fowler* (1840) 2 Beav. 302.
[36] *Aquis Estates* v. *Minton* [1975] 1 W.L.R. 1452.
[37] (1960) 12 P. & C.R. 66.
[38] [1974] 1 W.L.R. 148.
[39] (1975) 233 E.G. 845.
[40] See V. Callender [1979] *Conveyancer* 285.

[41] Development Land Tax Act 1976, s. 8(1)(*a*), Capital Gains Tax Act 1979, s.137.

[42] This is not stated expressly in either statute.

[43] Development Land Tax Act 1976, s.8(2)(3), Capital Gains Tax Act 1979, s.137 (which, unlike the DLTA provision, does not actually expressly state when the disposal is deemed to occur).

[44] [1979] 3 W.L.R. 868.

[45] See the letter from the Somerset House (Inland Revenue Policy Division) reprinted in [1978] *Conveyancer* 83.

[46] [1975] 3 All E.R. 416.

[47] [1968] Ch. 94.

[48] [1971] 2 W.L.R. 1149, (1971) 46 T.C. 687.

[49] Finance Act 1962, s.12(2) and Sched. 9, para. 1.

Obstruction—The Policeman's Best Friend?

R.C. AUSTIN

It is perhaps politically fashionable today to question and criticise the status, role and performance of the police and to castigate the police in particular for the breakdown in relations between sections of the community and the police. The "sus" laws campaign[1]; the allegations of serious assaults upon suspects in custody, (such as the Kelly case in Liverpool)[2]; the claims that the Brixton and Toxteth riots of last summer resulted at least in part from heavy-handed, insensitive policing of volatile areas; indeed that some of that volatility itself sprang from previous police harassment of ethnic minority citizens; the implicit confirmation of at least some of these claims by the Scarman Report[3]; the confirmation by the Royal Commission on Criminal Procedure[4] and the Confait Report[5] that certain "rights" such as the right of access to a solicitor, were made "dead letters" by police practice; the apparent failure of the police complaints system to ensure effective, independent treatment of complaints[6]; the general complaint that the police are neither sufficiently responsive nor accountable to the communities they serve[7]; these are some of the currently popular criticisms of the police.

But I do not in this paper wish to join that chorus which is largely a political one. Rather, it is my purpose to point out that in many cases, it is the vagueness and uncertainty, in content and scope, of some police powers and of some criminal offences, which may be a greater problem than those referred to above. If the police are not given clear limits within which to operate, and if definitions of offences are not clear and precise, then both police officers and criminal suspects have legitimate grievances against a legal system which does not fulfil those requirements. It is the duty of lawyers both academic and professional, to strive to ensure that the law does define both the powers of the police to interfere with the liberty of the citizen and the criminal liabilities of that citizen with clarity and precision.

The aim of this paper is to show that the offence of wilful obstruction of a police constable in the execution of his duty, contrary to s.51 of the Police Act 1964, is vague and uncertain, both as to the *mens rea* and the *actus reus* of the offence. Furthermore, as the *actus reus* of obstruction necessarily involves a consideration of whether the officer alleged to have been obstructed was acting within his duties or powers, it is also the purpose of this paper to demonstrate that those duties and powers are far from clearly defined.

If, as I believe they are, these propositions are proven, then a serious problem exists; if the citizen and the police officer alike are unable to ascertain the scope and content of the police officer's duties and powers, and if they are further unable to determine what constitutes an obstruction of the officer when performing those duties and exercising those powers, the potential for specific conflict between police officer and individual citizen and for the general conflict between the community at large and the police force, is enormous.

Some recent examples will suffice to demonstrate the lack of clarity in the law relating to police powers and the offence of obstruction and the difficulties thereby caused. In *Wershof* v. *Metropolitan Police Commission*,[8] the police officer erroneously believed that he had the power to seize the evidence without giving a receipt, and the power to arrest Wershof for obstruction of a police officer in the execution of his duty when Wershof refused to surrender the allegedly stolen ring. That police officer's ignorance of his powers has been criticised,[9] but was probably excusable. The principles laid down by Lord Denning M.R. in *Ghani* v. *Jones*[10] are far from clear. What is a "serious" crime? When is it "unreasonable" for an innocent person to withhold evidence or fruits of such a crime? Do those principles apply only when premises are being searched? Does *R.* v. *Waterfield and Lynn*,[11] though expressly put in doubt by *Ghani* v. *Jones*,[12] still apply in cases other than search of premises? These questions had not been given clear answers either by the Courts or Parliament at the time of *Wershof*.[13] Furthermore, the power to arrest for obstruction had generally been assumed, both by the police and the Courts,[14] (despite one clear authority to the contrary, *Gilberg* v. *Miller*[15]), because in most cases of obstruction, some other arrestable offence is committed, or a breach of the peace is anticipated giving rise to a power of arrest.

In those circumstances, the officer in *Wershof*[16] is hardly to be blamed for acting as he did, in good faith, to secure the recovery of stolen property and its preservation as evidence in any subsequent prosecution. If police powers are not clearly defined and limited, conscientious police officers seeking to protect persons and property by detecting crime, apprehending suspected criminals, obtaining evidence against them and recovering stolen property, will inevitably utilise their powers to the fullest extent. It is both unjust and unfair to criticise officers for exceeding limits which are retrospectively created or declared, as in *Pedro* v. *Diss*.[17] In that case the Divisional Court imposed upon the police officer's power to search persons for stolen or unlawfully obtained property, under s.66 of the Metropolitan Police Act 1839, an obligation to inform the suspect that he was being detained and of the reason for his detention, namely that the police officer wished to search him for stolen property he was suspected of conveying upon his person. Although an earlier authority[18] had assumed the existence of such an obligation, though at a much more rudimentary level, there was no clear rule establishing an explicit duty. The Divisional Court did not rely on that earlier authority, but argued instead by analogy from the same duty in cases of arrest, holding that there was no distinction for this purpose between arrest and detention for search and that *R*. v. *Inwood*[19] and *Christie* v. *Leachinsky*[20] therefore applied equally to detention for search as to arrest. The Divisional Court thus retrospectively created a new rule imposing conditions upon the exercise of the power to detain for search. The hapless police officer who in good faith had attempted to detain and search a suspect observed lurking in a doorway at night found himself physically attacked by the suspect. Yet the suspect was acquitted because the police officer had not observed the conditions subsequently imposed by the Divisional Court.

Similarly, the Courts have given little guidance in the past as to the meaning of "reasonable cause to suspect" the vague statutory test upon which most powers of arrest and of search without arrest are predicated.[21] Accordingly, conscientious police officers use such powers to their fullest extent. The near-random use, in certain areas, of stop and search powers, for drugs or stolen property,[22] is not particularly surprising, given the lack of any authoritative and detailed legal guidelines as to the scope of such powers.

We cannot legitimately blame the police for exercising these powers beyond their limits, when neither Parliament nor the Courts has seen fit to set such limits with any satisfactory degree of clarity or precision. Nor can we legitimately blame, and convict for an offence, the citizen who reacts against what he perceives as an abuse or excess of police power, if neither the power nor the offence are defined by Parliament or the Courts with any satisfactory degree of clarity or precision.

Perhaps then, some of the fault lies with the law and its institutions rather than wholly with the police, who seem recently to have been the exclusive target for criticism.

In relation to the offence of obstruction of a police officer in the execution of his duty, it is my thesis that the potential for excess and abuse of power by police officers and for conflict between police officers and citizens resisting what they perceive as unjustifiable intrusions upon their rights and liberties, is greater in this area than in most others.

Obstruction of or assault upon a police constable in the execution of his duty are frequent grounds for arrest and common charges prosecuted in the courts.[23] The offence of obstruction of a police constable in the execution of his duty did not exist until 1885,[24] yet our police constables seemed not to be unduly frustrated prior to that date in carrying out their duties.[25]

The growth of obstruction as a catch-all charge has caused some alarm among academic commentators.[26] The grounds for criticism of the offence of obstruction can be summarised as follows:

(1) Obstruction of or assault upon a police constable in the execution of his duty are selected as charges in order to obtain heavier sentences than those for the alternative available charge, *e.g.* binding over orders or charges of common assault.[27]

(2) Obstruction is charged because it is easier to prove than some other offences which require proof of additional elements, such as common intent or purpose in unlawful assembly.[28]

(3) In the context of public order, obstruction is commonly given as the ground for arrest and is frequently the charge brought, because of the benefit of the ambiguity between obstruction of the highway, which is arrestable, and obstruction of a police constable, which is not.[29]
Further, in procession cases, unreasonable user of the highway is more difficult to prove than the constable's reasonable apprehension of future breach of the peace.[30]

(4) The vagueness and generality of police powers, and the refusal of the courts to investigate closely the justification for a police officer's belief in the necessity to take action gives the police wide discretion the impeding of which will constitute the offence of obstruction.[31]

I now turn to examine the law, and preface my remarks with the general observation that whereas most of the earlier and some of the recent cases seemed to establish obstruction of a police constable as a broad catch-all charge, highly useful to the police, some recent authorities appear to be moving away from that position, and to be attempting a more precise, narrower definition of the offence. With respect, that attempt has not been wholly successful, though it is of course wholly welcome.

What constitutes the *actus reus* of wilful obstruction of a police constable in the execution of his duty, under s.51 of the Police Act 1964? There are, it seems, three possible definitions when looking at the cases: *First* that whenever the conduct of the accused, without lawful excuse makes the police officer's task more difficult, he has commited the *actus reus* of obstruction. *or*

Second that whenever the conduct of the accused makes the police officer's task more difficult, and the police officer is not acting unlawfully, *i.e.* not committing a crime or a tort, then the accused has committed the *actus reus* of obstruction. *or*

Third that the accused commits the *actus reus* of obstruction if and *only* if the police officer is exercising a specific power or duty conferred or imposed upon him by law, the police officer is acting strictly within the limits of that power or duty, and the conduct of the accused makes the exercise of that power or the fulfilment of that duty more difficult.

The first definition appears to receive support from the dictum of Lord Parker C.J., in *Rice* v. *Connolly*,[32] when he described obstruction as follows:

> " . . . to 'obstruct' in s.51(3) is to do any act which makes it more difficult for the police to carry out their duty."[33]

The last word of that statement is crucial, and his Lordship went on to describe the police officer's duty in the following words

> " . . . it is part of the obligations and duties of a police constable to take all steps which appear necessary for keeping the peace, for preventing crime or for protecting property from criminal injury . . . "

and later

> "the duty to detect crime and to bring an offender to justice."[34]

These may well be general descriptions of the functions of a police force, or even the tasks a police officer is required to perform by his superiors or even perhaps an accurate job description—but it is not a description of a constable's specific legal powers and duties. When seeking to justify an act which infringes the liberty or rights of a citizen, the constable must point to a specific legal authority—just as the Secretary of State in *Entick* v. *Carrington*[35] was not permitted simply to point to his general duty to protect the interests of the State or the Crown, so too the constable cannot simply rely upon some general duty to counter crime.

Furthermore, insofar as Lord Parker's words purport to be a description of specific powers, they are inaccurate. First, a constable has power to do only what is *reasonably* necessary (not "all steps which appear necessary") to prevent a reasonably apprehended breach of the peace.[36] Secondly, that power does not extend beyond breach of peace to all crimes[37]—though a police constable may use *reasonable force* to prevent crime, to effect or assist a lawful arrest, and to prevent an escape from lawful custody, under s.3 Criminal Law Act 1967.

One might ask whether there is any practical difference between breach of the peace and all crimes and between all necessary steps, reasonably necessary steps and reasonable force. The response must be that these conditions and powers decline successively in width. The practical effect of these differences may be considerable, in that they may determine for example, whether a police officer may commandeer the property of a private citizen, for example to erect a road-block with a lorry,[38] whether a police officer can require a private citizen to do certain acts of a hazardous or even unlawful character,[39] and whether a police officer may enter private property.[40]

It is clear, then, that Lord Parker was asserting a more general principle by so describing a police officer's duty, namely that the citizen who made the constable's job or task more difficult, was guilty of obstruction. It does not appear to be necessary under *Rice* v. *Connolly*[41] for the prosecution to establish that the constable allegedly obstructed was exercising any specific power or duty. The scope of the offence would thus appear to be unlimited—indeed it appears to confer untramelled powers upon the police and extensive liability upon the citizen.

But clearly such a position is untenable, and *Rice* v. *Connolly* is qualified by the requirement that the accused's conduct must be "without lawful excuse."[42] Two comments may be made here, the first being that such a requirement appears to reverse the burden of proof and cast upon the defence the onus of proving that the accused's conduct was excused by law, rather than the prosecution being required to prove that the accused's conduct was prohibited by law. This is contrary also to the general principle in English law that a citizen is at liberty to do anything which is not expressly forbidden by law.[43] Secondly, while this requirement that the accused's conduct must be "without lawful excuse" may in some cases be related to the accused's belief in the existence of a certain state of fact or even perhaps of law and fact,[44] in most cases this

requirement would be regarded as part of the *actus reus* of the offence[45] or as an element independent of both *actus reus* and *mens rea*, yet in *Rice* v. *Connolly*[46] it was introduced as a definition of "wilfully" or "wilful," which describes the requisite *mens rea* of the offence. There is therefore considerable judicial confusion in the reasoning of *Rice* v. *Connolly*.[47] Nonetheless, the Lord Chief Justice went on to say, applying his definition of wilful, that since the law recognised the citizen's legal right of silence (despite his moral or social duty to assist the police) the accused was not acting wilfully in refusing to answer the constable's questions. Further, that since the accused was not by law required to go with a constable unless arrested, the accused was not acting wilfully in refusing to accompany the constable to a police call box.[47] Neither of these legal excuses related to the accused's state of mind—they were objective facts—yet they made his conduct "not wilful." As I shall explain later, the decision in *Rice* v. *Connolly*[48] is correct, but, with respect, the reasoning is clearly erroneous. It will be my argument that the accused had not committed the *actus* of obstruction and therefore questions of wilfulness or *mens rea* did not arise. (On virtually any test, the accused in *Rice* v. *Connolly* had the *mens rea* for obstruction—he deliberately led the police constables on a "wild goose chase" around the town and he quite intentionally made their task more difficult by refusing to give his name, address and activities that evening, and by refusing to go with them).

The first definition of the *actus reus* therefore involves considerable difficulties—it is extremely wide; it imposes no clear limits to the scope of the offence; as applied in *Rice* v. *Connolly* it confuses the concepts of *mens rea* and *actus reus*; it reverses the normal burden of proof and it appears to be contrary to a fundamental principle of English law,[49] namely that unless an act is expressly prohibited by law, it is lawful.

Turning then, to the second definition, under which the accused commits the *actus* if his conduct makes the constable's task more difficult and the constable is not acting unlawfully, in the sense of committing a crime or, more usually, a tort, such as trespass. This definition preserves the wide scope of the police constable's general duties, but imposes a limitation that he must not commit an act specifically proscribed by law. This in some circumstances may be wider than the first definition, in that it can impose wider liability for omissions than the first definition, as demonstrated by the case of *Stunt* v. *Bolton*,[50] where the accused was convicted of obstruction for refusing to surrender to a police constable the keys to a motor vehicle. The vehicle was causing an obstruction of the highway, the driver was under arrest following a positive breathalyser test, and the accused, to whom the driver had given the ignition keys, was suspected of having consumed alcohol, but had not been breathalysed. The constable demanded the keys, the accused refused to comply.

It clearly was the constable's duty to remove the obstruction from the highway, and his power to use reasonable force to prevent the commission of the offence of obstruction of the highway. He could therefore have towed the vehicle away. He could have asked the accused to remove the vehicle (of which the accused was by implication the bailee), and if the accused refused, arrested him for obstruction of the highway. He could have obtained duplicate keys and removed the vehicle by driving it away. But prior to this case there was no specific legal power conferred upon a police constable to seize the ignition keys from a person to whom the keeper of a vehicle has given the keys, nor to require that person to give possession of the keys to the police constable. Nonetheless, the accused was convicted of the offence of obstructing the police constable in the execution of his duty. The police constable was acting within his general duty to prevent crime, though not within any specific legal power, authority or duty. He did not commit any crime or tort in demanding the keys, *i.e.* his conduct was not expressly prohibited by law. The court implied or inferred a duty on the accused to hand over the keys, but there was no previous authority in law to justify this infringement of the proprietorial rights of the owner of the keys and this intervention in the custodial duties of the bailee thereof. Nor I submit was there any good policy reason, given the alternative solutions open to the police constable. It was, however, necessary for the Court to create such a duty to overcome the plea that the bailee had a lawful excuse for his omission, namely his legal duties as bailee to protect the owner's proprietary rights in the keys.

The disadvantages of this second definition of *actus reus* are similar to those of the first definition, namely that the scope of the offence is enormous and uncertain if the courts are prepared to create specific ancillary powers (and their correlative duties) by inference from the existence of general duties and powers, qualified only by the requirement that the police constable's conduct is not expressly prohibited by existing law. Also, it again reverses the burden of proof and again infringes the principle that the citizen is entitled to do any act not expressly prohibited by law. The greatest disadvantage, however, lies in the power exercised by the court retrospectively to create new powers for the constable

and new correlative duties for the citizen. Retrospective penal legislation by the courts is contrary to fundamental principles of individual liberty and constitutional law.

The third definition is in my submission not only the correct definition in that it is supported by principle and strong authority, but is also the more desirable insofar as it clarifies and clearly limits both the scope of the offence and of police powers.

Halsbury[51] defines obstruction so as to require that the police officer be acting in the exercise, and strictly within the limits of a specific power conferred by law. More recently, three cases, two specifically on obstruction, and another on a statutory offence of refusing to comply with a police officer's request to provide a specimen of breath, have given considerable support for the view that an officer can be obstructed only if he is exercising some specific power or duty conferred by law and not merely general powers or duties arising out of his functions or office. In *Lindley* v. *Rutter*[52] the accused's conviction for assaulting a police constable in the execution of her duty was quashed on appeal by the Divisional Court because in attempting to remove the accused's brassiere by force, the woman police constable exceeded the strict limits of her power to search arrested persons and to seize property in their possession. Donaldson L.J. strongly asserted that

> "Police constables of all ranks derive their authority from the law and only from the law. If they exceed that authority, however slightly, technically they cease to be acting in the execution of their duty and have no more rights than any other citizen. This is a most salutary principle upon which all our liberties depend and it is not to be eroded merely because as in this case, the limits of the constable's authority may not have been clearly defined. . . ."[53]

The power to remove personal clothing did exist but only where there was reasonable cause to believe the arrested person would otherwise cause herself harm. Furthermore the Chief Constable's standing orders could not add to the authority conferred by law. *Lindley* v. *Rutter* is therefore strong authority for the limited definition of obstruction, since it is submitted that the phrase "in the execution of his duty" must bear the same meaning in cases of obstruction as in assault cases, given that the words appear in the same section of the same statute.

Further support for the limited definition is to be found in *Pedro* v. *Diss*,[54] which required the police constable to comply with strict conditions (informing the suspect of the detention and the reasons therefor) as to the exercise of a statutory power of detention and search. Failure to so comply took the constable outside the strictly limited scope of his powers and he was therefore not acting in the execution of his duty. *Morris* v. *Beardmore*,[55] though not an obstruction case, adopts a very similar approach in confining the exercise of a statutory power within strict limits, so as to narrow the criminal liability of the citizen for failing to comply with a police constable's request to provide a specimen of breath. Although breathalyser cases have hitherto been regarded as *sui generis*, the generality of the *ratio* in *Morris* v. *Beardmore*, that statutory powers must be strictly construed, and that officers exceeding the strict limits of their powers cease lawfully to execute their authority,[56] clearly takes the case out of that *genus* and renders it applicable to the definition of obstruction of a police constable in the execution of his duty. Furthermore, cases of assault upon a constable in the execution of his duty[57] were explicitly cited in *Morris* v. *Beardmore*.[58] It is important to note that whilst an unlawful act, whether at civil or criminal law, takes a police officer outside the execution of his duty,[59] it is not the unlawfulness *per se* which has that effect. Rather, it is because the statute is construed so as not to authorise the commission of unlawful acts in the absence of express provision to that effect. Thus it is the exceeding of authority which takes the constable outside the execution of his duty. This is made clear by Lord Edmund-Davies when he points out that the power to require the provision of a specimen of breath is exercisable only if the constable is in uniform.[59] The non-wearing of a uniform is not an unlawful act, yet the constable would not be acting in the execution of his duty, if he purported to require the provision of a specimen of breath when not wearing a uniform.[59]

Similarly, failure to produce a warrant in correct form when requesting entry for search of premises under s.23 of the Misuse of Drugs Act 1971, though not a tort, takes the officer outside the execution of his duty. The denial of the police constable's request, in *Syce* v. *Harrison*[60] could not therefore constitute an obstruction of the constable in the execution of his duty, since the constable was not complying strictly with the conditions upon which his power was dependent.

There is, therefore, strong authority supporting this third alternative definition of obstruction, that an officer can only be obstructed in the execution of his duty when he is acting strictly within the limits of a specific power conferred upon him by law.[61]

Further definitional problems (other than whether the constable was acting in the execution of his duty) exist, concerning both the *actus reus* and the *mens rea* of obstruction. The scope for committing the offence by omission remains wholly unclear. *Rice* v. *Connolly*[62] appeared to impose the burden on the accused of proving that his failure to comply with the officer's request was justified by some lawful excuse. Subsequent cases have not even granted that as a defence, since in both *Stunt* v. *Bolton*[63] and the notoriously difficult case of *Johnson* v. *Phillips*,[64] the accused had lawful excuses for refusal to comply with the officer's request, the first that to comply would be in breach of his legal duties as bailee, the second that compliance would constitute a criminal offence. The Courts appear willing in these cases to create duties and impose them on the citizen, not on the basis of any statutory authority but from the general functions of the police constable to keep the peace, protect life and property, detect crime and apprehend criminals. The creation from such broad powers of such duties, and the imposition of criminal liability for failure to perform them, without clear and explicit authority for so doing, is precisely the power denied to Parliament and the police by the House of Lords in *Morris* v. *Beardmore*.[65]

There is wide divergence between the authorities as to the requisite *mens rea* for obstruction. Although "wilful" was thought to encompass oblique intention,[66] recent authority appears to diverge on this issue. In *Willmott* v. *Atack*,[67] the accused was held on appeal not to have the necessary *mens rea* on the basis that although he intended to interpose himself between the police constable and the arrested man, his purpose in so doing was to calm the arrested man down and persuade him to go quietly with the police, thus avoiding unnecessary violence. *Willmott* v. *Atack* therefore clearly requires specific intent; the accused must intend that the police officer be obstructed as a consequence of the accused's conduct. It is not sufficient that the voluntary conduct of the accused does in fact obstruct the officer if the accused did not intend that to be the consequence of his conduct.

This position appears to be qualified somewhat by the recent decision in *Ostler* v. *Elliott*,[68] however, where the Divisional Court held that the accused could not have the necessary *mens rea* for wilful obstruction if he reasonably believed that the persons he obstructed were not police officers. This creates an objective test for *mens rea*, rather than the subjective test adopted by the House of Lords for mistake of fact in *D.P.P.* v. *Morgan*.[69] The requirement of reasonable belief is supported by *Albert* v. *Lavin*,[70] where the defendant genuinely but unreasonably did not believe that the person he assaulted was a police officer, and was convicted of assaulting a police officer in the execution of his duty.

The interesting consequence of *Ostler* v. *Elliott*[71] is that although for almost all purposes the non-wearing of a uniform does not affect the powers[72] of a police constable, whether a person has the necessary *mens rea* for obstruction of, or possibly, assault[73] upon, a police constable in the execution of his duty may depend upon whether the constable is wearing a uniform, if he takes no other adequate steps to identify himself as a constable.

CONCLUSIONS

The varying definitions of the *actus reus* of obstruction lead to considerable uncertainty as to the scope and content of the offence. In turn, the apparent width of the offence under some authorities confers wide, ill-defined powers upon the police and commensurate obligations and criminal liabilities upon the citizen. There is considerable uncertainty as to the mental element required, so that the citizen acting entirely in good faith and for wholly proper motives may incur liability. The scope for committing the offence by omission is not satisfactorily resolved in that the courts appear able and willing to create duties retrospectively and by implication only.

This wholly unsatisfactory position is reflected in two decisions reported since this lecture was delivered, in which the Divisional Court flatly contradicts itself as to the scope of the offence of obstruction. In *Ricketts* v. *Cox*,[74] the accused was convicted of obstruction in that he was abusive, unco-operative and positively hostile to two police constables questioning him, that he used obscene language and that he tried to walk away from the officers. The conviction was upheld, on the basis that the accused obstructed the police and had no lawful excuse for so acting. Yet in *Bentley* v. *Brudzinski*,[75] the Divisional Court appears to adopt the third definition considered above, by contrasting the "execution of his duty in the broad meaning of that term, but not in its technical meaning." The real question was whether the police constable had exceeded his specific legal powers of stopping and questioning a citizen, short of making an arrest. As the police constable had done so by placing his hand on the accused's shoulder in order to detain the accused, the accused's assault upon the constable was not an offence under s.51 of the Police Act 1964, though it almost certainly was a common assault, the force used to resist the detention being excessive. But it is the contrast between the constable's duty in the broad sense of investigating suspected crime and in the technical sense of exercising specific legal powers which makes *Bentley* v. *Brudzinski* wholly inconsistent with

Ricketts v. *Cox*,[76] thus adding to the uncertainty as to the definition of the offence of obstruction.

Such uncertainty may in practice mean that obstruction, far from being the constable's best friend, may well be his worst enemy. Some of the blame for the difficulties caused in individual cases and the friction in the community which may result from police use of wide, ill-defined powers, must rest with the Courts and Parliament for their failure to produce clear definitions of police powers and in particular of the offence of obstruction of a police constable in the execution of his duty.

Notes

[1] See the Third Report of the Select Committee on Home Affairs, H.C. 271 of 1980–81 which persuaded the government to introduce legislation to repeal that part of s.4 of the Vagrancy Act 1824 which created the offence of being a suspected person. See now the Criminal Attempts Act 1981.

[2] See Adjournment Debate, House of Commons, March 20, 1981. (H.C. Deb., Vol. 1, col. 604). See also The Police Complaints Board's Triennial Review Report, Cmnd. 7966 (1980), para. 69.

[3] Cmnd. 8427 (1981) Pt. IV, pp.64–71.

[4] Cmnd. 8092, (1981) pp.97–98.

[5] Report of Sir Henry Fisher into the Confait Case, HMSO 1977, para. 15. See also Baldwin and McConville, "Police Interrogation and the Right to see a Solicitor" [1979] Crim. L.R. 145.

[6] The Police Complaints Board's Triennial Review Report, Cmnd. 7966 (1980) while denying the feasibility of a wholly independent complaints investigation system, did voice concern at the public discontent over unexplained injuries sustained in police custody and suggested an element of independence in the investigation of such complaints. The Scarman Report, Cmnd. 8427 (1981), indicated a loss of confidence in the complaints procedure not only on the part of the ethnic minority communities, but generally see pp.65, 115–117.
Recently, the Council of Indian Organisations expressed its complete lack of confidence in the Police Complaints system and recommended its members to boycott the system until it was reformed. See *The Times*, January 25, 1982, p.3.

[7] Scarman Report, *supra*, pp.47–59, particularly paras. 4.43–4.46.

[8] [1978] 3 All E.R. 540.

[9] M.P. Furmston, "Ignorance of the Law" (1981) 1 L.S. 37, 42.

[10] [1970] 1 Q.B. 693, 708; [1969] 3 All E.R. 1700, 1705.

[11] [1964] 1 Q.B. 164; [1963] 3 All E.R. 659.

[12] [1970] 1 Q.B. 693, 707–708; [1969] 3 All E.R. 1700, 1704–1705.

[13] [1978] 3 All E.R. 540.

[14] For example, in *Rice* v. *Connolly* [1966] 2 Q.B. 414, the only issue considered was whether refusing to answer police questions was obstruction. The Court appears to have assumed a power of arrest if obstruction had occurred. In *Wershof* itself, counsel for the police officer argued that the police had a power to arrest for peaceable obstruction, [1978] 3 All E.R. 540, 548. In *Willmott* v. *Atack* [1976] 3 All E.R. 794, the accused was arrested for obstructing a police officer in the execution of his duty, and the Divisional Court made no comment, despite the finding by the Crown Court at first instance that there had been no assault. The only issue

considered was whether the offence of obstruction required specific intent. See also Leigh, *Police Powers in England and Wales*, (1975) p.72.

[15] [1961] 1 All E.R. 291.

[16] [1978] 3 All E.R. 540.

[17] [1981] 2 All E.R. 59.

[18] *Willey* v. *Peace* [1950] 1 All E.R. 724; [1951] 1 K.B. 94.

[19] [1973] 2 All E.R. 645.

[20] [1947] A.C. 573.

[21] *e.g.* Criminal Law Act 1967, s.2; Misuse of Drugs Act 1971, s.23(2); Metropolitan Police Act 1839, s.66.

[22] As in Brixton, during Swamp 81, when the police appeared to justify near-random stop and search of young male blacks on the basis that such persons were statistically more likely to be in possession of controlled drugs or stolen property. Statistical tendencies, even if proven, hardly constitute reasonable cause to suspect, yet some of the Metropolitan Police appear in practice to rely on such a test, despite the low success rates such searches produce. See Scarman Report, *supra*, paras. 4.37–4.40, 4.48, 4.63.

[23] Regrettably, precise numbers are not available since obstruction is subsumed into miscellaneous offences in police statistics. However, a brief glance through the law reports and at the press after political demonstrations, industrial picketing and other forms of potential public disorder, give some indication of the frequency of s.51 arrests and charges.

[24] Prevention of Crimes (Amendment) Act 1885.

[25] See *Humphries* v. *Connor* (1864) 17 Ir. C.L.R. 1; *O'Kelly* v. *Harvey* (1883) 15 Cox C.C. 435. *Contra, Beattie* v. *Gilbanks* (1882) 9 Q.B.D. 308, though it is arguable that in that case, the prosecution erred in their selection of accused, the real culprits being the Skeleton Army who, it is submitted, could have been successfully prosecuted.

[26] See, for example, the criticisms of *Duncan* v. *Jones* [1936] 1 K.B. 218; Brownlie, *The Law Relating to Public Order* (1968), pp.17–22; E.C.S. Wade, *Police Powers and Public Meetings* (1936–38) 6 C.L.J. 175; T.C. Daintith, *Disobeying a Policeman—A Fresh Look at Duncan* v. *Jones* [1966] P.L. 248; Leigh, *Police Powers in England and Wales* (1975), pp.90–93.

[27] *e.g. Duncan* v. *Jones* [1936] 1 K.B. 218; *Donnelly* v. *Jackman* [1970] 1 All E.R. 987; *Davis* v. *Lisle* [1936] 2 K.B. 434.

[28] Contrast *Beattie* v. *Gilbanks* (1882) 9 Q.B.D. 308 with *Duncan* v. *Jones* [1936] 1 K.B. 218.

[29] See Leigh, *Police Powers in England and Wales* (1975), p.93.

[30] Compare *Duncan* v. *Jones* [1936] 1 K.B. 218 and *Piddington* v. *Bates* [1960] 3 All E.R. 660, with *R.* v. *Clark* [1964] 2 Q.B. 315.

[31] See, for example, *Stunt* v. *Bolton* [1972] Crim. L.R. 561; 116 S.J. 803; *Duncan* v. *Jones* [1936] 1 K.B. 218; *Piddington* v. *Bates* [1960] 3 All E.R. 660; *Johnson* v. *Phillips* [1976] 1 W.L.R. 65.

[32] [1966] 2 All E.R. 649.

[33] *Ibid.* p.651.

[34] *Ibid.* A similar view of the police constable's duty to protect life and property was taken in *Johnson* v. *Phillips* [1976] 1 W.L.R. 65.

[35] (1765) XIX St.Tr. 1029.

[36] *Piddington* v. *Bates, supra*.

[37] *Thomas* v. *Sawkins* [1935] 2 K.B. 249.

[38] See Bennun, *The Duty to Assist the Police—Some Aspects in Fundamental Duties* (ed. Lasok, Jaffey, Perrott and Sachs.) (1980), p.124.

[39] *Johnson* v. *Phillips, supra*.

[40] *Thomas* v. *Sawkins, supra*; s.2(6), Criminal Law Act 1967.

[41] [1966] 2 All E.R. 649.

[42] *Ibid.* pp.651–652.

[43] See, for example, de Smith, *Constitutional and Administrative Law* (4th ed., 1981), p.447.

[44] *e.g. R.* v. *Denton* [1972] 1 All E.R. 65.

[45] See commentary on *R.* v. *Denton, supra* in [1982] Crim. L.R. 108.

[46] [1966] 2 All E.R. 649.

[47] *Ibid.* pp.651–652.

[48] [1966] 2 All E.R. 649.

[49] A principle recently re-iterated, though arguably wrongly applied, in *Malone* v. *Metropolitan Police Commissioner* (*No.* 2) [1979] 2 All E.R. 620.

[50] (1972) 116 S.J. 803; [1972] Crim. L.R. 561. *Davis* v. *Lisle, supra* also exemplifies this second definition.

[51] *Halsbury's Laws of England* (4th ed.), Vol. 11, p.559, para. 962.

[52] [1980] 3 W.L.R. 660. *Lindley* v. *Rutter* upholds an earlier ruling in the direction to the jury in *R.* v. *Naylor* [1979] Crim. L.R. 532.

[53] *Ibid.* p.663.

[54] [1981] 2 All E.R. 59.

[55] [1980] 3 W.L.R. 283; [1980] 2 All E.R. 753, H.L.

[56] [1980] 2 All E.R. 753, 759.

[57] *Davis* v. *Lisle, supra R.* v. *Waterfield and Lynn, supra.*

[58] Note 55 above.

[59] [1980] 2 All E.R. 753, 759.

[60] [1980] Crim. L.R. 649, report corrected at [1981] Crim. L.R. 110.

[61] Furthermore, most of the cases which appear to support the two alternative definitions are, on their facts, not inconsistent with this third definition *e.g.* in *Rice* v. *Connolly, supra*, the police officer may ask questions, but he has no power at law to require any person to answer those questions. In *Davis* v. *Lisle, supra*, the officer may investigate crime, but he has no authority at law to remain on private property as a trespasser in order to make enquiries. In *Ingleton* v. *Dibble, supra,* the officer did have the legal authority to require a specimen of breath, hence an act which prevented the appropriate specimen of breath being given did obstruct the constable in the exercise of that specific statutory power and hence in the execution of his duty.

[62] (1972) 116 S.J. 803; [1972] Crim. L.R. 561.

[63] (1972) 116 S.J. 803.

[64] [1976] 1 W.L.R. 65.

[65] [1980] 3 W.L.R. 283; [1980] 2 All E.R. 753, H.L.

[66] See *Arrowsmith* v.*Jenkins* [1963] 2 Q.B 561 where the defendant's continuation of a public speech in the knowledge that her conduct was causing an obstruction to the highway, was held to be sufficient proof of *mens rea* on the part of the defendant.

[67] [1976] 3 All E.R. 794.

[68] [1980] Crim. L.R. 584.

[69] [1976] A.C. 182.

[70] [1981] 3 All E.R. 878, H.L. The case also turned on a different point altogether, namely that even if the person restraining the accused had not been a constable, that person would still have been acting within the citizen's power and duty to prevent a breach of the peace or to prevent crime under s.3 of the Criminal Law Act 1967, and the accused's resistance to the detention would still have been unlawful. However, this misses the point, which is that even if the accused's conduct, if directed at a citizen, remained unlawful, it would not be an assault upon a constable in the execution of his duty, but merely a common assault. Their Lordships appear to have confused the issues of *mens rea* and *actus reus*, and to

have confused two distinct offences. But see *McBride* v. *Turnock* [1964] Crim. L.R. 456, which suggests that it is necessary to distinguish assault cases from obstruction cases on the issue of *mens rea*.

[71] [1980] Crim. L.R. 584.

[72] For exceptions, see Road Traffic Act 1972, ss.8 and 159.

[73] There is considerable doubt as to this defence in charges of assault; see *McBride* v. *Turnock* [1964] Crim. L.R. 456. Smith & Hogan, *Criminal Law* (4th ed.) p.364.

[74] [1982] Crim. L.R. 184 (decided in November 1981).

[75] The Times Law Report, March 3, 1982.

[76] [1982] Crim. L.R. 184.

Namibia and Zimbabwe: Decolonisation and the Rule of International Law

R.H.F. AUSTIN

Introduction: The United Nations' role in decolonisation

The relatively peaceful transformation of the vast European empires in Africa, Asia and the Caribbean into dozens of independent states has been one of the major successes of the international community since the ending of World War II. The legal and institutional framework for this task is the United Nations Charter and the norms evolved by the major organs of the United Nations—the General Assembly and the Security Council. During the 40 odd years of this process a significant body of international law has developed, which is of special and symbolic significance to the majority of United Nations member States whose very being was a part of this law. That law has also served the older and bigger member States, providing important guidelines towards decolonisation based on new legal concepts and perspectives which reduced the risks that this historic change in political, economic and social relations would not (in a dangerously bi-polarised world) be accompanied by major wars. The case of the decolonising process in Vietnam, which proceeded largely outside this United Nations framework might be regarded as the exception which proved the great value of this body of rules.

In fact this body of law and practice on decolonisation has been predominantly an African phenomenon, and the harmonious development of the norms involved has owed much to the constructive counter-point achieved between the United Nations and the Organisation of African States.[1]

The special case of Namibia

By far the most complex and legally interesting of the specific tasks of decolonisation in Africa has been case of Namibia.[2] This territory and its people commenced its unique legal status over sixty years ago, and owes more than most situations in international affairs to law and especially to the law of the United Nations. In a sense it was one of the original legal models for a multi-racial, non-imperial, and peaceful world of States based on the democratic idea of self-determination of peoples. For that reason it is especially remarkable that Namibia remains, in fact, one of the outstanding cases of a dependent people and territory still awaiting self-determination. It is all the more remarkable because this dependent status is maintained by South Africa (the pre-eminent racist State) as a standing and flagrant rejection of self-determination by means of a massive military machine which challenges the legal status of Namibia and resorts to the use of force to resist the United Nations decolonisation norms.

The problems examined

The object of this paper is to seek to expose, examine and explain some of the reasons for this contradictory situation. It also seeks to examine the relationship between the non-liberation of Namibia and the idea of the rule of law in the international system. In particular it is intended to examine the trends in this part of law revealed by the similar problem of the liberation of Zimbabwe, and two important phenomena which have emerged in both cases: the increased tendency to ignore the rules of international law and to resort to, or tolerate, the use of force to undermine the rules: the combined efforts being made to demote (if not to abolish) the role of the United Nations in these, the most difficult and painful cases of the historic conflict between racial paternalism and exploitation, (as colonialism is unambiguously seen by the Third World) and the desire for the achievement of freedom as independent nation States by all colonial peoples. The fact that both these tendencies, have been supported by States whose role in the promotion of the rule of law, and whose condemnation of the use of force, having been their proud boast adds to the interest of the phenomenon.[3] Likewise the contradiction between their long standing condemnation of racism and dictatorship and the "solutions" they now advocate for Namibia is discussed.

I. *THE LEGAL FRAMEWORK FOR THE CONTROL AND ELIMINATION OF COLONIALISM IN NAMIBIA*

Namibia is a poignant example of the complexities and contradictions which typify the grandeur and misery of international law.[4]

On the one hand it may be regarded as an impressive example of the resilience and imagination of international law, and its potential for providing a peaceful solution, within a normative framework, to the most fundamental conflicts of interests. On this view the Mandate System gave legal form, in 1919, to the ideal of self-determination[5] for even the most vulnerable and helpless people, at a time when few existing States would have endorsed it. The preservation, and later within the United Nations, the development of this ideal was a remarkable achievement of idealistic statesmen and lawyers. Thus there evolved a unique international institution which survived the League of Nations under whose protective cloak it was born. As the United Nations and the international community wrestled, in the aftermath of their victory over European racism and fascism, with the embarrassing assertion of similar policies by South Africa, their erstwhile ally, trading partner and, in some cases, kith and kin; the law continued to provide the major basis for the attempt to thrash out the problem, and the legal status of Namibia was further clarified. It would not take the relatively simple path to self-government and independence provided by the Trusteeship system, but would remain subject to the Mandate as modified by the realities of its actual control by a State which largely rejected the idea of governing subject to restraints imposed by international law.[6]

In this development legalism and international institutional sophistication played an unusually large role in preserving "the sacred trust of civilisation" which could be regarded as summing up the principles of non-annexation, government in the interests of the inhabitants, non-militarisation of the territory, and subjection to international administrative and judicial supervision, which were the essence of the Mandate undertaken by South Africa. This tendency, to employ international legal techniques continued, in spite of the remarkably clear proof of the pitfalls of this approach, afforded by the 1966 decision (or non-decision as it may be more accurately described) of the International Court of Justice.[7] To Third World, and especially the African States concerned with this problem, this was the orderly and peaceful means of proceeding. Respect for international law remained high, and the evolving *jus publicum Africanum*[8] provided a clear indication of the way ahead. So, on to the legal stock of the Mandate there was grafted a lush growth of norms and guidelines for the ending of colonialism, racism and the associated threats to peace which the United Nations had been created to eliminate.

From this body of law it followed, as night must the day that, in the face of decades of consistent breaches by South Africa of its obligations towards the mandated territory and its people, the agreement whereby South Africa administered Namibia must be terminated. In due course this legal action was taken by the General Assembly,[9] submitted to and endorsed by the Security Council,[10] and passed on for legal consideration by the International Court of Justice, which held it to be constitutional and effective.[11]

A. *The "Legal Answer": The Grand Design?*

The same enthusiasm for legal forms lead to Namibia having an additional, and again unique legal characteristic: it was made a territory governed directly by the United Nations.[12] The mystery of "World Government" was made real, albeit on a caretaker (and as it turned out) legally fictious basis! The crude, physical alternatives such as the recognition of a government in exile or perhaps an African military expedition to confront and eject the unlawful occupant was not assayed. Those methods would be too reminiscent of that old-fashioned, individualistic and power-centred international law, the law of the powerful. The United Nations' approach may be slow, but it was seen as saving on destruction of lives and property.[13] In essence this was the application of the ideal that the rule of law in the modern world is preferable to the rule of force. Thus the situation was reached in which the law of the United Nations, accepted by the overwhelming majority of its members, stated in clear terms, in essence that:

: the people of Namibia were entitled to self-government and independence,

: they should be allowed to move into that state of freedom after properly supervised elections on the basis of one man, one vote,

: until that time the government of Namibia would be conducted on behalf of its inhabitants by the Council for Namibia for the United Nations,[14]

: South Africa had no legal right to be in Namibia, and must withdraw its administration in favour of the United Nations,

: as long as it remained in control of Namibia, South Africa was unlawfully occupying the territory,

: as a result, all its acts in Namibia, with limited exceptions for humanitarian reasons, were illegal and invalid. This invalidity particularly included acts concerned with the exploitation and extraction of Namibian natural resources,

: South Africa would in consequence be internationally responsible for its illegal actions in relation to Namibia and be required to compensate the new State at independence.

: United Nations member States were obliged to refuse recognition to South Africa's illegal acts *vis à vis* Namibia, and if they insisted on relations, including commercial relations, with the illegal occupant, might also be internationally responsible for injury caused to Namibia.[15]

This was the grand climax of the legal solution of the Namibian problem. It provided a comprehensive code and, via negotiation a formula to end the problem. If it worked, even gradually, it would mark a major victory for the rule of law. The question which must be faced is: was it merely a facade? Were the Statesmen, international civil servants, and especially the lawyers not indulging in an elaborate hoax, to deviate and exhaust the energies of those concerned to end racism and colonialism in Namibia, by building a structure which was no more than a facade?

The answer it seems, must be a qualified—No. Most States did, and still do, accept this formula for solving the Namibian problem, and these include (at least until recently) the five Western Contact States whose potential contribution to a lawful, peaceful solution (by virtue of their especially close relationships with South Africa) is critical. For the same reason it is so important to observe these same States' approach to this, and the similar Zimbabwean problem, during the period since the "legal answer" to Namibia was so cogently (or was it merely glibly?) propounded by the United Nations and its major organs.

Without this massive United Nations legal structure there is no doubt that "the sacred trust of civilisation" would long since have evaporated in the heat of the intense (and traditionally typical) respect for "realism" and "effectiveness" felt by States. This atmosphere would have been all the more overwhelming for such a delicate ideal as the "sacred trust" given the combination of the immense and strategic mineral wealth of Namibia and the military strength and 19th century single-mindedness of South Africa. By now South Africa's occupation would have been elevated by acquiescence and recognition to legitimacy, and Namibia would have become either an integral part of the metropolitan State or one (or more) of a local form of that extraordinary South African neo-colonial invention: the Bantustan. The frustration of that "reality" by the international legal and institutional structure supporting Namibia, if only as an idea, deserves the description "Grand." The question is: has the "reality" been only temporarily frustrated by the law and can the legal design be implemented?

B. *The Factual Problem. The Miserable Achievement?*

1. *South Africa's continued illegal occupation of Namibia*

In spite of the elaborate legal norms and procedures for liberation in Namibia, the territory and its people are effectively governed not by the United Nations Council for Namibia, but as they have been since July 1915 when South African forces defeated the Germans, by Pretoria. The nature of this government reflects the fact that South African rule faces increasing resistance from the inhabitants.[16] By March 1981 the South African Defence Forces had an estimated 1,000,000 troops and paramilitary police in Namibia, providing a remarkable concentration of one South African soldier for every 12 Namibians.[17] This presence is by no means passive, as indicated by the fact that 80 per cent. of the Namibian population are living in martial law areas, and South African defence expenditure in Namibia had grown in 1981 to an estimated 2.8 billion Rand from approximately 0.5 billion Rand in 1976.[18]

This stark contrast between the law and reality is of course not unique to Namibia, in the decentralised international legal system it is common. However, Namibia is in common with others in the field of decolonisation, associated with a level of centralised and organised behaviour by virtue of its being dealt with by United Nations member States on a collegiate basis, through the United Nations. This means that apart from the question—How will South Africa's illegal occupation of Namibia be ended?, there are a range of problems associated with Namibia involving an unusually developed legal content. These problems touch the interests of States, apart from South Africa, including several which are members of the Western Contact Group.

2. *Embarrassing legal questions?*

If the Namibian problem is solved within this unusually intense legal context rather than on some highly political, "practical and negotiated" basis, it would expose several potentially embarrassing issues. These include questions of the potential international responsibility of States which have been associated with the South African armed forces' massive destruction of life and property in Front Line States, particularly Angola. These were attacked because of the material support they give to SWAPO in accordance with their obligations as United Nations members. There is the matter of the individual responsibility of South African statesmen, soldiers and policemen (and mercenary soldiers) for "crimes against peace," "acts of aggression," "crimes against humanity" and simple "war crimes" connected with these actions. Many of these questions and potential answers have been considered over the years by the United Nations and interested non-governmental bodies. The richness of the framework makes it convenient to pose them as legal rather than political questions, though here, as in all wars, the law has an important psychological use for all concerned. The airing of such embarrassing questions in a legal context would be avoided by any government,[19] and even the slightest possibility of such an event makes it all the more understandable that States wishing to maintain their reputation would seek to ensure an entirely "political" solution, or perhaps to change the rules of the game before such a final summing up by reference to the law takes place.

The latter of these two options—rule changing in mid-game—may seem a contradiction or an impossibility to the amateur sportsman, or the private lawyer in a municipal system. Indeed it may be regarded as the very negation of law and the rule of law. The Namibian problem illustrates that in the international system, which is traditionally less organised, less legalistic, more organic in its making, as well as its interpretation of norms, this may still be possible.[20] Its occurrence in relation to Namibia is however, especially important because decolonisation, and this case in particular, had been transferred, to be dealt with in a more orderly legal framework, and out of the rough "wheeler-dealer" world where might, violence and influence, rather than law, have decided the outcome of problems. There is a risk that manipulation of the rules in the Namibian case will result in a loss of faith in the law, and a tendency to rely—even among weaker States upon the "old-fashioned," practical methods, including the use of force.

3. *The use of force to achieve decolonisation*

This tendency was already apparent in the law of decolonisation.[21] As the most recalcitrant champions of racial supremacy and colonialism resorted to increasingly violent means to suppress demands for democratic representation and self-determination, and learned how to maximise their remaining influence with important Western States to prevent the centralised enforcement of decolonisation by the United Nations, so, especially in Africa, the right to resort to the use of force against such regimes was increasingly asserted. Whether this was a good or bad development can be judged in a variety of ways. One of the results, in my view, was to bring super-power politics to the centre of the stage on which decolonisation was being acted out and thus to interconnect (or confuse?) the struggle for self-determination with the conflict between East and West. Given the contradictions inherent in the idea of the capitalist system re-organising, and risking the destruction, of one of its most profitable and politically reliable sectors, (the Southern African white controlled territories), this may have been inevitable. The connection between this development and the pressures on the law examined below is obvious. The use of force in the decolonisation of Portuguese territories resulted in a situation over which Western States, convinced of their natural right to continue to influence affairs in South-Central Africa, found they had little or no control. This may have convinced them of the need to create a situation in which they would have more control, and it is to this end that the modification of the norms for Namibian independence seem to be directed.

C. *Redesigning the Decolonised State*

The creation of an independent sovereign State by a predetermined process is an interesting idea. The assumption is that the new entity will be effectively sovereign and capable of self-determination and not some "clone" incapable of independently deciding its own fate. Yet we know that the new State will operate within and be shaped by practical limitations as well as within the limits of international law. Can this "shaping" be done more effectively, and with less resistance and complaint, during the foetal stage of the State's creation? Is this what Zimbabwean and Namibian independence illustrate? Has international law played a role in this?

Contemplating Namibia, and the recent independence of Zimbabwe, one is acutely aware of the degree to which sovereign independence is fictional. At the same time, the relativity of effective sovereignty is almost too obvious to dwell upon. But it seems worthwhile to investigate the attempts apparently being made by the influential States involved, to adjust the legal framework for independence, and to create a new State which would be both legally and functionally more dependant than the existing colonial entity! This phenomenon has probably always been associated with the creation of new States in practice. But Namibia may represent a new dimension. First there are the methods (including the use of force) to create the necessary pressure on the supporters and beneficiaries of the existing legal formula, to change it and accept a new formula. Second, there is the new formula itself, which in this case has been progressively set out, and in different ways, including a remarkable document sponsored by the Contact Group, and described as a Non-Paper.[22]

1. *Time and the law in Namibia*

In form, the original formula, Security Council Resolution 435, is still the basis for a solution. In practice important changes are being sought, in both the internal arrangement of political and military affairs in Namibia, and in the relationship of Front Line States to the process of achieving independence. Time is of the essence in all respects. Had Resolution 435 been implemented shortly after its adoption the shape of independent Namibia would predictably have been a SWAPO government, committed like other Front Line States to the completion of the task of freeing the black majority in South Africa from *Apartheid* and minority rule. Its delayed implementation provides time for changing the facts[23] and the rules. As General Magnus Malan, the South African Minister of Defence remarked to the United States Assistant Secretary of State, Chester Crocker, "The longer it takes to solve the Namibia question, the less South African presence will be required there. We will reach a stage where internal forces in Namibia can militarily defeat SWAPO."[24] This was one of the facts for the creation of which time was needed. A major fact, externally, was the necessity to force the Front Line States, particularly Angola to stop supporting SWAPO, or at least to reduce its support for SWAPO on the basis of the United Nations formula.

2. *Force and the law in Namibia*

This could only be done by military means because Angola is unique in the region for its economic and political independence of South Africa. The problem was the United Nations condemnation of such pressure as "aggression" and the danger of the imposition of sanctions for such grossly illegal action. The answer lay, as in the past in Southern Africa, in the willingness of the West to restrict the Security Council's response to purely verbal condemnation. Even, as in the case of the South African invasion of Angola in August 1981, this minimal judgment of the use of force could be effectively frozen (and the action legitimised?) by the United States' veto of the draft Security Council resolution which would have condemned the action as aggression, though it refrained from calling for sanctions against South Africa.[25]

The effective suspension of the rules prohibiting the use of force by South Africa in Namibia and Angola set the scene for creating a state of mind among the Front Line States in which the basic rules for independence might be changed.[26] Such a scenario might seem too fantastic to be real. But to statesmen and lawyers concerned with the problem there are many questions to be answered. Would States which had themselves helped create and elaborate a legal system for decolonisation, and which still formally support it, undermine it? Is it possible to merely reverse the rules? Is the tolerance of South Africa's overt use of force sensible behaviour by States prepared to risk a great deal unilaterally to condemn and sanction both its external use (by the Soviet Union in Afghanistan) and its internal application (by the martial law authorities in Poland)? Could the United Nations which had so central a role in protecting Namibian self-determination be excluded from its predominant position? Could arrangements and undertakings be made to modify the United Nations Charter and perhaps make Namibia more vulnerable than ever before to the strength of the neighbour which had dominated it for over sixty years? Surely an impossible task? The ground rules are too well known, no State with a respect for the rule of law would attempt it. Yet a model of sorts, for such a dramatic manipulation of the rules already exists. It is the case of Zimbabwe, and a brief consideration of the final stages of that State's progress to independence is instructive and relevant to the Namibian saga.

II. *REDESIGNING DECOLONISATION AND REDUCING THE ROLE OF THE UNITED NATIONS*

A. *The relevance of Zimbabwe and Lancaster House*

Important changes in the rules for the decolonisation of Rhodesia and the creation of Zimbabwe emerged in the preparations for the Lancaster House conference to end the war of national liberation there.

1. *The original model for the decolonisation of Zimbabwe*

(a) *The legitimacy of the National Liberation Movement.* The basic situation by mid-1979 was that by the combined processes of the United Nations and the relevant regional organisation, the O.A.U., the Patriotic Front had gained the status of the "authentic representative" of the disenfranchised majority. (As SWAPO does in relation to Namibia.)[27] In this capacity they enjoyed United Nations support for both their diplomatic and military efforts to achieve majority rule. Britain in relation to Rhodesia retained its legal, but largely passive, responsibility for the territory. No exact equivalent to it exists in Namibia, although the United Nations Council for Namibia may be seen as the formal sovereign of that territory.

The opponents of the Patriotic Front, whether the Smith or the Smith-Muzorewa authorities were regarded as having no legal right to govern or represent the territory, nor to use force in defence of their usurped authority against either the Patriotic Front nor United Nations Member States assisting it. (The South Africans and their protegees in Namibia, though for different reasons, are in a similar situation in Namibia).

To this extent, the United Nations guided by the *Jus Publicum Africanum* proclaimed by the O.A.U., had judged the Patriotic Front (as it does SWAPO in Namibia) to have aims consistent with those of the Charter and the United Nations' interpretation thereof. The incumbent regime (as South Africa in Namibia), was seen as being opposed to the United Nations' objectives.

(b) *The electoral basis for independence.* However, as regards the final achievement of independence the United Nations scheme required that the choice of the new State's first government be made by neither the O.A.U. nor the United Nations, but by the people of the territory. Thus the rule to be applied was that a free, properly supervised election on the basis of one man, one vote be held in conditions of peace and order. This would preclude the automatic elevation of Liberation Movements to government, and preserve the principle of self-determination. It was very much in line with the ideals proclaimed by the influential Western States.[28]

2. *Techniques for the evasion of the United Nations' model*

The opponents of the United Nations inside both Rhodesia and Namibia, once it appeared to them that decolonisation was a serious probability, sought means of evading it or alternatively of providing an imitation of it which would be acceptable to the international community, or at least to the Western States whose support they needed. Their methods, like those of the Liberation Movements' combined internal political efforts, diplomacy and the use of force (both internal and external).

POLITICAL. The political methods ranged from the creation of Bantustans (alleged to be perfect expressions of self-determination by separated black ethnic groups) to the establishment of multi-racial governments combined with some form of popular election by black voters. Liberation Movements were identified as "Communist" and the hope was that this, combined with a flavouring of election and black participation, would satisfy at least the Western States' interpretation of the decolonisation norm. Ideally they hoped for full acceptance by the international community and membership of the United Nations for their creations.

MILITARY. In addition Rhodesia resorted to the use of armed force against Front Line States supporting the Liberation Movement. It was initially presented under the legally false but cleverly chosen title of "hot pursuit" of Patriotic Front combatants into these States. As it became clear that major United Nations action in response to this would be suppressed by the friendly veto of some Western States, and that effective strikes could be carried out against economic and transport targets in the Front Line States (dramatically escalating the cost of their support of the Patriotic Front) the real objective of these attacks became more obvious. Indeed the attraction of this technique as a means of pressuring these States to persuade the Patriotic Front to end the war and subject itself to almost any form of settlement was so great that it was used (virtually as a negotiating method) by the Rhodesians (and indirectly exploited by the United Kingdom) during the Lancaster House Conference itself.[29] The prospect of being refused bases in the Front Line States, combined with its conviction that it could win at the polls, led the Patriotic Front (in spite of its dissatisfaction with the ceasefire arrangements, the arrangements for the supervision of the elections and especially the constitution which had been decided—largely by Britain—for the new State), to acquiesce in the settlement plan.

EXCLUSION OF THE UNITED NATIONS. The extraordinary achievement of the Rhodesians, combined with South Africa and the United Kingdom was the total exclusion of the United Nations (the authority which had kept open the possibility of Zimbabwean independence and whose members had designed the norms by reference to which the decolonisation was to be achieved) from the final stages of the process: the conference, the ceasefire and the elections.[30] The United Nations was regarded by the Rhodesian authorities, as it is by South Africa in Namibia, as totally incapable of even-handedness in these areas, and they insisted upon its exclusion. This fear, and more particularly that the involvement of the United Nations would preclude the possibility of a "moderate" black government in Zimbabwe was apparently shared by Britain, which took considerable pains to persuade the Commonwealth, and especially the African members thereof, that the United Nations was unsuited to the task.

THE COMMONWEALTH ALTERNATIVE. The idea that the Commonwealth was the appropriate agency no doubt helped those Commonwealth States who did not share fears of the election of a less than "moderate" government. This imaginative revival of the Commonwealth created a critically important lobby in the O.A.U. and thus the United Nations, for the plan to exclude it from the final stages of Zimbabwe's decolonisation. As a result efforts during the Lancaster House conference by the Patriotic Front to retain some United Nations role in the ceasefire and election process were totally unsuccessful, both in London and in New York. The formula had been dramatically changed.[31]

THE SUCCESS OF THE LANCASTER HOUSE FORMULA. In essence then, the expectation of a United Nations role in this process was totally and dramatically reversed by Britain in the final stages of the Rhodesian problem. In essence the shape of the solution and the rules by which it would run were agreed at the Lusaka Conference of Commonwealth Heads of State. The *substance* of the rules however; the holding of one man, one vote elections, the presence of independent observers and the attempts to ensure a ceasefire and peaceful conditions for the elections, were in line with United Nations' expectations and norms. The major role of African Commonwealth States no doubt accounted for this, as did the intervention of the Commonwealth Secretariat which was particularly insistent upon the presence in Rhodesia of a large and independent body of international observers during the election.[32]

The important substantial rule change which was secured at Lusaka (applicable for at least 10 years to post-independence Zimbabwe), and which would have been resisted easily in the United Nations context, is the disproportionate, and purely racially determined, representation of the white minority.

The factor perceived at that time (1979) as most likely to distort the process (by ensuring election of a government which was less than friendly to the West) namely the physical involvement of the United Nations was totally excluded by the Lancaster House formula. In this sense, the pressures created by the Rhodesians' attacks on the economic infra-structure of both Zambia and Mozambique were effective in persuading these States that a less than perfect solution was preferable to continued war and destruction. Lancaster House achieved a great deal for its architects in Zimbabwe, apart from the peace it achieved for the people of Zimbabwe. The potential victory, by armed revolution, of the Marxist-Leninist Liberation Movement was effectively aborted. The economic structure of Rhodesia was preserved almost intact for Zimbabwe.

3. *The critical omission of Lancaster House: misjudging the potency of the United Nations' electoral formula*

Many different techniques to avoid "unrestrained" self-determination and decolonisation were experimented with in Rhodesia,[32] and many lessons learned in the course of the 14 years of the Smith regime.[33] But perhaps the most important lesson was only learned *after* the Lancaster House Conference and the election. This was that the United Nations' *formula* for achieving self-determination, the holding of one man, one vote elections was more critical to ensuring an accurate reflection of the will of the majority than the *presence* of the United Nations itself. Thus, in spite of the eleventh-hour changes at Lancaster House, the election resulted in an overwhelming victory for the parties of the Liberation Movement. The Prime Minister and the governing party turned out to be the men who until the day of the results were reviled and feared by white Rhodesians and Whitehall alike as "Marxist Terrorists." The use of the United Nations formula had successfully avoided armed revolutionary change on the Angolan-Mazambiquean model, but had failed to produce a "moderate" government, in spite of the exclusion of the United Nations itself from the ceasefire and the election. Pretoria's pause for thought over Namibian independence in the wake of the Zimbabwean election may have been shared in Western capitals. Could they create rules to ensure a more dependent Namibia?

An African perspective: Zimbabwe as a constructive example

On the other hand, African statesmen have long urged that African National Liberation Movements, whoever they receive military or other support from, and whatever ideological label is attached to or adopted by them, are autonomous entities entitled to their sovereign choice of friends, methods or ideologies in the achievement of the supreme necessity: national self-determination.

They should not be automatically regarded as unfriendly by Western States merely because they associated with Socialist States or were described as Communists by their opponents or as Marxists by themselves. That after all is the essence of sovereignty and co-existence. They are no more necessarily "communists" and perpetual enemies because of their wartime alliances, than Western States are necessarily so by reason of their World War II alliance with the Soviet Union. The record of the new State is the proper basis to judge.[34] The ability of Zimbabwe so far to balance its ideals against the realities of the region suggests that if the United Nations formula for independence is applied in Namibia and SWAPO, as is expected at present by all (including South Africa), becomes the government, it too would be capable of balancing ideals with realities and govern in the interests of its people. The United Nations formula achieved self-determination in Zimbabwe, in spite of the distortions of Lancaster House. Namibia is *a fortiori* the next appropriate case to take the final steps to independence on that basis.

III. *NAMIBIAN DEVELOPMENTS*

Events in relation to Namibia since Zimbabwe's independence in April 1980 do not suggest that the lesson drawn by either South Africa or the Western States is such a positive one. These include the escalation of the use of force by South Africa, and Western (especially the United States) responses thereto, and the attempt by Western States to change both the legal basis upon which Namibian independence will be achieved and the international legal environment in which the future State will have to survive.

A. *Military*

1. *The use of force inside Namibia*

South Africa's continued presence in Namibia is based on force. It occupies the territory by virtue of its military strength, and its use against the population, 80 per cent. of whom live under martial law.

This occupation has no legal basis, and has been characterised as illegal. It is based on armed force but is not, on the face of it, belligerent occupation, which would make it legitimate and temporary. South Africa gives no indication of limiting its use of force in Namibia, indeed indications suggest that, as in the case of Rhodesia (but with greater military resources) it will use force to coerce its opponents into accepting its preferred solution. Far from dismantling its forces to pave the way for a negotiated settlement South Africa has increased its military presence.

2. *The Use of Force against Front Line States*

Here again the pattern is that established by the Rhodesian action against the Front Line States, but more so.[35] South Africa has in all but name been fighting a war against Angola since 1975. It also gives military support to the UNITA, the insurgent military opponents of the MPLA government of Angola. In addition it has made attacks on Zambia and Botswana.

The war against Angola was quiescent after the South African invasion was repulsed in 1976. It was intesified in mid-1979 since when well over 50 per cent. of the known attacks on Angolan targets have been made. Damage to Angola over the years to mid-1981 amounted to over U.S.$7 billion. By the end of 1980 South African forces had killed 1,800 Angolans, mainly civilians, and wounded 3,000. This was apart from major attacks and casualties inflicted upon Namibian refugees and SWAPO bases in Angola.[36]

South Africa has made it clear that it is prepared to conduct its war against SWAPO inside Angola. By its actions, and its choice of targets in Angola, it has demonstrated that it regards the technique of destroying the Liberation Movement by attacking its supporting Front Line States as the most effective and, to it, the most acceptable means of ensuring that the decolonisation process (particularly its furtherance by the military action of PLAN (the armed wing of SWAPO) is halted. More important perhaps for the law on this topic, has been the paralysis of the Security Council's role as the fortifier of the rule prohibiting such South African military action. The Security Council has never been prepared to take "enforcement action" under Chapter VII against this "aggression" but has consistently maintained at least the normative defence of Namibian self-determination. The United States veto suspended even this support.

B. *Diplomatic*

1. *Delaying the Implementation of Security Council Resolution 435*

South Africa's tactics indicate that military pressure on the Front Line States will be maintained until they are prepared to abandon SWAPO and accept almost any solution to end the war. It is no surprise in view of the dividends it paid in the case of Zimbabwe.

The most intensive action of this war has been in fact in the period after the Comprehensive United Nations plan for the settlement of Namibia's independence was accepted, by all parties including South Africa, and adopted in the form of Security Council Resolution 435 in September 1978. South Africa's refusal to implement the plan, combined with the military action and the Security Council's inability to act to stop attacks (even when it has condemned them) has already partly achieved the desired effects. By the time of the abortive Geneva Pre-Implementation meeting in January 1981, South Africa had demanded and obtained important changes of the United Nations plan, including the total exclusion of SWAPO forces from the proposed Demilitarised Zone and the concentration of the bulk of the United Nations military personnel in that zone.

South Africa has repeatedly delayed implementation, while

SWAPO has consistently sought the early implementation of the plan. The general reaction of the critical Western States has been to offer further negotiations, combined occasionally with veiled threats to South Africa that they must not delay indefinitely. Nevertheless, the indications are that South African delays will continue to be tolerated.

But the most alarming reaction by the Western States, which suggests that the real solution to their minds is a more substantial modification of the formula to meet South Africa's desire for, in effect, a perpetually dependent Namibia, plus a guarantee from Namibia not to support the claim of the black majority in South Africa to self-determination, nor to support the war of national liberation already being waged for this cause inside South Africa. That this may be the Contact Group's new approach appears from an ingeniously described "non-paper" (set out in full below) left by them with the various interested States and organisations involved in the search for a Namibian solution. Similar indications may be found in their outline of the principle for a constitution for an independent Namibia.

The Non-Paper on Namibia

"The attached is an untitled non-paper which the Contact Group has left with your Organisation during its mission to Africa.

The five are not seeking formal replies to this suggestion in Phase 1. The suggestion, if agreed to by the parties, would only be implemented at a later stage in the process.

The Contact Group believes parties may wish to consider voluntary undertakings to ensure the peaceful future and genuine independence of Namibia, undertakings which would also contribute to stability of the region.

Namibia and its neighbours might thus wish to provide reciprocal assurances of non-interference and non-resort to force. These could be included in a declaration which would reaffirm elements in the UN Charter and the Declaration on Friendly Relations between States (UNGA Resolution 2625). The attached is a possible text of such a declaration.

The five are not seeking to impose their views but would be ready to help the parties come to an agreement.

One way of pursuing this might be for the parties to inform the Secretary-General of their agreement/commitment to the proposed declaration and their statements could then be incorporated in a report endorsed by the Security Council; but there may be other ways of proceeding.

If international recognition of the following principles were desired they could be embodied in reciprocal undertakings among the parties concerned. These principles could be formalised later in a form to be determined, possibly in the context of an endorsement by the Security Council.

1. All States will respect the independence, the sovereignty, the territorial integrity and the policy of non-alignment of Namibia, in particular by refraining from the unlawful threat or use of force, or from any other act inconsistent with the purposes of the United Nations. All States are urged to manifest their will to respect these principles.

2. The State of Namibia will live in peace and develop friendly relations with other States in accordance with international law. It will therefore not permit organised activities within its territory directed towards the commission of any act of aggression or any other act which involves an unlawful threat or use of force against any other State. The neighbouring States will follow the same principle regarding their relations with Namibia.

3. The State of Namibia will not permit within its territory the installation of foreign military bases or the presence of foreign military units except by virtue of a decision of the UN Security Council or in accordance with the exercise of its rights of self-defence if an armed attack occurs against it, as provided for in the Charter of the United Nations."

IV. *THE NON-SOLUTION OF COLONIALISM IN NAMIBIA AND THE NON-PAPER OF OCTOBER 26, 1981*

A. *The Form and Formalities of the Non-Paper*

The non-paper is presented very much as an idea, rather than a proposal. It is worth considering both its substance and form. It is an interesting technique to achieve legal changes in the short term (if it were actually accepted) or in the long term (by establishing it as a new negotiating position and a measure against which some future compromise formula might be reached). It is presented against a background of the continued formal acceptance by the Contact Group that it is the four-year-old Resolution 435 which is still the formula for independence.

Its preliminary paragraphs, preceding the proposed declaration of principles, seem to suggest a legally binding undertaking between the parties involved in Namibia and in the region. This includes SWAPO, as (like the constitutional proposals) they have been put to SWAPO, but the actual identity of the Namibian participant is merely described as "Namibia," as if it were a State. The implication is that the declaration, if made, would be binding upon the newly independent Namibian State. Is it a treaty?[37]

Those involved in the declaration do not include the Contact Group States, and are restricted to "Namibia and its neighbours." The object appears to be to obtain undertakings from SWAPO of considerable significance to the future Namibia, and to seek to make them enforceable.

The declaration appears to be intended to become, via its notification to the Secretary-General of the United Nations a part of the formal plans of that organisation for the Namibian settlement. Yet it will not be a Security Council resolution, but by being endorsed by the Security Council it would become a part of the basic United Nations law, making significant changes to the terms of Resolution 435, the present "charter" for Namibian independence.[38]

B. *The Substance of the Non-Paper*

1. *Namibian integrity and sovereignty*

The first paragraph appears to provide no extra rights or duties beyond those Namibia would enjoy as a party to the United Nations Charter. The declaration gives the misleading impression that it will achieve an obligation upon "all States" to respect Namibian sovereignty etc. Since they will not be parties, "all States" are not bound by this undertaking, which suggests that it is pretentious and probably bogus. Its only real value might lie in South Africa's participation and thus its reaffirmation of the duty not to use force against Namibia. Given the existing fact that the Namibian problem stems from South African force being used in and against Namibia, the proposal of the declaration for the future, rather than the Contact Groups insistence upon its immediate application and compliance therewith by South Africa, suggests an ulterior motive for the proposal.

It is also clear that the Contact Group members, not being parties, are not offering themselves as guarantors of Namibian independence.[39]

The reference to territorial integrity raises the problem that South Africa insists that the sole effective seaport of Namibia (Walvis Bay) will not become independent when the territory does, but will remain South African.[40] This position contradicts the United Nations position on Walvis Bay, and it is unfortunate that the declaration does not endorse that position, and make it clear that Namibian territorial integrity (including Walvis Bay) must be respected from the start.

The reference to the non-alignment of Namibia is vague and undefined. It may imply an obligation on Namibia not to associate with either power bloc in its future political or economic relations, which could be a considerable limitation.[41] It is either so vague as to be meaningless, or it is an unreasonable undertaking to seek to impose before independence in this vague form.

2. *The restriction of organised aggressive activities in Namibia*

On the face of it this again restates the situation under the Charter and general international law. In the context of Southern Africa however, it is probably intended to prohibit support for or tolerance of the activities of South African national liberation movements by Namibia.

The reciprocal obligation on neighbouring States contained in the final sentence may suggest that a breach by Namibia would entitle a neighbour (South Africa is the most obvious candidate) to act by using force to suppress such a breach. This is ambiguous, and it would appear to be contrary to existing international law to purport to issue a licence to attack on this basis. In any case the action be "legislated" against, by a South African liberation movement, may be regarded, because it is aimed at the *Apartheid* system (which is characterised as a crime under international law), as lawful and not aggressive. If that is the intention, the provision should make it clear. As it stands it may "legitimise," military action by South Africa which would otherwise be clearly illegal. The outcome could be the absurd situation in which a post-independence South African occupation of Namibia could be legal, when its present occupation is not.

3. *The restriction of foreign bases in Namibia*

Experience in the region suggests that any African State which is a member of the O.A.U. and at the same time a neighbour of South Africa, may need foreign military help to avoid South African action against such State's support for national liberation in South Africa. Without such help independent Namibia would have little choice but to do as it is required by South Africa and in practice to play down its obligations on African liberation under the O.A.U. Charter. There is no comfort to be gained in this regard by the exception for units present as a result of a Security Council decision. The veto of Western States is unlikely to allow a United Nations (much less O.A.U.) action against South Africa to be launched from Namibia. The provision would seem to be an attempt to create a conflict of obligations of an O.A.U. member, and to seek to frustrate the likely operation of the *jus publicum Africanum* in the field of liberation.

There is however, the fact that by virtue of Security Council Resolution 432 (1978), South Africa, if it remains in Walvis Bay and is occupying Namibian soil, can be regarded as a legitimate target of an operation by Namibia (with foreign aid) to seeking to enforce that decision (if such it is) of the Security Council.

It is arguable that the decision must be one taken under Chapter VII and involving United Nations enforcement "action." It seems unlikely that such freedom to use force assisted by foreign forces was intended by the Contact Group, and it is another indication of the dangerously vague nature of this declaration.

The overall danger of the declaration is that it might be used by the only State in the region capable of the effective use of force, namely South Africa, to disguise action against Namibia with an spurious "legal" cloak. A similar danger is inherent in the other major proposal of the Contact Group—the principles of the proposed constitution for Namibia.

V. *THE CONSTITUTION PROPOSED FOR IMPOSITION UPON NAMIBIA*

The following is the full text of the revised Western proposals for the constitution made on December 17, 1981.

> "Principles concerning the Constituent Assembly and the constitution for an independent Namibia.
>
> A. Constituent Assembly
>
> 1. In accordance with U.N.S.C.R. 435 (United Nations Security Council Resolution 435), elections will be held to select a Constituent Assembly which will adopt a Constitution for an independent Namibia. The Constitution will determine the organisation and powers of all levels of government. Every adult Namibian will be eligible, without discrimination or fear of intimidation from any source, to vote, campaign and stand for ballot, with provisions made for those who cannot read or write. The date for the beginning of the electoral campaign, the date of elections and the electoral system, the preparation of the voters rolls and other aspects of the electoral procedures will be promptly decided upon so as to give all political parties and interested persons, without

regard of their political views, a full and fair opportunity to organise and participate in the electoral process.

Full freedom of speech, assembly, movement and press shall be guaranteed. The electoral system will seek to ensure fair representation in the Constituent Assembly to political parties which gain substantial support in the election. To this end, half the members of the Constituent Assembly will be elected on a national basis by proportional representation and half on the basis of single member constituencies. These constituencies will be de-limited so that they have as nearly equal a number of inhabitants as may be reasonably practicable.

2. The Constituent Assembly will formulate the Constitution for an independent Namibia in accordance with the principles in Part B below and will adopt the Constitution as a whole by a two-thirds majority of its total membership.

B. Principles for a Constitution for an independent Namibia

1. Namibia will be a unitary, sovereign and democratic State.

2. The Constitution will be the supreme law of the state. It may be amended only by a designated process involving the legislature and/or the votes cast in a popular referendum.

3. The Constitution will determine the organisation and powers of all levels of government. It will provide for a system of government with three branches: an elected executive branch which will be responsible to the legislative branch, a legislative branch to be elected by universal and equal suffrage which will be responsible for the passage of all laws: and an independent judicial branch which will be responsible for the interpretation of the constitution and for ensuring its supremacy and the authority of the law. The executive and legislative branches will be constituted by periodic and genuine elections which will be held by secret vote.

4. The electoral system will be consistent with the principles in A1. above.

5. There will be a declaration of fundamental rights, which will include the rights to life, personal liberty and freedom of movement, to freedom of conscience, to freedom of expression, including freedom of speech and a free press: to freedom of assembly and association, including political parties and trade unions: to due process and equality before the law, to protection from arbitrary deprivation of private property, without just compensation, and to freedom from racial,

ethnic, religious or sexual discrimination. The declaration of rights will be consistent with the provisions of the Universal Declaration of Human Rights. Aggrieved individuals will be entitled to have the courts adjudicate and enforce these rights.

6. It will be forbidden to create criminal offences with retrospective effect, or to provide for increased penalties with retrospective effect.

7. Provision will be made for the balanced structuring of the public service, the police service, and the defence services and for equal access by all to recruitment to these services. The fair administration of personnel policy in relation to these services will be ensured by appropriate independent bodies.

8. Provision will be made for the establishment of elected councils for local and/or regional administration."

A Negation of a Fundamental Aspect of the Right of Self-Determination

In late 1981 it emerged that the Western Contact Group favoured another important modification of the United Nations formula for Namibian independence. The original scheme assumed that a sovereign elected Constituent Assembly would produce the independence constitution of Namibia. Given the general expectation of an overwhelming SWAPO victory, this would produce a predictably unsatisfactory Constitution as seen by South Africa and its associates. An answer, not as complete as the Lancaster House version, but better than allowing Namibians total freedom to decide their own fate, was to set down the basic principles of the Constitution and obtain the agreement thereto of all concerned during these final stages, when South African room for military and diplomatic pressure, is greatest.

This in effect is what has been done in Namibia. The Principles would in most respects be acceptable to the parties seeking decolonisation:

— that Namibia be a unitary sovereign State:

— that the Constitution be sovereign and not freely amendable;

— that there be separation of powers of the three branches of government, and that it be based upon universal suffrage exercised at periodic elections;

— that there be a judicially enforceable Bill of Rights based on the United Nations Universal Declaration;

— that there should be an independent body to control public service recruitment, and that public institutions be open to all without discrimination;

— and, that there should be an elected local and regional administration.

But, apart from the irritating irony that these principles are in part the result of the insistence of South Africa (which will accept no similar restrictions upon its freedom to govern South Africa in contradiction of United Nations Human Rights standards), they contain the seeds of significant changes to the original United Nations' formula. These include the proposal that both the Constituent Assembly and the eventual government of Namibia be elected in part (50 per cent.) by a nationally based system of proportional representation. This may be intended to avoid an overwhelming victory for SWAPO, which favours the traditional Westminster model. In the first Zimbabwean elections the British insisted upon national proportional representation, which though it preserved a small representation by black supporters of the settler government, did not prevent a clear victory by the Liberation Movement parties. Lancaster House (reflecting the comparative weakness of the international status of both the United Nations and the Liberation Movements in Zimbabwe, compared with the clear international status achieved by Namibia and SWAPO) also imposed the additional colonial remnant of racial representation of the white community in the National Assembly.

There is specific provision for the protection of private property on the basis of "just compensation" to be paid in the event of its "arbitrary deprivation." The model of the United Nations Universal Declaration is chosen, rather than that of the 1966 United Nations Covenant on Political and Civil Rights, which does not include this protection. Again this is probably unexceptionable, as SWAPO has frequently indicated its acceptance of the principle, but it reflects the special interest which South Africa and the Western States have in investments in Namibia. What is more significant is that it makes no explicit reference to potential conflicts between this provision and the right of Namibia to expropriate illegal investments and unlawfully transferred property, done since the South African presence in Namibia became illegal. Is the implication that this, along with other awkward legal questions are intended to be "reconciled" away in the euphoria of Namibia's long delayed independence, or that the constitution is intended to override established international norms?

There is also a noteworthy provision that the future public service will have a "balanced structuring." This reminder of the

European system for the protection of minorities between the wars is interesting, and may indicate a growing, as yet undeclared, desire for more specific provision of minority protection in Namibia. As it stands it may be uncontroversial, but there is a long standing suspicion in Africa of the desire of Western States to ensure minority rights, given their tolerance of the denial of rights to the majorities in former colonial territories, and in South Africa today.

CONCLUSION

The management of the decolonisation of Namibia, like Zimbabwe, demonstrates the considerable potential of international law for achieving the solution of major problems within the international system. However, it also raises the question of the way in which the norms involved are used or manipulated and the consequential results for the credibility of international law and consequently its capacity to rule the behaviour of its subjects.

Is the fact that Namibia, which has been so thoroughly *legally* prepared, for independence, is now in fact being condemned to snatch its freedom from the flames of an escalating international armed conflict not a fundamental denial of the rule of international law in this field? Or does the persistence of legal discussion in these circumstances confirm the resilience and importance of law even in the midst of such destructive activities? Is the last minute manipulation of the rules in Namibia a threat to the role of international law and its credible operation, or proof that international law (in spite of lawyers' attempts to straitjacket it) is still as flexible as is necessary to meet the demands of contemporary international affairs? Even if the most positive answer is given to these questions, many States will only be encouraged to accept the rule of law if powerful States, which often preach that ideal in international affairs, are prepared in practice to treat international law as more than mere expressions of policy which can be arbitrarily changed. This is the test in Namibia.

Notes

[1] This is true of both the norms establishing the right to self-determination and independence in this region, and the norms establishing the methods, both peaceful and military, to implement that right. See R. Higgins, *The Development of International Law Through the Political Organs of the United Nations*; (1963) J. Dugard, The O.A.U. and Colonialism, *I.C.L.Q.* (1967); The *ius ad bellum* and the *ius in bello*, 93 *S.A.L.J.* (1976) 144, N. Ronzitti, Resort to Force in Wars of National Liberation, in A. Cassese (ed.) *Current Problems of International Law*

(1975) 319 *et seq.*; C. Theodorapoulos, Support for SWAPO's War of Liberation, 26 *Africa Today* 1979.

[2] See J. Dugard, *The South West Africa/Namibia Dispute* (1973) S. Slonim, *South West Africa and the United Nations* 1973. In this paper the territory will be referred to as Namibia, the United Nations title given to the territory in 1968 in General Assembly Resolution 2372 (XXII).

[3] The United States of America in particular has made dramatic contributions in the past to these ideals. In relation to Southern African decolonisation, and especially Namibia, it has now almost entirely reversed its role to become in effect South Africa's most important ally. The other members of the Western Contact Group make equally odd supporters of *Apartheid*. It is the thesis of this paper that that, in substance, is the outcome of their recent role in the attempt to secure the legal solution of the Namibian problem.

[4] See G. Schwarzenberger, The Misery and Grandeur of International Law, 18 *C.L.P.* (1964), p.284. In this, his inaugural lecture, Schwarzenberger used contemporary and controversial issues, including *Apartheid*, to test the working of principles of international law concerning active and peaceful co-existence. To guard against the danger of hidden partiality he urged the need for the teacher to articulate his *a priori* assumptions. Agreeing with this admission of the existence of bias, I must make it clear that my own perspective of international law is based *inter alia* on my conviction as an international lawyer from Africa, that it must be applied and studied with a sensitivity to its vital role to develop and preserve peace with humanity in Africa and elsewhere.

[5] Albeit in a limited form, it nevertheless spoke of "peoples not *yet* able to stand by themselves." (Italics added) Article 22 of the League Covenant.

[6] Several land-marks in this process must be noted. The judicial contributions: The Advisory Opinion on the *International Status of South-West Africa* 1950 I.C.J. Reports, 128, which confirmed the continued existence and binding nature of the Mandate upon S. Africa, and the right of the U.N. to supervise this, but rejected the idea that S. Africa must subject it to the Trusteeship system. The Advisory Opinion on *Voting Procedure* [1955] I.C.J. Reports, 67, and on the *Admissibility of Hearings of Petitioners* [1956] I.C.J. Reports, 23. The *Preliminary Objections* and *merits* of the contentious cases brought by Ethiopia and Liberia against S. Africa, *South West Africa Cases*, [1962] I.C.J. Reports, 319 and [1966] I.C.J. Reports, 6. See Bin Cheng, The 1966 South-West Africa Judgement of the World Court, 20 *C.L.P.* (1967), 181, J. Dugard *op. cit.*, Chapters 6, 7 and 8. The Advisory Opinion on the *Legal Consequences for States of the Continued Presence of South Africa in Namibia (South West Africa) notwithstanding Security Council Resolution 276* (1970). 1971 I.C.J. Reports 16. See J. Dugard, Namibia: the Courts Opinion, South Africa's Response, and the Prospects for the Future 11 Columbia Jnl. of Transnatl. Law 1972, p.14; R. Higgins, The Advisory Opinion on Namibia: Which Resolutions are Binding under Article 25 of the Charter? (1972) 21 I.C.L.Q. p.270; and E. Landis, Namibia: The Beginning of Disengagement, 2 *Studies in Race and Nations* (1970–71) no.1, p.1. There is a vast amount of literature on the subject, which is thoroughly surveyed (to 1973) in Dugard's book, where, *op. cit.* p.566; U.N. Resolutions of both the General Assembly and Security Council are also catalogued.

[7] See Bin Cheng, *op. cit.*

[8] This term, used by Professor Konrad Ginther of the University of Graz, identifies the potential role of regional international organisations, co-operating with the U.N., for developing and clarifying norms of special significance within the region. The O.A.U. Charter and its work must be understood if, for example, the law relating to decolonisation in Africa is to be seen as an integral part of the universal system rather than an eccentric code adopted by some States in breach of

International law and the U.N. Charter.

[9] G.A. Resol. 2145 XXII, Oct. 1966. S. Africa maintained this action was illegal, while France, Portugal and the U.K. (none of whom voted for the Resolution), also expressed doubts as to its legality.

[10] S.C. Resol. 264 (1969), passed by 13 votes to none, with France and the U.K. abstaining.

[11] [1971] I.C.J. Reports, 16 at p.58.

[12] G.A. Resol. 2248 (S–V) 1967.

[13] In view of the asymmetry of the military and economic strength of African States and S. Africa, it was also clear that (unless there was great power intervention) there was no alternative. The law provided a sense that something was being done, as indeed *in law* there was. Did it however create expectations the disappointment of which would destroy the faith of these States in the law? In this regard the, even minimal, approval or acquiescence in this legal approach by Western States is relevant when judging their behaviour in the recent stages of the problem.

[14] Decree No. 1 of the Council for Namibia, and G.A. Resol. 1514 XV 1960. The U.K. has taken the view that the Decree is without legal validity. See H.C. Debates, 4 Aug. 1976, and H.G. Schermers, The Namibian Decree in National Courts (1977) 26 I.C.L.Q. Nevertheless even the U.K. acts in a manner suggesting that it accepts the Namibian claim to independence and the legitimacy of the U.N. role therein.

[15] See the 1971 Advisory Opinion and S.C. Resol. 301 (1971) in which the S.C. "adopted" the opinion.

[16] In part this resistance is encouraged by a belief in the right to be free. But it is also true that the assertion of self-determination through SWAPO, supported by the O.A.U., was an essential basis of the formation of an international conviction that Namibians were entitled to liberation. This is the other reality which plays a vital role in the law of Namibia.

[17] International Defence and Aid Fund (I.D.A.F.) Fact Paper No. 10 *Apartheid's Army in Namibia*, January 1982, p.3. See also the Sunday Telegraph March 22, 1981.

[18] I.D.A.F. *op. cit.* p.15.

[19] The possibility of Namibia being resolved in the context of intense judicial activity comparable for example to Nuremberg is most unlikely. The necessity of the consent of States to the jurisdiction of any arbitral or similar proceedings makes it almost impossible. The circumstances of newly won independence with the associated instability of the new State, make such structured solutions even more remote. Bearing this in mind it is interesting to observe how much of the argumentation surrounding the excesses which are often associated with decolonisation (especially when armed conflict is involved) is conducted by references to rules of international law which are only fully meaningful in the rarely accepted judicial context.

[20] Or is it merely that without enforcement machinery (and the constant call for, and unique if limited use of, sanctions against South Africa underlines this), for even such sophisticated norms as those of the U.N. on decolonisation, international law must live with law-breakers?

[21] See G. Abi-Saab, Wars of National Liberation and the Laws of War 3 *Annales D'Etudes Internationales* (1972) p.93, J. Dugard, SWAPO. The *jus ad bellum* and the *jus in bello*. 93 *S.A.L.J.* (1977) N. Ronzitti, Wars of National Liberation—A Legal Definition (1975) I *Italian Y.B.I.L.* p.192.

[22] The document, like the proposals for the constitutional principles for Namibia (see p.223 below) has not as yet been published in full in source materials easily available. They are therefore set out in full, below. It is interesting that information

and comment on them in Western newspapers has been scant, though the remarkably active and liberal press in Windhoek has given them coverage. This might suggest that to talk of "perspectives" of international law has a practical, physical, as well as a cultural and intellectual aspect.

[23] An important technique being used in Namibia by South Africa, as it was in other essentially colonial situations for the purpose of avoiding total liberation, is the "indigenisation" of the colonial structure. (The creation of Zimbabwe-Rhodesia is the best example, terminologically speaking. "Vietnamisation" was another.) It takes the form of the Democratic Turnhalle Alliance (D.T.A.) in Namibia, created on the basis of elections unilaterally organised by S. Africa. It has an additional significant element in Namibia, the creation of an indigenous military structure. This has the further objective of providing a S. African trained and orientated internal force which will remain mobilised even if the terms of S.C. Resol. 435 are eventually implemented unchanged. See further, *I.D.A.F. Fact Paper No. 10* Jan. 1982, Chapters 2, 3, 4 and 7.

[24] Notes on the conversation between U.S. Asst. Sect. of State, Chester Crocker and S. African representative on April 15/16, 1981, and leaked to the press. *op.cit.* p.3.

[25] The Reagan Administration has since its inception indicated its desire to support South Africa. Secretary Haig, welcoming the South African Foreign Minister, "Pik" Botha, the first African foreign minister to visit the White House after the election, spoke of the two States' "shared interests" and the need to "talk as friends" and expressed the hope for a "new beginning of mutual trust and confidence between the U.S. and S. Africa." These may be normal platitudes for such occasions, but is such a policy capable of being legally implemented? Are there no legal limits? For the Third World, after S. Africa's refusal at Geneva in Jan. 1981 to implement the U.N.'s 1978 plan, it appeared, in the words of Ambassador Munoz Lopez, the P.R. of Mexico to the U.N., speaking in April 1981 on the call for sanctions, that "practically everything has been said and practically everything has been tried . . . What prevails is a feeling of deep frustration . . . The U.N. can scarcely retreat before those who violate its resolutions and do harm to its principles."

[26] See *I.D.A.F. Fact Paper No. 10*. Chapter 6, on the dimensions of S. African action. My own *in loco* inspection of the action in the Southern Cunene Province of Angola (in October 1981) indicates that the prime target of S. African air and land forces is not SWAPO being pursued on the basis of a non-existing right of "hot-pursuit," but the Angola civilian population and its infrastructure. See the forthcoming publication of U.N. Committee Against Apartheid of the Report of the Special Mission of the International Commission of Inquiry into the Crimes of the Apartheid Regime.

[27] G.A. Resol. 31/146 XXI (1976).

[28] See the support of this principle by the International Court of Justice in the Advisory Opinion on *The Western Sahara* [1975] I.C.J. Rep. Its rather crude frustration by Morocco was the subject of vigorous criticism, but not by the States now playing the role of honest brokers in Namibia. See T. Frank, The Stealing of the Sahara (1976) 70 *A.J.I.L.* Is Namibia to be a more subtle example of the same thing?

[29] Likewise the use of force by the Liberation Movements continued. Far from accepting its legitimacy however the U.K. characterised it as the reason for Rhodesian "defensive" action, even when the targets were not the Liberation Movements but the Zambian railways or the Mozambiquean food distribution system. A parallel can be found in the persistence of the Contact Group with their mobile negotiations while refusing to make their pursuit of this peaceful alternative conditional upon an end to S. African attacks and virtual occupation of Southern

Cunene. The rules, that such defence of colonialism is unlawful, seemed clear, how much more tolerance of illegality is needed to indicate a reversal of the *opinio juris* of at least the key Western States? See D. Bowett, Reprisals Involving Recourse to Armed Force (1972) 66 *A.J.I.L.* p.1, for an interesting study of the idea that armed reprisals prohibited by the U.N. Charter, may have been re-instated by U.N. practice in relation to Israeli action against its P.L.O. supporting neighbours. S. Africa has links with Israel on counter-insurgency techniques, and it would not be surprising if these were extended to include "normative" matters.

[30] This was a dramatic and deliberate reversal of the policy adopted in earlier attempts to achieve liberation and independence (Geneva 1976, Malta 1977). The failure of such attempts (which took place in a context of much less transborder violence) was given as one reason for the change.

[31] The diplomacy which achieved this before and at the 1979 Lusaka Commonwealth Heads of State Conference is worthy of a study of its own.

[32] In relation to Namibia, the Contact Group seem, in essence, to have taken on the role of Britain as the surrogate (?) imperial power, while S. Africa with the D.T.A. may be seen to parallel the "Smithorewa" regime. The present plan, based as it still is upon S.C. Resol. 435 retains the U.N. element. This includes the U.N. Force (UNTAG), though it is being increasingly squeezed out of Namibia into the proposed Demilitarised Zone (DMZ). What concerns those observing the constant whittling away by S. Africa and its allies-cum-arbitrators (the Contact Group), is whether the U.N. will be entirely eliminated. There will be no Commonwealth African States to provide even a modest balance in that case and the Namibian Liberation Movement would find itself on its own, which is where its opponents would prefer it to be.

[33] The story of the ongoing tussle between successive British governments (of both parties) on the one hand, to arrive at a settlement with the Smith regime—the various "Talks" on "Tiger," "Fearless" amongst other venues—and the combined efforts of the Commonwealth and the U.N. on the other, to ensure that the black majority were at least equal parties to any settlement and that the final arrangement was acceptable to the U.N., is an important and early indication of the very different interpretation of self-determination by Western and Third World States.

[34] Here it is worthwhile noting the inextricable connection between the liberation of peoples subjected to a history of colonial exploitation and deliberate underdevelopment, and the problem of development. There is a sense of inevitability (which may not be shared, but needs to be understood) that some form of State control by the newly established democratic government (socialism in some form or other) is the only way to meet the expectations of liberty and make up for the lost years. Freedom through development, the next stage of decolonisation, is now an international problem seeking a solution by legal as well as other means. States and statesmen with a power to influence the law should seek means to ensure that it meets, rather than frustrates this equally worthy desire for freedom from poverty. Of course there is a balance to be struck between conflicting interests, but it needs lawyers informed of all the circumstances to help shape it. Short cuts, achieved in general by coercion, will merely preserve the conflicts for another day. The constitutional protection of the existing maldistribution of land in Zimbabwe, which is part and parcel of the international legal/political operation surrounding Lusaka and Lancaster House, is an example of a legal solution which does little to solve the problem.

[35] See *Financial Mail* (Johannesburg) November 21, 1980 which shows how S. Africa's defence expenditure has risen from 707 million Rands in 1974, to an estimated 2,800 million Rands in 1981.

[36] See *I.D.A.F. Fact Paper No. 10* (Jan. 1982) Chapter 6.

[37] The Lancaster House Agreement, which is a very different document to this proposal, also presents a question as to its exact legal status.

[38] This amounts to a devious attempt to oust, or at least reduce, the development (or in this case preservation) by the U.N. of the critical legal framework of post-independence Namibia. It smacks of secret treaty-making in disguise, and it is difficult to understand (if it is not merely innocent "kite-flying") why the proposal should not be openly discussed and incorporated into the U.N. formula.

[39] The experience of the U.K.'s reaction to its obligations resulting from the Turkish invasion of Cyprus and the Treaty there, suggests that this is a welcome omission.

[40] The U.N. General Assembly has voted by 119 to none, with 21 abstentions, that Walvis Bay is an "integral part of Namibia." G.A. Resol. S.9/2. See also Goeckner and Gunning, Namibia, South Africa and the Walvis Bay Dispute (1980) 89 Yale L.J. 903.

[41] There has been vigorous canvassing for States in this region, including Angola and Mozambique which have existing relations with Comecon, to join the Lomé Convention States. There is also the crucial Southern African Development Conference, involving the existing Front Line States and intent *inter alia* upon achieving their economic independence of South Africa. This is strongly supported by EEC States, and it would be difficult to understand why Namibia should be excluded from such an arrangement.

The Great Transfer of Employee Rights Hoax

R.W. RIDEOUT

"Euro-jargon sometimes goes well into the law of France and of Germany. It rarely goes well into English law."[1]

The problem of the harmonisation of law

It must be rare for a government to announce that it is legislating with "remarkable lack of enthusiasm."[2] Nevertheless the British government scarcely needed to state this in the case of the Transfer of Undertakings (Protection of Employment) Regulations.[3] Not only will they become effective three years later than required by EEC Council Directive 77/187, commonly referred to as the Acquired Rights Directive, thus making the United Kingdom the last EEC member to comply. Even a cursory glance at the Regulations reveals that they do not comply with the Directive and in the debate in the House of Commons employers were told not to worry about one of the major provisions of the Directive because the Regulations purporting to implement it would have no effect in practice. Civil servants, moreover, had spent two years trying to convince the Commission that there was good reason not to apply the Directive in Britain.

If there are any constitutional lawyers still talking of Parliamentary Sovereignty the problem they have is eclipsed by the more practical problem of the use of delegated legislation to enact a law which nobody wants in language so ambiguous that its judicial application is likely to require (whether or not such a requirement is actually met) amending legislation on almost every judgment.

Lawyers concerned with the EEC, however, have a problem which dwarfs any facing the constitutional lawyer. How is one to approximate the laws of the member nations? The need for such approximation is obvious in Labour Law although, no doubt, that area is not the leader in the field. Labour law also provides an excellent example of the difficulties besetting harmonisation by reason not of its deviating from member to member but of the diversity of labour practice which underlies that law.

Much of the demand for approximation of laws arises as a matter of economics. Section 6 of the Health and Safety at Work, etc., Act 1974 imposes obligations on manufacturers, designers, suppliers and importers of any article for use at work to ensure, so far as is reasonably practicable that the article is so designed and constructed as to be safe. British industry is apt to complain that this, among other alleged examples of highly safety-conscious law in this country, imposes upon it an added cost unfair in terms of its competitiveness with other Common Market countries which have less rigorous requirements and show little desire to pursue approximation by advancing, as against retreating, along such a path. At least the mechanics of approximation of this type of requirement, if the will were there, would be relatively simple. It is otherwise when one comes to consider the complex ways in which varying law and practice affects other aspects of the cost of labour.

One is bound to admit that on occasion it is impossible to see how legislation could achieve the desired effect, since instinctive reaction governed by differing attitudes of mind will operate to frustrate the purpose. In Britain, for instance, industrial tribunals decline to examine whether an employer's decision to declare a redundancy is economically justified.[4] At present they will only go so far as to consider whether the employer's decision, once taken, does create a diminution in requirement.[5] Beware the British employer who thinks his prerogative to decide this extends to his subsidiary in Holland. He will find that the affected trade union can refer the matter to a tribunal which will almost certainly order a public examination of the employer's financial position and prospects in order to decide, as a matter of social policy, whether he is to be allowed to close down. Even if it were politically feasible to produce legislation to achieve such an incursion on management prerogative in this country it is doubtful whether there could be found words sufficiently specific to stand against the instinctive feeling existing in this country, but apparently not in Holland, that even a mixed economy demands such freedom.

The situation which we are about to examine, however, reveals that the early warning systems and forward defences of government rarely allow such a possibility to be tested. One such forward defence ensures that the process of agreeing to an EEC Directive on the part of a government not convinced of its desirability shall resemble in objective collective bargaining on British Railways. (This is unfair to BR. Much British Collective Bargaining is of the same nature.) A form of words is devised sufficiently vague or ambiguous to absorb as many differing interpretations as it can and to leave those who can agree to one such interpretation uncommitted unless and until a single precise meaning is required. Nothing else can explain the ambiguity of the "Acquired Rights"

Directive which would be unbelievable had it not been easily surpassed by the Transfer of Undertakings Regulations—unless, of course, one believes that quite a lot of uncertainty can be introduced by translating French into English.

Had it not reflected somewhat badly on them, the government would no doubt have ordered Lord Wedderburn's finest quotation yet to be similarly published whenever his name is mentioned. "They snatch away," he said, "the rights which were intended by the directive, like some bicycle thief snatching purses in the night." The pure beauty of this concept somewhat obscures its unfairness. Lord Wedderburn would be hard pressed to say what was intended by the Directive, and the government cannot be accused of snatching anything. They had long made it clear that they had every intention of leaving the purse but ensuring that it contained very little of value. No doubt the government is intending to deceive most of the people some of the time but then it could be said that Lord Wedderburn, who on this occasion advocated the transferability of collective agreements did so with his tongue in his cheek. That path leads straight to the enforceability of collective agreements. One hopes that the government had other reasons than lack of appreciation of the point to miss this opportunity to introduce what their predecessors in 1971 were so keen upon.

Scope of the regulations

The Directive is plainly not intended to apply to a transfer of control of an undertaking by means of a change in the ownership of shares. No doubt the representatives of the British government had not taken too much trouble to point out to the EEC that this is the more usual means of transfer of undertakings in the United Kingdom whereas it is by no means so common in most other EEC countries. Although Lord McCarthy made something of this in the House of Lords debate, however, the fact that the Regulations do not apply to the majority of transfers of undertakings in the United Kingdom is in many respects not as serious as it sounds. If the name of the employing company does not change then nor do its contractual obligations to its employees. There is no termination of the contracts of employment occasioned by the transfer. Consequently there is no need to make any special provision for the continuation of contractual and statutory rights. The failure to include such transfers will, however, have a substantial effect upon the benefits which would otherwise have been derived from prior consultation with and information to employees concerning the effects of the change. These are just as likely to be far-reaching in a share transfer as they are in any other form of takeover. Usually employees are wholly unaware that the share transfer is pending until after it occurs. By that time the plans of the transferee are normally well advanced. The employee lacks both the opportunity to influence them and the advance warning to make alternative arrangements for his own future.

The reference to transfer of an undertaking only includes an undertaking in the nature of a commercial venture. There is nothing in the words of the Directive to support such a limitation or in the earlier draft which purported to exclude more specific categories such as government bodies and charities. No EEC member would interpret the Directive as applying to public employees in the sense of those employed by the government. On the other hand, few would exclude the public sector of industry. If a commercial venture is one in which capital is invested against a chance of profit and a risk of loss there must be some doubt whether the regulations apply to transfers from this sector. Certainly they would appear not to apply to transfers from local authorities. The fact that some exclusion is justified only serves to emphasise the point made by Lord McCarthy[6] that resort to a term like "commercial venture" is bound to lead to dispute and litigation. Apart from the possibility that the Regulations will be regarded by general agreement as a semantic disaster of such magnitude that they are best ignored altogether one can imagine many examples of such dispute. As the House of Lords was reminded at the time, the Court of Appeal had shortly before castigated the Greater London Council for not running London Transport as a commercial venture. But even if London Transport were run so as to break even it could be argued that it is not a commercial venture. Quite apart from this, however, a transfer by the Crown to the private sector is likely to be excluded. As Lord Lyell for the government pointed out he had not in the past been too good at paying attention in Lord McCarthy's tutorials and he chose not to explore this point.

There is, however, a deeper seated and more intractable problem in the nature of problems of overcoming established attitudes which we mentioned earlier. The Directive refers to the transfer of an undertaking and it is obvious from the later requirements that this is not intended to apply to a mere transfer of assets. In case there was any doubt about this the Regulations may be taken to have indicated their position by a side-wind. It is provided that when they refer to part of an undertaking they mean a part being transferred as a business. This must be taken to infer the same requirement of a total transfer. In *Melon* v. *Hector Powe Ltd.*[7] the concept of a business was construed restrictively. A factory which made suits mainly for one set of retail outlets was held not to carry on the same business after it had changed hands and begun making suits for the wider wholesale market. It seems inconceivable that the EEC Commission could have contemplated the inclusion of only so narrow a range of transactions as United Kingdom law has already established in the case of longer standing statutory provisions for continuity of employment. Yet it seems inevitable that United Kingdom law will apply that restrictive approach.

No doubt those who drafted the Directive in rather general terms expected individual governments to ensure that these general provisions applied to more particular situations. It seems unlikely that the British government and its servants were unaware that it is common in large groups of associated companies for one of those companies to act as employer of all the group's personnel. The Directive would be capable of covering the situation which would arise if one of the non-employing companies was transferred outside the group because it provides for the transfer of the "transferor's rights and obligations arising from a contract of employment. . . . existing on the date of a transfer" (Art. 3111). The Regulations (Para. 5(1)), however, render this as

> "A relevant transfer shall not operate so as to terminate the contract of any person employed by the transferor . . . but any such contract. . . . shall have effect after the transfer . . . "

It cannot be argued that an employing company which is not the transferor is transferring part of its undertaking when it transfers employees to the transferee since its undertaking (a) does not involve such an activity and (b) remains intact.

Hiving-down

The British government might have been able to argue that it had only failed in a genuine endeavour to re-word in a meaningful fashion the somewhat ambiguous generalisations of the Directive were it not for its treatment of hiving-down. This, however, is so clearly an intention to limit the operation of the Directive so as to exclude the practice that more significantly than any other detracts from the transfer of employee rights. It would have been pointless to attempt to conceal the intention to produce a set of Regulations so full of large holes as to catch very little.

The device of hiving down enables a receiver to transfer the assets of an insolvent company to an intermediate owner who is usually a wholly-owned subsidiary of the insolvent. The insolvent company retains the liabilities, including the employees. Employees are a liability at this stage because they have accumulated some quite valuable entitlements. Most important among those entitlements is compensation for redundancy. If the employees were transferred with the assets the intermediate company would pick up liability for that entitlement. The final purchaser would then have the task of dismissing the employees he did not want and meeting the liability. Hiving down, however, enables the receiver to offer a potential purchaser a bundle of assets. The liabilities will be a charge on the purchase price and in the case of employee remuneration and redundancy compensation may even be met by the Secretary of State from the central redundancy fund.[8] It is even possible[9] that as the law stood before the Regulations hiving down would destroy the continuity of employment even of those employees who are ultimately transferred by the insolvent company to the final purchaser since that transfer of employees will not also involve a transfer of business. The transfer of business takes place between the intermediate owner (to whom, incidentally, the insolvent company will probably hire out the required employees) and the purchaser.

As we shall see, the effect of the rest of the Regulations if allowed to operate on this situation would be to effect an automatic transfer of all rights and obligations to the intermediate owner followed by a further similar transfer to the final purchaser. Such destruction of one of the major attractions of hiving down the British government purports to see as likely seriously to reduce the chances of disposing of an insolvent business as a going concern thus preserving at least some of the jobs. Even if the result is that central funds have to meet a liability which has not been transferred this is less undesirable than having to meet the same liability and be faced with more unemployed.

It is, therefore, provided in the new Regulations (Reg. 4) that where there is a transfer to a wholly-owned subsidiary no transfer for the purposes of the Regulations shall be deemed to take place until immediately before that transferee ceases to be a wholly-owned subsidiary or further transfers the undertaking to another person. It is the obvious intention of the paragraph to imply that the single transfer deemed then to take place shall be regarded as one made by both the insolvent and the intermediate owners so that the references to the transferor of the business in subsequent paragraphs shall also be a reference to the insolvent company which is still the employer. Since this is vital to the operation of all the subsequent paragraphs upon the rights of employees who do ultimately transfer to the final purchaser it is a pity it is not stated more clearly. The government describes regulation 4 as providing a "suspended" transfer. (This concept was originally suggested by Davies and Freedland 1980 I.L.J. 95. They, however, proposed to safeguard the employees dismissed during the suspension.) By this it means that employees not wanted by the final purchaser can get lost on the way. They may be dismissed in the timeless zone. When the transfer takes place they are no longer employed so no rights transfer. Their rights lie in claims against the insolvent company. Lord McCarthy asked[10] whether there was any necessary right to re-engage in a hiving down situation. He knew that the answer he never received was negative. In fact, however, this poses a much more complex question, which we shall deal with in the next section, of whether there is any obligation to re-engage in any transfer situation. In other words, does an employee who is dismissed before a direct transfer have any rights against the transferee as distinct from the transferor? If he does not the Regulations would seem to have effected a novation of contract without consent. That, however, is the most likely conclusion.

If this is so the claims of employees who were not required in future could, even without the special provision, be kept off the assets by dismissing them before transfer to the intermediate owner. The trouble is, of course, that at that point the requirements of the final purchaser are not known. Regulation 4, therefore, provides a breathing space in which such employees can be selected and dismissed without any liability falling upon the ultimate purchaser.

It is only fair to add that Regulation 4 does not remove hiving down entirely from the scope of the Regulations. Those employees who are ultimately transferred will have their rights and obligations transferred under Regulation 5.

Extent of the rights transferred

The instrument applies to transfer the rights of employees of the transferor and, to a limited extent, to provide protection for affected employees of the transferee. Where the contracts of employment with the transferor would otherwise have been terminated, it is provided that after the transfer the contract shall have effect as if originally made with the transferee. (Reg. 5(1)). The next paragraph, although expressed to be without prejudice to this is, in fact, far wider. It states:

(a) all the transferor's rights, powers, duties and liabilities under or in connection with any such contract shall be transferred by virtue of this Regulation to the transferee [except as regards occupational pensions schemes]; and

(b) anything done before the transfer is completed by or in relation to the transferor in respect of that contract of a person employed in that undertaking or part shall be deemed to have been done by or in relation to the transferee [except as regards the imposition of criminal liability].

It seems certain that these words are wide enough to ensure the all-important continuity of employment for the purpose of safeguarding accrued entitlements to statutory benefits. Provisions in other parts of the Regulations clearly indicate that such was the intention (*e.g.* Regulations 8(1) and 14(1).) Nevertheless it remains strange that the words in every earlier draft of sub-paragraph (a) above extending it to "rights etc. otherwise arising in connection with the employment" should have been deleted. Those words reflected more closely those in the EEC Directive covering rights and obligations arising "from an employment relationship." Their deletion leaves the critical issue of transfer of statutory rights to be effected by the highly ambiguous words of sub-paragraph (b) above. Nevertheless it would be nonsense not to provide for the transfer of statutory rights which form the most immediately beneficial of all the incidents of employment and there seems little doubt that tribunals and courts would regard them as included in the transfer.

It is presumably on this mixture of common sense and apparent intention that the government declared itself in no doubt that statutory rights would be transferred.[11]

Effect upon termination of the contract

This concept of the involuntary transfer of contractual rights and obligations to one who was not a party to the contract is new to English jurisprudence but would not seem as theoretically revolutionary in any Continental system. Statute has previously provided that a transfer shall not operate as a dismissal[12] but this assumes transfer with the consent of both parties and implies no suggestion that the content of the contract must remain the same.

Subject to the possibility of a claim for unfair dismissal or wrongful dismissal the contract of employment may be terminated by the transferor before the transfer so that none of the employee's rights transfer. The corresponding right in the employee, strictly speaking, is that if transferred he may terminate the contract by due notice. It is said that those who framed the Directive did not intend to interfere with the rule in *Nokes* v.

Doncaster Amalgamated Collieries Ltd.[13] which has its counterpart in a number of Continental systems, so as to impose automatic transfer of the contract upon an employee against his will. Lord Wedderburn seems to have been correct, however,[14] to state that the United Kingdom Regulations do exactly that. It is provided (Regulation 5(5)).

> Paragraph (1) above is without prejudice to any right of an employee arising from these Regulations to terminate his contract of employment without notice if a substantial change is made in his working conditions to his detriment; but no such right shall arise by reason only that, under that paragraph, the identity of his employer changes unless the employee shows that, in all the circumstances, the change is a significant change and is to his detriment.

This appears quite clearly to remove the right of the employee to treat his contract as terminated by the transfer alone. He now has either to terminate the contract himself (*i.e.* by proper notice) or show a detrimental change in his working conditions arising from the transfer. In other words the employee loses the right to complain of the transfer as a dismissal both under common law and statute law unless it amounts to a constructive dismissal. It is probable that such a detrimental change could not be supplied by changes in the occupational pension rights inherent in the transfer. This is the one part of the contract which both the Directive and the Instrument permit to be excluded from the contractual transfer. The British government took advantage of the entitlement to exclude all reference to pension claims. Unfortunately Regulation 7 which effects this exclusion provides that the whole of Regulation 5 (including 5(5)) does not apply to such schemes. This appears to mean that the absence of such a scheme cannot be invoked as a detrimental effect of the transfer. On the other hand all the rest of the contract is transferred by Regulation 5 so that the employee is unable to claim that the cessation of business by the transferor itself operates as a termination.

The words in Regulation 5(1) "any such contract which would otherwise have been terminated by the transfer shall have effect after the transfer as if originally made between the person so employed and the transferee" make it clear that if neither party takes whatever steps are necessary to terminate the contract that same contract is unbroken by the transfer. In short, the mere change of employer will not, as now, operate as a dismissal by the transferor and a re-engagement by the transferee. It is unlikely that there will be any problems in practice where the contract would not otherwise have been terminated by the transfer. This situation seems to arise where a receiver is appointed by a company in voluntary liquidation.[15] But when the receiver further transfers the business the Regulations will operate normally.

Redundancy

The employee who leaves his employment before the transfer and is able to show that the change is detrimental to him, will, presumably, be able to claim a constructive dismissal by reason of Regulation 5(5). He is likely, therefore, in common with those actually dismissed before the transfer, to claim redundancy compensation. The employee who does not wish to transfer but who is not dismissed and is unable to show such detriment and the employee who transfers to a different job which he accepts will have no such recourse against their former employer. They will be in no worse position in that respect than at present but will lose their present statutory right to a trial period. Regulation 5, in other words, has the same effect as section 84(1) of the EPCA 1978 but eliminates the need for consent to achieve that effect.

Unfair dismissal

The Regulations deal with rights to claim unfair dismissal in a most interesting way. Paragraph 8(1) provides a rebuttable presumption of unfair dismissal wherever any employee either of the transferor or the transferee is dismissed wholly or principally for a reason connected with the transfer. Not only does this cover a wide array of reasons but it clearly applies to employees of the transferee who are displaced as a result of the transfer. At first sight, however, it would appear to be considerably restricted in its effect by paragraph 8(2) which provides that the presumption may be rebutted by an economic, technical or organisational reason for dismissal entailing changes in the workforce of either the transferor or the transferee. Where such is the reason or principal reason for the dismissal it will form a sustantial reason of a kind such as to justify the dismissal. It will still be necessary to establish that it was reasonable to proceed to dismissal for such a reason. This is the Euro-jargon to which Lord Wedderburn referred. The trouble is that its translation into English seems to produce the word "re-organisation." That, however, is the word applied to the much criticised "other substantial reason" which plays on the technicality of the statutory definition of redundancy. Is there not a danger that the Regulations have produced a situation in which dismissal to which they apply is either unfair or is by reason of re-organisation but cannot be for redundancy alone? Whether the provision is wide enough to destroy the effect of the presumption in practice depends on one critical question of the significance of which English law has not so far shown much realisation. It appears to have been the intention of those who drafted the EEC Directive—and a number of member states have made the point more clearly than the UK in their complying legislation—that economic, technical or organisational reasons should be established as an objective fact to cause the dismissal. If this is held to be the effect of the UK Regulations it will radically alter this aspect of the law of dismissal. That law has hitherto accepted the employer's subjective judgment as conclusive of the existence of a redundancy or, for that matter, a re-organisation. The difficulty in applying any objective assessment of economic, technical or organisational reasons will lie in the extent to which industrial tribunals feel equipped to make such judgments. Without such a standard, however, it is obvious that the very fact of the transfer will afford such justification. The employee's safeguard will then lie only in a decision as to whether the way in which the employer has reacted is reasonable. This may be a difficult matter to decide especially if the dismissal (which may, of course, be a constructive dismissal) is separated by a considerable period of time from the transfer.

It should be noticed that paragraph 12 of the Regulations renders void any agreement purporting to exclude or limit the operation of these provisions. An employee, therefore, who agrees to transfer to a different job with the transferee employer actually retains the contractual right to insist on his former terms and conditions including the former job definition. If the employee resiles from his agreement, therefore, the employer who does not agree to provide the former job will be faced with the possibility of a claim for actual or constructive dismissal which he would first have to justify within the terms of paragraph 8(2) and then establish as a reasonable response to these circumstances.

The obligation to consult

The obligation to consult the representatives of recognised trade unions prior to a proposed redundancy[16] is generally considered minimal. Continental countries are, in many instances, well aquainted with much more extensive obligations, and the present Regulations applying the Directive do indeed extend the previous obligation in cases of transfer of business which, of course, will often involve redundancy. In some circumstances, as for instance where every employee is taken on in suitable alternative employment by the transferee, no right to consultation would arise under the 1975 Act and the right granted by the Regulations will be wholly new.

The Directive requires both transferee and transferor to inform representatives of employees of the reason for the transfer, the legal, economic and social implications of the transfer for the employees and the measures envisaged in relation to them "in good time" before the transfer is carried out and, in the case of the transferee, in any event before the conditions of employment of his employees are directly affected by the transfer. If either transferor or transferee envisages measures in relation to his employees he is required to consult the employee representatives in good time and with a view to seeking agreement on such measures.

This appears to be intended to be an absolute obligation. The United Kingdom Regulations would seem, therefore, to fall short of the requirement by allowing the usual statutory dispensation where the employer can show that it was not reasonably practicable for him to comply with either duty and that he took such steps towards compliance as were reasonably practicable. The Regulations undoubtedly fall short of the requirements of the Directive in requiring only information to and consultation with recognised trade unions. The Directive speaks of employee representatives. No doubt it had in mind the Works Councils common in many Continental countries but the absence of any obligation to maintain such bodies should not justify exclusion of the obligation to consult with informally appointed employee representatives or unrecognised trade unions.

The Regulations leave out the words "with a view to agreement" which had been included in every previous draft of them. When asked to explain this omission Lord Lyell[17] said that it was because these words did not appear in any other legislation and were considered unnecessary. It is a surprising thought that in a country where no obligation even to bargain in good faith is recognised it should be thought that it was not necessary to state that consultation should be conducted with a view to agreement. This is especially true since the Regulations re-translate the words "in good time" to require information "long enough" before the transfer "to enable consultation to take place." The process of agreement might conceivably take a little longer so that "long enough before to enable consultation" envisages a considerably shorter period than "in good time to consult with a view to agreement."

It is a point of no consequence but there is actually no power to include in the Regulations (Regulation 10(2)(a)) the requirement of information as to when the transfer is to take place. The Directive does not require this information and there is no power, as Lord Wedderburn pointed out,[18] by this type of Regulation to impose obligations that the government is not actually required to impose. It is interesting to observe that the Regulations only require information as to the approximate date. No doubt this is because no provision is made to ascertain the actual date. It is quite probable that in some claims it will be necessary to determine this date with precision.

It is difficult to know what to say about the sanction available to enforce the duty to inform and consult. It is, at the instance of the trade union concerned, limited to a maximum sum equivalent to two weeks' wages for each of the employees concerned. In aggregate this could be quite a large sum but it is scarcely likely to have the compulsive effect of some Continental sanctions for similar failures. In any event it is not obtainable in addition to a protection award. Worst of all no special provision is made to recover it in the case of insolvency from which precisely it will normally arise.

On the whole it might have been thought that a government which was genuine in its assertions of a desire to improve the quality of voluntary bargaining would have taken an opportunity like this to take a larger step forward. If Lord Wedderburn is right to be sceptical of the practical effect of "Euro-jargon" such as "legal, economic and social implications," the only clear advance is the imposition of an obligation on the transferee to inform and consult his employees likely to be affected.

Transfer of the benefit of collective agreements

Wherever the transferred undertaking maintains, after the transfer, "an identity distinct from the remainder of the transferee's undertaking"[19] then any independent trade union recognised to any extent by the transferor in respect of any description of transferred employees shall be deemed to have been recognised by the transferee to the same extent. (Regulation 9). The Regulations then provide enigmatically that "any agreement for recognition may be varied or rescinded accordingly." United Kingdom law, as we have seen, would allow most recognition agreements to be varied or rescinded at will. The agreement itself might provide for unilateral termination by notice or alternatively not envisage such termination. The critical question is whether the Regulation intended to provide as a matter of law that the agreement could only be terminated according to its own terms or, in other words, to make it contractually enforceable. On the one hand it is clearly the intention of the EEC Directive that such agreements should not be compulsorily transferred merely to be rescinded at will. On the other hand it would be a little surprising if UK law permitted most recognition agreements to be terminated at will but entrenched those recognition agreements which had passed a barrier of transfer of business.

It has been argued that since it is obviously possible by legislation to provide for the enforceability of collective agreements (*e.g.* Restoration of Pre-War Trade Practices Acts 1942 and 1950) the Regulations should be construed as impliedly having this effect. It seems very unlikely whether the courts would be prepared to make an implication directly contrary to an earlier statutory provision, especially as the Regulations refer to the existence of that provision.[20] Moreover in both Houses[21] the government stated that an employer was free to ignore (not merely to cancel by proper notice) any such collective agreement if he could get away with it. There seems little doubt that this is a correct statement of the law. It may not seem to some of our Continental colleagues a particularly responsible attitude to an industrial society which is supposed to be regulated by collective agreement.

The provisions relating to the transfer of other collective agreements (Paragraph 6) are no more clear in this respect. It is provided that wherever there is in existence in relation to any employee whose contract is transferred by reason of these Regulations a collective agreement with a recognised trade union that agreement shall have effect after the transfer as if made by or on behalf of the transferee with that trade union. Anything done in relation to that agreement by or in relation to the transferor before the transfer shall be deemed to have been done by the transferee. Any order (for instance one made by the CAC) shall have effect as if the transferee were a party to the agreement.

Much of the apparent effect of this provision is unnecessary save as removing anomalous effects. The substantive parts of such agreements so far as they have individual application will almost certainly have been incorporated in the contracts of employment which have been transferred. Most procedure agreements will merely be the outward manifestation of recognition. If recognition is conceded the procedure is bound to be accepted until properly amended. The doubtful points arising from this provision apply, therefore, to a small but important selection of clauses in collective agreements which are more than expressions of intention but less than matters of individual contract or recognition procedure.

Perhaps the most obvious example would be union membership agreements. It seems unlikely that British trade unions will wish to fight hard for contractual enforceability of these, or any other, aspects of collective agreements and it is unlikely that the EEC will wish to bring much pressure to bear for the contractual enforceability of closed shop agreements. It seems most likely, therefore, that if there is to be an attempt to read contractual enforceability into the Regulations it will stem from the provisions as to transfer of recognition.

CONCLUSION

It may not be difficult to imagine a certain irritation among trade unionists and employers in other EEC member countries if they read the House of Lords Debate on these Regulations. One is bound to ask whether the EEC Commission will tolerate so flagrant an example of failure to comply with a Directive if, as must surely be the case, the failure gives United Kingdom employers an economic advantage.

This Directive is directed to member states and it is unlikely, therefore, that courts would hold that an individual could claim rights under the Directive where those rights did not exist under the Regulations. In the end, therefore, it seems likely that pressure will be placed upon the British government to require it to comply with the Directive. There is only one, somewhat unlikely, possibility of improving upon the Regulations. It will be apparent from the preceding discussion that several of the most significant provisions and exceptions are highly ambiguous. Since the Regulations are intended to give effect to the Directive then, notwithstanding statements on behalf of the British government, making it apparent that such was not its intention, it would seem proper to resolve ambiguities by reference to the intention of the Directive. In this way some of the shortcomings might be removed. This method, however, could not, for instance, correct the exclusion of hiving down or the non-enforceability of collective agreements. Moreover, the Directive itself is by no means clear of ambiguity. If the next British government decides that, with or without enthusiasm, it must stay in the Common Market it might be a good idea to start again on this particular exercise.

If such a new start is made it is suggested that the proper way to proceed would be to absorb the requirements of the Directive into the main body of the law. No provision is made in the present Regulations to repeal or amend any of the law. Once again, for this to arise, the continuity provisions[22] must be read in conjunction with another set of provisions affecting the same subject which, if they refer to the same concepts, use different words to do so. The government was obviously afraid to do this for fear that the Regulations would be *ultra vires* the enabling Act. In the result, however, United Kingdom legislation has taken another step in its recent rapid progress towards incomprehensibility and unworkability.

Notes

[1] Lord Wedderburn of Charlton H.L. Deb. 1166 (10.12.81) col. 1491. This quotation is published at the express wish of Lord Lyell H.L. Deb. 1166 col. 1498.

[2] H.C. Deb. (9.12.81) 679–681.

[3] 1981/1794.

[4] *Sanders* v. *Ernest A. Neale Ltd.* [1974] I.C.R. 565; *Moon* v. *Homeworthy Furniture (Northern) Ltd.* [1977] I.C.R. 117.

[5] *Ranson* v. *G.W. Collins Ltd.* [1978] I.C.R. 765; *O'Hare* v. *Rotaprint Ltd.* [1980] I.R.L.R. 47.

[6] H.L. Deb. 1166 (10.12.81) col. 1486.

[7] [1980] I.R.L.R. 80.

[8] See Employment Protection Act 1978 s. 122.

[9] See *Pambakian* v. *Brentford Nylons Ltd.* [1978] I.C.R. 665.

[10] H.C. Deb. 1166 (10.12.81) col. 1487.

[11] Lord Wedderburn had plainly assumed that there was grave doubt about this—H.L. Deb. col. 1492.

[12] See Employment Protection (Consolidation) Act 1978 s. 84 (1).

[13] [1940] A.C. 1014.

[14] H.L. Deb. col. 1490.

[15] *Re Foster Clark Indenture Trusts* [1966] 1 W.L.R. 125.

[16] Employment Protection Act 1975 s. 99.

[17] H.L. Deb. col. 1496.

[18] H.L. Deb. col. 1494.

[19] The EEC Council Directive 77/197 from which the Regulations spring refers to maintenance of autonomy.

[20] Trade Union and Labour Relations Act 1974 s. 18 (1).

[21] H.C. Deb. (9.12.81) 679–681; H.L. Deb. (10.12.81) col. 1493.

[22] EPCA 1978 schedule 13.

INDEX